The ascent of globalisation

Manchester University Press

The ascent of globalisation

HARRY BLUTSTEIN

Manchester University Press

Copyright © Harry Blutstein 2016

The right of Harry Blutstein to be identified as the author of this work has been asserted by him in accordance with the Copyright, Designs and Patents Act 1988.

Published by Manchester University Press
Altrincham Street, Manchester M1 7JA

www.manchesteruniversitypress.co.uk

British Library Cataloguing-in-Publication Data
A catalogue record for this book is available from the British Library

Library of Congress Cataloging-in-Publication Data applied for

ISBN   978 1 7849 9289 7   hardback
ISBN   978 0 7190 9971 7   paperback

First published 2016

The publisher has no responsibility for the persistence or accuracy of URLs for any external or third-party internet websites referred to in this book, and does not guarantee that any content on such websites is, or will remain, accurate or appropriate.

Typeset by
Servis Filmsetting Ltd, Stockport, Cheshire
Printed in Great Britain by
Bell & Bain Ltd, Glasgow

Contents

Acknowledgements   vi
Abbreviations   vii

Prologue   1

Part I: The liberal foundations of globalisation   7

1. A better tomorrow   13
2. Last best hope for peace   24
3. Dawn over Bretton Woods   42
4. The European experiment   59

Part II: Sovereignty of global markets   79

5. The war of ideas   83
6. The new globalists   99
7. The anatomy of an insurgency   113
8. Accelerated development   127
9. Free trade follies   141
10. Global Fifth Amendment   157

Part III: The human face of globalisation   173

11. When the saints come marching in   179
12. Assault on the summit   192
13. Civilising globalisation   209
14. Health of nations   225

Epilogue   242

Index   252

Acknowledgements

I would like to particularly thank those many people who struggled through draft after draft of the manuscript. In particular, Jim Wilson who, over many a Yum Cha, provided constructive comments, as did Quynh-Nhu Nguyen, whose humour, patience and insights helped me improve the book, and she did so without the need to be fed. As well as commenting on the contents, Dave Mercer, Chris Burnup and Peter Ellyard often made me uncomfortable, as they challenged my arguments, and while we're unlikely to ever agree on every issue, they helped me tighten sloppy arguments and seek out more evidence to back the major themes explored in this book. Many other people have been generous with their time and advice, among them Estevão Mabjaia, Harris Gleckman, Frank Penhalluriack, Nicole Krause, John Mooney, Patrick Longfield, Lawrence Molloy, Brian Gold, Lynn Murrell, Eric Walker, Fred Funnell (senior and junior), Greg Foyster, Rob Williams, Kate Richards, Di Websdale-Morrissey, Jesse Samulenok and the indomitable Bette Oldis, who sadly is no longer with us. Special thanks go to the RMIT Document Delivery team, in particular Marina Zovko, Tony Foley and Anna White, who went to extraordinary lengths to track down primary and obscure documents for me. Finally to my favourite wife, Carol Lawson, for her love, support and encouragement. This work simply would not have been possible without her.

Abbreviations

BCSD	Business Council for Sustainable Development
BIT	bilateral investment treaty
CSR	corporate social responsibility
EU	European Union
FCTC	Framework Convention on Tobacco Control
GATS	General Agreement of Trade in Services
GATT	General Agreement on Tariffs and Trade
GAVI	Global Alliance for Vaccines and Immunization
ICC	International Chamber of Commerce
IEA	Institute of Economic Affairs
IIPA	International Intellectual Property Alliance
IMF	International Monetary Fund
IP	intellectual property
IPC	Intellectual Property Committee
ITO	International Trade Organization
LOTIS	Liberalisation of Trade in Services
MAI	Multilateral Agreement on Investment
MDG	Millennium Development Goals
NAFTA	North American Free Trade Agreement
NATO	North Atlantic Treaty Organization
NGO	non-governmental organization
OAS	Organization of American States
OECD	Organization for Economic Co-operation and Development
SEATO	South East Asia Treaty Organization
TPP	Trans-Pacific Partnership
TRIMS	Agreement on Trade-Related Investment Measures
TRIPS	Agreement on Trade-Related Aspects of Intellectual Property Rights
TTIP	Transatlantic Trade and Investment Partnership
UN	United Nations
UNDP	United Nations Development Programme

UNEP	United Nations Environment Programme
UNICE	Union of Industrial and Employers' Confederations
UNICEF	United Nations Children's Fund
WBCSD	World Business Council for Sustainable Development
WHO	World Health Organization
WSSD	World Summit on Sustainable Development
WTO	World Trade Organization

Prologue

How distances become less and less; and this rapid approach, what is it but the commencement of fraternity? Thanks to railroads, Europe will soon be no larger than France was in the middle ages. Thanks to steam-ships, we now traverse the mighty ocean more easily than the Mediterranean was formerly crossed. Before long, men will traverse the earth, as the gods of Homer did the sky, in three paces! But yet a little time, and the electric wire of concord shall encircle the globe and embrace the world. (Victor Hugo, 1849)

In the public's imagination, globalisation might well have begun in 6 November 1872, when Jules Verne published the first instalment of *Le Tour du monde en quatre-vingts jours*, soon translated to *Around the World in Eighty Days*. It was first serialised in the popular newspaper, *Le Temps*, and then published as a book the following January.

This novel was a departure for Verne, who was best known for his science fiction; speculations on the impact of future technologies. For once he found that the present had caught up with his imagination, as he built his adventure story around the revolution in international transport and communications that was happening around him.

Verne's novel opens at the Reform Club in London, where, over a game of whist, six friends discuss an item in that day's *Morning Chronicle*, which proclaimed the possibility of circumnavigating the world in eighty days. Challenging the scepticism of his companions, Phineas Fogg wagers £20,000 that he can complete the journey in that time.

With first-class tickets for Paris, he and his man-servant, Passepartout, set out on their adventures. Travelling by train, steamship, sledge-bearing sails and even an elephant, they overcome storms, kidnappings, natural disasters and Sioux attacks. As an added complication, Inspector Fix mistakes Fogg for a bank robber and begins to tail him. During the pursuit, Fix keeps Scotland Yard abreast of his progress through the telegraph system, which by the late nineteenth century linked three continents. While incidental to his story, Verne takes obvious pleasure showcasing the latest technologies, using their ability to compress both space and time to drive the action.

At the end of the book, Verne asks his hero, 'What had he gained from all this commotion? What had he got out of his journey?'[1] The answer: the hand of a pretty princess, whom Fogg saved from certain death in India. Had Verne put the same question to his readers, they would have undoubtedly confided that they had not only been handsomely entertained, but learned just how small the world had become as well.

As instalments appeared in France, they were wired to England and the US, where some newspapers treated Phineas Fogg's progress as straight news. People even wagered whether Fogg would succeed in circumventing the world in eighty days.

Verne happened on the idea when he read an article in *Le Tour du Monde*, a popular weekly journal devoted to travel and exploration. In its 12 November 1869 issue, the journal used a story on the opening of the Suez Canal, due five days later, to include a schedule on circling the earth using commercial transcontinental trains and ocean-going steamers, concluding that the journey could be done in eighty days.

The opening of the Suez Canal was important as all the other forms of transport that girdled the globe had been finished just a few years earlier. The Cunard Steamship Company opened up the trans-Atlantic route in 1840 to paying passengers, while the Pacific Mail Steamship Company launched the first regular trans-Pacific steamship service between San Francisco, Hong Kong and Yokohama in 1867. The introduction of propeller driven steamships on these routes made these journeys safe and fast. Travelling across the US had been possible after 10 May 1869, when Central Pacific and Union Pacific railway lines joined up at Promontory Summit, Utah Territory.

Verne's novel was a commercial success, as was the play adapted from his book, which ran in Paris for three years, and after that in Vienna, Brussels, London and New York. Enjoying the windfall from his literary efforts, Verne went out and acquired a larger yacht as well as a mistress, de rigueur for any self-respecting French author. Verne's success undoubtedly owed much to his talent for telling a rollicking good tale, but he also cleverly tapped into the zeitgeist – the idea of the world getting smaller excited his readers.

The revolution in fast international transport also reduced the cost of foreign goods and stimulated a massive movement of migrants from Europe and Great Britain to the New World. For this reason, scholars refer to the period from 1870 to 1914 as the first wave of globalisation.[2]

The first wave was ended by the First World War, but was not forgotten. In 1919, a young economist by the name of John Maynard Keynes wrote a pamphlet, *The Economic Consequences of the Peace*, calling for 'not only ... [a] return to the comforts of 1914, but to an immense broadening and intensification of them'. He went on to paint a seductive picture of a possible future.

> The inhabitant of London could order by telephone, sipping his morning tea in bed, the various products of the whole earth, in such quantity as he might see fit, and reasonably expect their early delivery upon his doorstep; he could at the same moment and by the same means adventure his wealth in the natural resources and new enterprises of any quarter of the world, and share, without exertion or even trouble, in their prospective fruits and advantages; or he could decide to couple the security of his fortunes with the good faith of the townspeople of any substantial municipality in any continent that fancy or information might recommend. He could secure forthwith, if he wished it, cheap and comfortable means of transit to any country or climate without passport or other formality, could dispatch his servant to the neighbouring office of a bank for such supply of the precious metals as might seem convenient, and could then proceed abroad to foreign quarters, without knowledge of their religion, language, or customs, bearing coined wealth upon his person, and would consider himself greatly aggrieved and much surprised at the least interference. But, most important of all, he regarded this state of affairs as normal, certain, and permanent, except in the direction of further improvement, and any deviation from it as aberrant, scandalous, and avoidable.[3]

Keynes also warned of a multi-headed 'serpent to this paradise'. He was referring to virulent nationalism, manipulation of markets by cartels and myopic protectionism.

Sadly, Keynes's fears were realised over the next twenty years, as the Great Depression led to the outbreak of an international economic war. During the 1930s, governments employed destructive weapons like high tariffs, trade discriminations and obstructions, and currency devaluations to give them an unfair trade advantage. These foolhardy policies resulted in high unemployment and poverty, providing an ideal environment for the rise of nationalist, fascist and militarist regimes, while in the USSR, Stalin consolidated his brutal brand of communism. These conditions, in turn, precipitated the disaster of the Second World War.

Even as the allies prosecuted the war, their governments started to plan the postwar reconstruction. At the centre of this planning was Keynes, now a world-famous economist. He was among a group of well-placed internationalists working for the governments of the US, Great Britain and Europe. Keynes's influence reached further, as his economic theories would cast a benevolent shadow over the postwar order in what became the second wave of globalisation.

At the back of their minds were lessons learnt from the first wave; its successes and failures. Technology would once again be an important enabler, but not the laissez-faire environment that they believed had led to the downfall of the earlier period of globalisation. This time round, the postwar planners decided to make globalisation more robust by actively designing and building a superstructure around institutions, rules and shared expectations of appropriate behaviour, otherwise known as 'norms'. This architecture would, they hoped, provide the political, social and economic stability needed to protect the second wave from the serpent that Keynes had identified some thirty years earlier.

Postwar globalisation, therefore, can be defined as a sustained period of institution and rule building, which formally started in 1944 at the Bretton Woods conference and continues until this day.

The Ascent of Globalisation uses the lives of the postwar generation of architects to present an intimate history of globalisation. The book describes the beliefs that they imbibed in their youth, examines the experiences that sculpted their ideas, delves into the dreams that inspired them, follows their struggles, and reflects on their legacies.

I chose architects who were either indispensable to creating parts of the global superstructure or innovators who introduced design features that have enjoyed lasting impact. Their stories also provide insights into how flaws in the architecture contributed to the global financial crisis, the ineffectiveness of the UN, instability within the European Union, the rising influence of transnational corporations, unfair trading systems and the inability of the international community to reach treaties to tackle environmental risks like climate change.

Part I examines the architects of the foundation institutions that appeared in the years after the end of the Second World War. They comprise of the World Bank, International Monetary Fund (IMF), United Nations (UN) and the European Union (EU, which started life as the European Coal and Steel Community). This period of institution building saw the establishment of the *international liberal order*, the blueprint of which was largely influenced by Keynes and his economic ideas.

The glue that held this order together was unparalleled cooperation between nation-states. International institutions afforded them the opportunity to deal with problems that extended beyond the jurisdiction of individual countries and which each could not solve by acting alone.[4] Thus, rather than sacrificing parts of their sovereignty, this new order presented nation-states with the ability to deliver economic and political benefits to their citizens by cooperatively dealing with issues previously beyond their reach.

An important feature of these arrangements is how they skilfully balance central authority with 'the proper liberty of each country over its own economic fortunes', as Keynes explained.[5] He envisioned that governments would possess the ability to re-distribute the benefits of economic globalisation by actively promoting employment and bringing in social security systems, safety nets and other programmes that moderated the harsh impacts of global markets.

While the international liberal order addressed economic and political security, it also created institutions and rules to tackle other risks to global welfare. For example, the World Bank is charged with helping poor countries tackle poverty, and UN agencies address threats to human rights, health, food security, crime and the environment, just to name a few.

Part II describes how the private sector, and particularly executives from transnational corporations, challenged government hegemony over the nature and governance of globalisation. Armed with the ideas of neoliberals, with Friedrich Hayek being a major influence, they advocated a new model of globalisation in which markets are central. This was not a return to laissez-faire policies that had dominated the first wave. Instead, the *neoliberal global order* was built around the 'international Rule of Law', which Hayek described as possessing 'mainly a negative kind' of power that necessitated the ability 'to say "no" to all sorts of restrictive measures' that governments might want to impose on international commerce. Thus, the neoliberal vision sought to protect the individual, by whom Hayek means market actors like transnational corporation and consumers, against the 'tyranny of the state' by severely limiting 'unfettered sovereignty in the economic sphere'.[6] The emergence of the neoliberal order led chairman and CEO of Citicorp, Walter Wriston, to suggest that its ascendency marked the 'twilight of sovereignty'.[7]

Part III sees leading figures within the UN instigate programmes to soften the impact of neoliberal policies, arguing that the international community had a role in moderating the downsides of globalisation and spreading its benefits more widely. The approach was inspired by the ideas of political scientist John Ruggie, who mapped a new role for international agencies, which is to promote policies, programmes and norms that would cushion the dislocations, insecurity, inequality and other downsides of economic liberalisation. This required a major shift in the way international agencies interacted with globalisation.

> Simply put, postwar institutions, including the United Nations, were built for an inter-*national* world, but we have entered a *global* world. International institutions were designed to reduce *external* frictions between states; our challenge today is to devise more *inclusive* forms of global governance.[8]

While it has been convenient to divide postwar globalisation into three phases, there are no distinct boundaries between them, nor has one approach replaced what came before. The result has been a sometimes uncomfortable amalgam, which led political scientist, Richard N. Gardner, to observe that the 'house of global order' is a great 'booming, buzzing confusion'.[9] At least by exploring its various strands, some sense can be made of the nature of globalisation and how it affects the world today.

Notes

1. J. Verne, *Around the World in Eighty Days*, translated by Geo. M. Towle (Boston: James R. Osgood and Company, 1876), p. 214.
2. The identification of the period 1870 to 1914 as the first wave of globalisation is contested, with some scholars arguing it started much earlier. See Robbie Robinson's *The Three Waves of Globalization* (London: Zed Books, 2003) and Nayan Chanda's *Bound Together* (New Haven, CT: Yale University Press 2007).
3. J.M. Keynes, *The Economic Consequences of the Peace* (London: MacMillan and Co., 1920).
4. A.-M. Slaughter, *A New World Order* (Princeton, NJ: Princeton University Press, 2004).
5. D.E. Moggridge (ed.), *The Collected Writings of John Maynard Keynes* (Cambridge: Macmillan/Cambridge University Press, 1980), Vol. XXV, p. 11.
6. F.A. Hayek, *The Road to Serfdom* (London and Henley: Routledge & Kegan Paul, 1944, reprinted 1979), pp. 175 and 172.
7. W.B. Wriston, *The Twilight of Sovereignty* (Bridgewater, NJ: Replica Books, 1992).
8. J.G. Ruggie, F. Douglas Gibson Lecture in Political Economy, Queen's University, Kingston, Ontario, delivered on 20 November 2000. Italics in the original.
9. R.N. Gardner, 'The Hard Road to World Order', *Foreign Affairs*, 52:3 (1974), 556–76.

Part I
The liberal foundations of globalisation

After Pearl Harbor, many of Hollywood's finest joined the army. One was Darryl F. Zanuck, the cigar-chomping president of Twentieth Century Fox. As a colonel in the Army Signal Corps, he served in the Aleutians in the Northern Pacific as well as North Africa.

On his return to civilian life in 1943, he became fixated on the failure of the League of Nations, which he saw as a lost opportunity for permanent peace. If only, he speculated, the US had listened to President Woodrow Wilson and joined the League in 1919, then the Second World War might have been avoided. And so, Zanuck decided that he would use his position to convince the movie-viewing audience to embrace Wilson's dream of a 'better, saner world'.[1]

In a project dear to his heart, on 1 August 1944, Twentieth Century Fox released a motion picture celebrating the life and dreams of the twenty-eighth president, simply titled *Wilson*.

Zanuck's timing was perfect – the war was nearing its end, and political leaders had just finished meeting in Bretton Woods and would soon be gathering in San Francisco to finalise the charter for the United Nations. Together, these international summits would lay the foundations for the postwar liberal order.

While Zanuck sold *Wilson* as a piece of popular entertainment, he also hoped that the movie would rally public support behind these endeavours, completing the project that Woodrow Wilson had started twenty-five years earlier.

The film's budget of $5.2 million made the movie Hollywood's most expensive production up until that date. Having bet heavily on the success of *Wilson*, Zanuck wryly quipped that unless it was 'successful from every standpoint, I'll never make another film without Betty Grable'.[2]

The project was always going to be risky, and to scotch rumours that he was making a 'message' movie – Hollywood code for a movie that would have no chance at the box office – Zanuck told a reporter that *Wilson* would appeal to 'the regular mugs and bobby-sockers, and we don't want them getting the idea that it's highbrow'.[3]

To this end, Zanuck lavished money on sets to make the film a Technicolor spectacular. But to succeed, the picture also needed a likeable hero. Unfortunately, the president had the reputation as an aloof, dour and somewhat scholarly man. To humanise Wilson, the flick treated audiences to glimpses into his private life: coaching the football team at Princeton; sing-alongs with his three adorable daughters, as their father tickled the ivories; and later, his courtship of Edith Galt, who became First Lady in December 1915. The celluloid president even displayed a playful sense of humour, a quality Wilson lacked in real life.

The movie drew drama from Wilson's clashes with the political foxes of Old Europe: Lloyd George of Britain, Vittorio Orlando of Italy and Georges Clemenceau of France. They were mainly interested in fighting over the spoils of war, keen to extract territory and treasure from the defeated nations. Wilson valiantly struggled to convince them to support the League of Nations, which he argued passionately would create a lasting peace. After winning that fight, he faced off against Henry Cabot Lodge, who proved to be his nemesis by persuading the US Senate to reject the treaty.

As one would expect from Hollywood, Woodrow Wilson's journey is portrayed as heroic, his shortcomings papered over and his opponents became one-dimensional villains. Nevertheless, the critics loved *Wilson*, with the *Washington Post* gushing that it was 'one of the most distinguished films in the whole history of the cinema'.[4] Hollywood also took to *Wilson*, and it won five Oscars.

It was not, however, a commercial success, losing the studio $2.2 million. With no marquee stars and running an epic two-and-a-half hours long, it struggled at the box office, particularly in the Midwest, where Wilson's presidency had never been popular.

For most of the movie, Zanuck restrained himself. But in its last scene, he indulged in some heavy-handed proselytising. As the president's term winds down, his Secretary for the Treasury (played by the debonair Vincent Price) asks Wilson whether the cause is now lost.

> I'm not one of those who have the slightest anxiety about the eventual triumph of the things I've stood for. The fight's just begun. You and I may never live to see it finished. But it doesn't matter. The ideals of the League aren't dead just because a few obstructive men now in the saddle say they are. The dream of a world united against the awful waste of war is too deeply imbedded in the hearts of men everywhere.[5]

The message was clear. By putting words into the president's mouth, Zanuck was urging the current generation to embrace Woodrow Wilson's dream and complete the project he had started.

As it turns out, a number of the men who would take up Wilson's baton in the 1940s happened to have attended the Paris Peace Conference in 1919. While they all admired Wilson's idealism, they criticised his strategy and performance during negotiations, determined not to repeat the same mistakes.

One of those men was Franklin Delano Roosevelt, whom Wilson had appointed assistant secretary of the navy in 1912. In February 1919, FDR happened to be on the same ship as Wilson, who was also bound for Washington, DC. Roosevelt was delighted when the president invited him and Eleanor to lunch in his cabin. Assuming the role of mentor to the younger politician, Wilson explained the importance of the League, 'The United States must go in or it will break the heart of the world, for she is the only nation that all feel is disinterested and all trust.'[6] This conversation transformed Roosevelt from a lukewarm supporter to an enthusiastic Wilsonian internationalist.

When Roosevelt became the Democrat's candidate for vice president in 1920, he used his acceptance speech to offer public support for the League of Nations.

> Modern civilization has become so complex and the lives of civilized men so interwoven with the lives of other men in other countries as to make it impossible to be in this world and not of it.[7]

During the subsequent campaign, when FDR saw isolationism reassert itself in the American psyche, he decided to soft-pedal his rhetoric. Nevertheless, over the next twenty years, he quietly worked behind the scenes to sow the seeds for internationalism, which he hoped would take root when the circumstances were more auspicious.

That time came during the Second World War, and as president, Roosevelt employed his considerable political wiles to bring the United Nations to life. He applied those same skills to ensure that the International Monetary Fund and World Bank were supported at Bretton Woods. Together, these institutions formed the foundation of the liberal international order.

The only gap was the International Trade Organization (ITO), which was left to President Truman, after FDR's death, to shepherd through the Senate. Lacking the same commitment and political savvy of his predecessor, he failed that challenge. It would nearly take another fifty years before an international trading system was in place, but it would be quite different from the liberal model pursued in the 1940s.

John Maynard Keynes, who would work closely with the Roosevelt Administration a quarter of a century later on the international economic order, was, in 1919, a relatively unknown, although quite senior treasury official. His brilliance as an economics expert, however, had secured him a ticket to Paris, where he advised the British delegation.

A keen observer, Keynes believed that Wilson was out of his depth among the skulk of political leaders from Old Europe. Keynes put Wilson's failure down to his naivety, gormless idealism, a 'slow and unadaptable' mind. 'He had no plan, no scheme, no constructive ideas whatever for clothing with the flesh of life the commandments which he had thundered from the White House', wrote Keynes.[8] As much as Keynes deplored Wilson's ineptitude, he conceded that there was 'substantial truth in the President's standpoint'.[9] If nothing more, Keynes admired Wilson's ambition to forge the League of Nations, even though Wilson was unable to vest the organisation with the authority it needed to enforce the peace.

Never one to sit on the side-lines, soon after the Paris Conference, Keynes travelled to Amsterdam to meet key European and American financiers. At its first meeting, held on 13–14 October 1919, Keynes proposed an international currency to facilitate international trade, which the League of Nations would manage.[10] But, unable to attract political support, this proposal went nowhere.[11]

The Anglo-American model of liberal internationalism had more success during the latter half of the 1940s, when the international community embraced rules and institutions designed to promote productive and responsible behaviour among nations. Its success or failure, however, depended on the ability of countries to voluntarily cooperate. What makes this new order remarkable is that it established the principle that all countries, whether powerful or not, would be governed by the rule of law.

Europe showed that another model existed. Its prime architect, Jean Monnet, also happened to have attended the Paris Peace Conference, where he advised the French prime minister.

Monnet's ideas were shaped by his experiences working for the League of Nations, where he was its deputy secretary general between 1919 and 1923. While Monnet enjoyed some successes, he found the reasons for his failures more instructive.

> In Geneva I was impressed with the power of a nation that can say no to an international body that has no supranational power. Goodwill between men, between nations, is not enough. One must also have international laws and institutions.[12]

During the 1950s, Monnet helped develop economic and political institutions that would bring Europe closer together. This experiment took the liberal order into new territory by subjecting nation-states to the authority of supranational rules.

These two variants of the international liberal order represent the first phase of globalisation.[13]

This principle became a guiding light for liberal internationalists who emerged from the Second World War determined to complete Wilson's dream, but this time around, they worked hard to construct a robust institutional framework around this principle that would willingly sacrifice the purity of the vision against the realpolitik of the times.

Notes

1. D. Zanuck, 'Preface to 'Wilson', in John Gassner and Dudley Nichols (eds), *Best Film Plays of 1943–1944* (New York: Crown Publishers, 1945), p. 2.
2. Darryl F. Zanuck quoted by Thomas J. Knock in '"History with Lighting": The Forgotten Film *Wilson*', *American Quarterly*, 28:5 (1976), 523–43, quote on p. 531.
3. C.R. Koppes and G.D. Black, *Hollywood Goes to War* (New York: Free Press, 1987), p. 320.
4. Review that appeared in the *Washington Post* on 8 September 1944. It is quoted by Thomas J. Knock in '"History with Lighting": The Forgotten Film *Wilson*', p. 533.
5. L. Trotti, *Wilson*. This screenplay was published in J. Gassner and D. Nichols (eds), *Best Film Plays of 1943–1944*, p. 86.
6. A.E. Roosevelt, *This Is My Story* (New York: Harper & Brothers, 1937), p. 289.
7. F.D. Roosevelt, acceptance speech for vice president of the United States, delivered on 9 August 1920 on front steps of his Hyde Park residence in New York State.
8. J.M. Keynes, *The Economic Consequences of the Peace* (New York: Harcourt, Brace & Howe, 1920), p. 43.
9. Letter from John Maynard Keynes to Mr Kerr, dated 19 May 1919 and published in *The Collected Writings of John Maynard Keynes*, ed. E. Johnson (Cambridge: Macmillan/Cambridge University Press, 1971), Vol. XVI, pp. 441–2.
10. D.J. Markwell, *John Maynard Keynes and International Relations* (Oxford: Oxford University Press, 2006), p. 93.
11. In a series of private meetings of economists held in Amsterdam in October and November 1919, Keynes unsuccessfully proposed an international currency to facilitate international trade and extend the League's powers so that it provided a forum for economic cooperation. For more on these meetings see Donald Moggridge's account in *Maynard Keynes: An Economist's Biography* (London and New York: Routledge, 1992), pp. 354–5.
12. M. Bromberger and S. Bromberger, *Jean Monnet and the United States of Europe* (New York: Coward-McCann, 1969), p. 19.
13. The term 'globalisation' first appeared in a dictionary in 1961 (Webster's *Third New International Dictionary of the English Language*, unabridged, Springfield, MA: Merriam, p. 965), but took root in the public imagination during the 1980s and the concept is distinguished by attracting a large number of definitions. For the purposes of this book, globalisation refers to the creation of ideas, institutions, rules and norms that have promoted the integration of economies, industries, markets and policymaking around the world. In the interwar period and up until the 1970s, the concept was referred to as 'internationalism', and even 'interdependence'. It was only in common use after the fall of the Berlin Wall, when it developed what seemed to be unstoppable momentum.

1
A better tomorrow

> Now comes the final era by Cumae's Sibyl sung;
> The great order of the ages is born afresh.
> And now justice returns, returns old Saturn's reign;
> With a new breed of men sent down from heaven. (Virgil, *Eclogue*)

The education of a maverick

Wendell Willkie's natural stage was the world, but for a short period during 1940 he settled for running for president of the United States against Franklin Delano Roosevelt, who was seeking an unprecedented third term.

After his defeat, Willkie found a new cause that demanded his attention. As the US entered the war, Willkie worried that Americans were not looking ahead to when the war was won. Having seen the opportunity squandered after the First World War, he set out to convince the public of the necessity of a strong international order to underwrite postwar security and prosperity. His success helped pave the way for the creation of bodies like the United Nations, World Bank and International Monetary Fund, making Willkie an important pioneer in the history of globalisation.

Wendell was born in Elwood, Indiana, on 18 February 1892, to second generation German immigrants, Herman and Henrietta Willkie. When Wendell did not have his nose buried in a book, he was anticipating dinnertime, when everyone sat down to discuss their current reading, debate recent events or explore new ideas. This thirst for knowledge stayed with Wendell, and he remained a voracious reader his whole life.

The father's politics were liberal, which he passed on to his son. From his mother, who carved a career for herself as a lawyer in a male-dominated profession, Wendell acquired his drive and ambition.

His father held a firm view that all his children should learn the value of hard work and self-reliance. Once each child decided where he or she wanted to spend summer vacation, Herman handed them a one-way ticket and twenty dollars, leaving them to fend for themselves for the next two months. Wendell laboured as a vegetable picker in California, worked on a threshing crew in Oklahoma, and sweated on the shop floor of a tinplate factory. Every year he would return home, a little wiser in the ways of the world, but usually with just a few dollars in his pocket. That changed when he got a job as a barker for a flophouse in Aberdeen, South Dakota. Showing a natural aptitude for business, he negotiated a 30 per cent share of the profits. To keep all the beds full, even on slow nights, he dragged in derelicts who paid fifty cents for a bed. That year, he came home with $300 in his pocket.

At Indiana University, where he enrolled on a Bachelor of Arts degree in 1910, rumours spread that he might be a communist when he convinced his economics professor to give a course on the ideas of Karl Marx, Herbert Spencer and Edward Bellamy. He encouraged this fiction when he later famously said, 'Any man who is not something of a socialist before he is forty has no heart. Any man who is still a socialist after forty has no head.'[1] While this comment exemplifies Wendell's self-deprecating humour, there can be little doubt that he never strayed far from classical liberalism. Nevertheless, he remained throughout his life intellectually curious and ready to test his own ideas against those of important thinkers, regardless of their political complexion.

In 1915, Willkie took six months off to earn some money and see something of the world. Landing a job in Puerto Rico, he worked as a chemical analyst on a sugar plantation. During his stay, farm workers went on strike. One day, while out riding with the plantation manager, he witnessed a half-starved worker suddenly emerge from the sugar canes. Wendell watched in horror as the manager hacked at the worker with his cane knife without breaking stride or even interrupting what he was saying to Wendell. Years later, after he had become a wealthy businessman, Willkie would reflect that this incident 'kept him from thinking like a typical American millionaire'.[2]

In the fall, he returned to Indiana University to complete his law degree, graduating in 1916. As luck would have it, his first case pitted him against his father, a veteran attorney of more than twenty-five years. It was a hopeless case, but Wendell gave it his all, addressing the jury for three hours. Afterwards Herman Willkie, with tongue firmly planted in cheek, apologised to the judge: 'I believe that my son will be a very great lawyer. He can make so much out of so little.'[3] The judgment went against the novice lawyer.

Although he enlisted in 1917, Willkie did not see active service. After leaving the army, he married Edith Wilk in 1919 and they settled in Akron, Ohio, where Willkie worked as a trial lawyer.

Public limelight

A liberal Democrat, Willkie found time in the early 1920s to campaign for the League of Nations, delivering hundreds of speeches at schoolhouses, county fairs and street corners. However, he was flogging a dead horse, as interest in the League had waned. He enjoyed more luck with his campaign against racism, helping drive the Ku Klux Klan out of Ohio.

In 1929, Willkie was lured to New York by the chairperson of Commonwealth and Southern, a major utility company, to be its in-house lawyer. By January 1933, he had become president and then, eighteen months later, CEO.

Now in his forties, the relatively young executive stepped into the political arena to challenge Roosevelt's plan to create the Tennessee Valley Authority, which he believed unfairly competed with private enterprise. Willkie proved to be a natural, and the public quickly took to him.

A good-looking man, he possessed pale blue eyes, a square Prussian jaw and black curly hair, which he disdained to keep combed. An inch over six feet and weighing in at 220 pounds, most of it brawn, he exuded a strong physical presence during debates. His secret weapons consisted of his candour, self-effacing wit, subversive intelligence and homespun charm. His charisma seduced those who met him, and according to his friend Stanley Walker, Willkie 'is about as anonymous and inconspicuous as a buffalo bull in a herd of range cattle'.[4]

As war approached, Willkie's attention turned to America's resurging isolationism, which he condemned in speeches and magazine articles. Already well known for his opposition to the New Deal, his name started to crop up as a possible candidate for the 1940 presidential elections. But there existed three major stumbling blocks to his ambition.

First, he had been a Democrat all his adult life, but would certainly lose the nomination against the sitting president, also a Democrat. He solved this problem by switching parties and joining the Republicans in 1939, eighteen months before the election.

The second complication was that he was a businessman, not a well-regarded profession in the wake of the Wall Street crash. Nevertheless, Willkie refused to apologise for his business background. 'I'm in business and proud of it', he declared. 'Nobody can make me soft-pedal any fact in my business career. After all, business is our way of life, our achievement, our glory.'[5]

The final obstacle could not be so easily brushed aside. Since 1937, he had been having an affair with Irita Van Doren, who edited the book review section of the *New York Herald Tribune*. If this affair leaked out, his campaign would sink before it was launched. Willkie, however, did not care. Besotted by Van Doren, he described her in private correspondence as the person 'I admire inordinately and love excessively.'⁶ Their relationship was based on their shared interests in literature and history, and, in time, he came to depend on her advice on political matters. When asked what might happen if news of the affair got out, Willkie shot back that his private life was his own. 'Everybody knows about us – all the newspapermen in New York', he told friends. 'If somebody should come along to threaten or embarrass me about Irita, I would say, "Go right ahead."'⁷

To their credit, Roosevelt and the press kept quiet. The public only became aware of the affair when, in 1948, the film *State of the Union* was released. Directed by Frank Capra, it is loosely based on the 1940 presidential campaign. Willkie is wonderfully portrayed by Spencer Tracy, with Angela Lansbury playing the role of Irita Van Doren. Katherine Hepburn plays Willkie's long-suffering wife (as opposed to real life where she was Tracy's long-suffering mistress). While he courted danger by continuing his affair with Van Doren, she turned out to be a source of strength during the campaign, helping Willkie frame his ideas and polishing his prose and speeches.

On 12 June 1940, Willkie officially announced his candidature before the Washington Press Club. Unwilling to enter the primaries because he had precious little support among traditional Republicans, Willkie decided to wait until the convention to throw his hat into the ring.

As soon as he announced his candidature, James E. Watson, former chairman at the Republican Conference, told him: 'It's all right if the town whore joins the church, but they don't let her lead the choir the first night.'⁸

It was not just Willkie's impudence that got up the noses of Republican stalwarts. He was a free trader in a party of protectionists, a liberal in a predominantly conservative party, a vocal civil rights advocate in a country that had turned a blind eye to the mistreatment of African-Americans, and most remarkably, an internationalist in a party that had championed isolationism for as long as anyone could remember. Moreover, he was the antithesis of a politician in a party of professional politicians. One journalist described him as a 'breath of mountain air in a hot, stale room'.⁹ While he was not popular with the Old Guard of the Republican Party, he was wildly popular with the rank and file, who put pressure on delegates. Against the odds, Willkie saw off his better-credentialed opponents and after six ballots, Willkie secured the nomination.

Once on the campaign trail, Willkie attracted large crowds. What they saw in the GOP candidate was a man who looked anything but presidential. While at the start of each day he was supplied with a new suit and fresh shirt, after a couple of hours, his clothes looked crumpled and his jacket was covered by a fine patina of ash, the result of a 30-cigarettes-a-day habit. This did not necessarily work against him. One newspaper photo captured the essence of the man: it shows Willkie sitting on a platform, waiting his turn to speak, with his legs crossed, revealing a hole in the sole of one of his shoes. For working people who had lived through the Depression, this showed them that Willkie was just a regular guy, thrifty in his habits, and nothing like the well-heeled and well-shod politicians the public expected to find in the Republican Party.

Travelling around the country by train, Willkie was at his worst reading prepared speeches. Despite possessing a splendid, baritone voice, he would stumble over the words, losing his audience in the process. Frustrated, on occasions, he would stop and theatrically throw his unstapled speech into the air, explaining to his audience: 'Some damn fool told me I had to read a speech to you. Now let me tell you what I really think.'[10] This earned him the reputation as a straight shooter, willing to argue for unpopular ideas.

Despite putting together a good campaign, Willkie lost by a shade under 5 million votes.

Over the next few years, Willkie became the unofficial leader of the Republican opposition, unafraid to present his views on the course of the war and the need for formal agreements to consolidate postwar cooperation. He also continued to promote internationalism within the Republican Party, which remained the stronghold for isolationists. In August 1942, as candidates were gearing up for a mid-term election, Willkie called on Republicans to pledge: 'When the war is over, we must set up institutions of international political and economic cooperation and adjustment among nations of the earth' and 'devise some system of joint international force'.[11]

Such support from the other side of the political fence undoubtedly emboldened Roosevelt, who was weighing how ambitious he could be in the new international order, which was being planned within the bureaucracy of his administration.

Global odyssey

Despite beating his Republican opponent in the election, President Franklin Roosevelt held Willkie in high regard. And so, in a meeting held on 7 August 1942, Roosevelt asked Willkie to visit major allied leaders around the world as his personal envoy. While the stated reason was to assess their commitment to the war effort, the president's real objective was to show the world that US foreign policy was bipartisan, and what better way than to have the unofficial leader of the GOP opposition assure its allies that the US was steadfast in their support? FDR also hoped that the trip would arm Willkie with the first-hand knowledge necessary to counter isolationists, who he anticipated would cause problems when his plans for a postwar international order came before the Senate.

Willkie had his own agenda. He intended to use this opportunity to educate himself about the war effort and to publicly voice his own ideas regarding the nature of the postwar world. For these reasons, he insisted on paying all of his own expenses. The government only picked up the tab for the plane and the crew.

Willkie took off from Mitchel Field, New York, on 26 August 1942, on an army air force C-87 christened *Gulliver*. In a trip lasting forty-nine days, he covered 31,000 miles in 160 hours of flying time. During that period, he circled the globe, visiting Africa, the Middle East, Central Asia, Russia and China.

One of his early stops included Ankara, where he immediately ran into trouble when the German government accused Turkey of breaching its neutrality. When Willkie was told that the German authorities had protested his visit, he cheekily replied: 'Invite Hitler to send to Turkey, as a representative of Germany, his opposition candidate.'[12]

The trip also generated an opportunity for Willkie to describe his ideas of the postwar world order and to assure allies that the US bore no hegemonic ambitions. Giving a press conference before leaving Ankara, he explained his position:

> I think the American people are looking for a peace of no territorial conquest, a peace in which the basic raw materials of the world are made available to all nations, and that the old idea of isolation and a disregard for other countries will pass out. They feel that small nations as well as large must have the right to aspire to democracy.[13]

With some variations, he repeated this message throughout his odyssey.

In the Soviet Union, he met twice with Stalin, whom Willkie described as 'a hard man, perhaps a cruel man, but an able man'.[14] Willkie made a favourable impression on Stalin, who described his American guest as 'a plain-speaking man'.[15] They got on well, in no part due to Willkie's ability to put away fifty-three vodkas at a banquet at the Kremlin, where the American guest showed Stalin that he could not be bested in a drinking contest.

His next stop was China, where Generalissimo Chiang Kai-shek hosted Willkie at his wartime capital, Chungking (modern Chongqing). Willkie soon fell under the spell of Soong May-ling, the stunningly beautiful wife of his host. After excusing themselves from a banquet, they disappeared to her secret penthouse apartment. At 9 p.m. a furious Generalissimo, accompanied by three bodyguards toting tommy guns, searched Willkie's apartments, much to the alarm of Gardner 'Mike' Cowles, who shared accommodations with Willkie. After opening closets and peering under beds, the cuckolded husband left in a huff. Cowles could not sleep and stayed up drinking scotch. He was relieved when Willkie slipped in at 4 a.m. as 'cocky as a young college student after a successful night with a girl'.[16] Without further incident, Willkie left China on 9 October, flying across the Gobi Desert to southern Siberia, then to Alaska, Edmonton, and back home.

As a diplomatic mission, Willkie's trip was a splendid success. He certainly left a favourable impression with most of those he met, from the highest in the land to ordinary folks in the street, whom he particularly made an effort to seek out. He displayed bravery visiting the front whenever the opportunity arose, and on state occasions, he both unsettled seasoned diplomats and charmed his hosts by his plain speaking and sense of humour.

A day after his return, Willkie conferred with FDR in the White House. 'I know that you are president and you could throw me out', Willkie told Roosevelt, 'but until you do I'm going to say a few things to you and you are going to listen'.[17] Willkie was not asked to leave, but the discussion sometimes heated up, as Willkie used the occasion to tell the president some home truths about his conduct of the war.

Selling 'One World'

On 26 October 1942, Willkie delivered a half-hour 'Report to the People'. Broadcast over four national radio networks, it reached an audience of around 36 million listeners. In undoubtedly his greatest speech, he used this opportunity to share his dream of a global unity.

> There are no distant points in the world any longer. The myriad millions of human beings [in] the Far East are as close to us as Los Angeles is to New York by the fastest railway trains. I cannot escape the conviction that in the future what concerns them must concern us, almost as much as the problems of the people of California concern the people of New York. Our thinking and planning in the future must be global.[18]

He ended by daring his audience 'to accept the most challenging opportunity of all history – the chance to help create a new society in which men and women the globe around can live and grow invigorated by freedom'.[19]

The speech had an immediate impact. Journalist and playwright, Clare Boothe Luce, said, 'Last night the world heard the message of a global Abraham Lincoln.' Renowned newspaper editor, politician, and author, William Allen White, commended Willkie for his courage to speak out against colonialism: 'For the first time in human history, the major leader of the great Republic spoke out specifically, naming names of nations and races, and demanding in terms definite and certain, freedom for all mankind.' The *Christian Science Monitor*, unaware that one was a fictional character, claimed, 'Mr. Willkie's trip may turn out to be more important than Phineas Fogg's and Marco Polo's put together.'[20]

After this broadcast, friends urged Willkie to put his ideas into a book. With the help of Irita Van Doren, he produced a lively account of his trip, with descriptions of exotic locations, fascinating vignettes, vivid pen pictures of his encounters with world leaders, including Joseph Stalin, Zhou Enlai and Charles de Gaulle, and acute analyses of the political situations in the countries he visited.

The book, *One World*, was published by Simon and Schuster on 8 April 1943, quickly becoming a bestseller. Its initial print run of 40,000 copies sold out within forty-eight hours and over the next seven weeks it sold 1 million copies. By the end of the year it had reached the 2 million mark, topping the *New York Times* bestseller's list from May to September. Eventually, *One World* sold 3 million copies, breaking all records for a nonfiction book. A digest version was published in several national magazines and syndicated in 107 daily newspapers.

One World was translated into major foreign languages, and copies of it were smuggled into occupied Europe and distributed by the Underground. Future Indian prime minister, Jawaharlal Nehru, read Willkie's book while in jail, and, after his release, told a radio audience in 1946, 'It is for this *One World* that free India will work, a world in which there is the free cooperation of free people, and no class or group exploits another.'[21] After he became prime minister, Nehru held hopes that the United Nations would, one day, be transformed into 'One World'.[22] No other book produced during the war years resonated with a truly international audience.

The book was also an opportunity to present his ideas for the new global order, so at the end of this narrative, Willkie developed the theme that 'men's welfare throughout the world is interdependent'.[23] While using *One World* articles and speeches to proselytise for a new world order, Willkie did not try to offer a blueprint. All he wanted to do was sell the message that peace and prosperity would be delivered by a liberal international order, based on political and economic cooperation between free and democratic nations.

Central to his vision of a new international order was a permanent body. '[T]he United Nations must become a common council', he argued, 'for the future welfare of mankind', which would 'sit in common council of strategy, of common economic welfare, of planning for the future'.[24] This central institution would govern the new order. What made it new was 'the creation of a world in which there shall be an equality of opportunity for every race and every nation'.[25] Behind this simple statement is a very subversive idea. The new order would not be based on power, like the old order, but would treat all nations alike.

Knowing how sensitive Americans were about their sovereignty, Willkie addressed this issue in an article that appeared in *Foreign Affairs* in April 1944.

> I want to see our Government and people use the sovereign power of the United States in partnership with the sovereignty powers of other peace-loving nations to create and operate an international organization which will give better protection to the rights of all nations, on a wider political, economic and social basis, than has ever yet been attempted in history.

In this article he went on to make the case for a permanent international body that could exercise effective authority, which would require its members to turn their backs on 'sterile formulas of exclusive national sovereignty'.[26]

To support his case, he pointed out that the two world wars of the twentieth century proved that every country was vulnerable in global instability, and therefore pooling sovereignty was the only way to guarantee political stability, peace and prosperity. For any international organisation to protect collective rights, Willkie argued, it would need to 'use force to maintain the rule of law'.[27]

Willkie also pursued another important principle: the new order needed to be based on cooperation between free people, which meant dismantling colonialism. Dismissing vague assurances of reform once the war was won, Willkie wanted firm timetables produced without delay, accompanied by 'ironclad guarantees, administered by all the United Nations jointly, [so] that they shall not slip back into colonial status'.[28]

During his trip, Willkie had discovered a 'reservoir of goodwill' towards America 'built on confidence in us, in our integrity of purpose, our honesty in dealing, our ability in performance'. This led him to conclude that the US was the only country with the moral authority to take the lead, and he hoped his country would fulfil its destiny of 'creating a new society, global in scope'.[29] Willkie also clarified that American leadership did not mean US hegemony based on a new sort of global imperialism. To counter this threat, Willkie hoped that the United Nations would 'safeguard the rights of small nations'.[30]

The other pillar of Willkie's vision of *One World* was the need for free trade between nations.

> Economic freedom is as important as political freedom. Not only must people have access to what other peoples produce, but their own products must in turn have some chance of reaching men all over the world. There will be no peace, there will be no real development, there will be no economic stability, unless we find the method by which we can begin to break down the unnecessary trade barriers hampering the flow of goods.[31]

Willkie was not the only voice advocating a new order, but he was one of the loudest and most effective. And it paid off. By early 1944, the tide was turning sharply towards liberal internationalism. A Gallup Poll showed that 74 per cent of the American public supported 'a world organization with police power to maintain world peace',[32] and even vocal isolationist leaders in the Republican Party, Taft and Vandenberg in particular, were ready to entertain the creation of some sort of international organisation.

Willkie's legacy is particularly notable because he emerged as an effective salesman of *One World*. Through his speeches and writings, Willkie helped attract public support for the creation of the postwar international order, which saw the establishment of institutions like the United Nations, the International Monetary Fund and the World Bank.

Sadly, Willkie never lived to see the blossoming of the postwar economic and political order. He died of a massive coronary thrombosis on 8 October 1944, at just fifty-two years of age.

Notes

1 Wendell Willkie quoted by Roscoe Drummond in 'Wendell Willkie, a Study in courage', from *The Aspirin Age, 1919–41*, ed. Isabel Leighton (New York: Simon and Schuster, 1949), p. 447.
2 J. Barnes, *Wendell Willkie* (New York: Simon and Schuster, 1952), p. 28.
3 E. Barnard, *Wendell Willkie: Fighter for Freedom* (Marquette, Michigan: Northern Michigan University Press, 1966), p. 46.
4 S. Walker, 'This is Wendell Willkie: A Biographical Introduction', in *This is Wendell Willkie*, a collection of Willkie's speeches and writings (New York: Dodd, Mead & Company, 1940), p. 37.
5 J. Barnes, *Wendell Willkie*, p. 165.
6 J.H. Madison, 'Thinking about Wendell Willkie', in *Wendell Willkie – Hoosier Internationalist*, ed. J.H. Madison (Bloomington: Indiana University Press, 1992), p. xv.
7 S. Neal, *Dark Horse* (New York: Doubleday & Co., 1984), pp. 43–4.
8 S. Neal, *Dark Horse*, p. 89.
9 J.M. Jordan, 'A Small World of Little Americans: The $1 Diplomacy of Wendell Willkie's One World', *Indiana Magazine of History*, 88:3 (1992), 173–204.
10 J. Barnes, *Wendell Willkie*, p. 168.
11 Wendell Willkie quoted by Stewart Patrick in *The Best Laid Plans* (Lanham, Maryland: Rowman & Littlefield Publishers, 2009), p. 61.
12 W.L. Willkie, *One World* (New York: Simon and Schuster, 1943), p. 38.
13 S. Neal, *Dark Horse*, p. 238.

14 W.L. Willkie, *One World*, p. 83.
15 E. Barnard, *Wendell Willkie*, pp. 359–60.
16 G. Cowles, *Mike Looks Back: The Memoirs of Gardner Cowles, Founder of Look Magazine* (New York: Gardner Cowles, 1985), pp. 88–9.
17 M.E. Dillion, *Wendell Willkie 1892–1944* (New York: Da Capo Press, 1972), p. 288.
18 W.L. Willkie, 'Report to the American People: Our Reservoir of World Respect and Hope', *Vital Speeches of the Day*, 9:2 (1942), 35–9.
19 W.L. Willkie, 'Report to the American People', 39
20 Quotes taken from Steve Neal's *Dark Horse*, p. 261.
21 Jawaharlal Nehru, broadcast from New Delhi when Nehru was president of the Indian National Congress delivered on 7 September 1946 in New Delhi. Reprinted in *India's Foreign Policy, Selected Speeches, September 1946–April 1961* (Delhi: Government of India, 1946), p. 2.
22 Jawaharlal Nehru, broadcast from Lake Success, New York on the United Nations Radio network, delivered on May 5, 1950. Reprinted in *India's Foreign Policy, Selected Speeches, September 1946–April 1961* (Delhi: Government of India, 1950), pp. 167–8.
23 W.L. Willkie, *One World*, p. 2.
24 W.L. Willkie, *One World*, p. 145.
25 W.L. Willkie, *One World*, p. 165.
26 W.L. Willkie, 'Our Sovereignty: Shall We Use It?', *Foreign Affairs*, 22:3 (1944), 347–61.
27 W.L. Willkie, 'Our Sovereignty', 347–61.
28 W.L. Willkie, *One World*, p. 150.
29 W.L. Willkie, 'Report to the American People', 35–9.
30 W.L. Willkie, 'Fiscal Program for War and Post-War Period', speech delivered 2 February 1944 in New York City. It was the first of a series of three meetings under the general title of 'America Plans and Dreams', arranged by *The New York Times*.
31 W.L. Willkie, *One World*, p. 167.
32 G.H. Gallup (ed.), *The Gallup Poll: Public Opinion 1935–1971* (New York: Random House, 1972), Vol. 1, pp. 387–8.

2

Last best hope for peace

> For I dipt into the future, far as human eye could see.
> Saw a Vision of the world, and all the wonder that would be ...
> Till the war-drum throbb'd no longer and the battle-flags were furled
> In the Parliament of man, the Federation of the world.
> There the common sense of most shall hold a fretful realm in awe,
> And the kindly earth shall slumber lapped in universal law. (Tennyson, *Locksley Hall*)

The invisible man

When the United Nations was created at an international meeting in San Francisco in the summer of 1945, its principal architect was just about invisible. He liked it that way.

Leo Pasvolsky was one of the United States government's main planners for the postwar world and 'probably the foremost author of the UN Charter', concluded historian Stephen Schlesinger.[1] Senator Tom Connally, a member of the US negotiating team, wrote in his memoirs: 'Certainly he [Pasvolsky] had more to do with writing the framework of the charter than anyone else.'[2] Joe Johnson, who worked at the State Department, said, 'there is no question in my own mind, no question at all, that the Charter is more Leo's document than it is anybody else's'.[3] Another State Department insider, Easton Rothwell, remarked:

> the idea of a new international organization at the end of the war came up as soon as we were in the war, actually before we got in, in the mind of Leo Pasvolsky. And the real architect of the United Nations is not Franklin Roosevelt. It's not Cordell Hull [secretary of state]. Leo Pasvolsky was the man who did it.[4]

While Pasvolsky is credited as the principal architect of the United Nations, he would not have succeeded without the commitment of President Roosevelt, patronage of Secretary of State Cordell Hull[5] and political support of influential senators – Arthur Vandenberg, a Republican and Tom Connally, a Democrat – who shepherded the United Nations Charter through the Senate in 1945.

It is a quirk of history that while the creation of the United Nations was chiefly an American project, its leading architect was a White Russian émigré.

Leo was born in Pavlograd (now part of the Ukraine) on 22 August 1893. His father, a historian, was expelled from Russia in 1905 for opposing the Czarist regime. The Pasvolsky family made its way to Philadelphia, where Leo excelled at school. In 1916, he gained admittance to the College of the City of New York, where he majored in economics. He then went on to study political science at Columbia University.

A talented journalist, Pasvolsky freelanced for several US newspapers during a trip he took through Europe after the First World War. Arriving in Paris in the winter of 1919, the young journalist suffered badly, owning just one pair of thin French kid shoes that did little to keep out the cold. His assignment with the *New York Tribune* was to cover the Paris peace conference, which turned out to be a formative experience, as were his observations of Woodrow Wilson's campaign to create the League of Nations. As a result of what he heard, Pasvolsky became a Wilsonian internationalist, joining the American Peace Society and attending annual meetings of the League of Nations.

Tiring of journalism, in 1922 Pasvolsky became an economist on the staff of the Brookings Institution (then called the Institute of Economics). At Brookings, Pasvolsky attacked isolationism, which dominated US policy during the 1920s and 1930s. His research argued that America would benefit from integrating its economy with the rest of the world.

Pasvolsky's articles on free trade brought him to the attention of Secretary of State Cordell Hull, who had long campaigned to reduce tariffs. Pasvolsky had the expertise that Hull was looking for. Having spent most of his career in Tennessee county courthouses and then as an up-and-coming politician in Washington, Hull's knowledge of international affairs was shallow, and he came to depend on Pasvolsky. 'Pasvolsky was the perfect public servant for Hull, endowed with a sharp analytical talent, a non-confrontational but principled personality, a library-like mind on global issues, a faith in free trade, and a passion to remain invisible', observed Stephen Schlesinger.[6]

Hull affectionately called Pasvolsky his 'Friar Tuck', an apt description of a man who was five foot six inches tall and weighed in at just under 200 pounds. He possessed an almost perfectly spherical face with a neat moustache and wore horn-rimmed glasses with thick lenses. A colleague referred to him as 'a round-eyed, round-tummied, little owl-like man ... An ostrich egg with a billiard ball on top of it.'[7] Constantly sucking on his pipe, Pasvolsky possessed a puckish sense of humour.

After working for Hull for two years, in 1936, Pasvolsky returned to the Brookings Institute. In the summer of 1939, as Pasvolsky was holidaying in

Maine, Hull surprised him with a phone call: 'Leo, ... they tell me I'm a damn fool ..., but I think Europe is going to have a war, and I think it's very important for US to be prepared for our role in relation to that war, and I want you to come back to Washington and work with me on postwar planning.'[8]

With an office next door to Hull's, Pasvolsky was in and out all day long. He used his privileged access to convince Hull that permanent peace required more than free trade, and that he should also explore international political arrangements that might avoid future conflicts. As a result of these discussions, on 16 September 1939, Hull appointed Pasvolsky his special assistant primarily to work on problems of peace.

Realising that he needed to build expertise and commitment within the Department, Pasvolsky convinced Hull to create a committee to explore the principles that would 'underlie a desirable world order'.[9] The result was the Advisory Committee on the Problems of Foreign Relations. It was succeeded by a number of other committees, all with similarly uninformative names, to keep the project secret. It was within these committees that the architecture of the United Nations took shape. While the composition of these committees changed, Pasvolsky remained a constant, using his close relationship with Hull to get his way, as Donald C. Blaisdell, who worked in the State Department between 1941 and 1947, observed:

> Leo Pasvolsky was pretty much writing his own ticket, that Hull was philosophically disposed to this whole idea, but that he wasn't particularly interested in it. International cooperation was a shibboleth of Cordell Hull I think. I don't think he really understood, or was very much interested in what this really involved, in terms of American sovereignty or American independence, and I think FDR [President Franklin Roosevelt] was so absorbed with winning the war that he was glad to have somebody give attention to this postwar period, but as long as it was under Cordell Hull, and then after Hull left it was Ed Stettinius [Hull's successor as secretary of state], well, that was all right.[10]

By the time the United Nations was a reality, Pasvolsky was accepted as its unchallenged architect, but he had to fight off a rival within the State Department, and the history of the United Nations might have been quite different had he not prevailed.

Competing dreams

If Pasvolsky was the invisible architect of the United Nations, Sumner Welles might be considered its forgotten architect. As Hull's undersecretary, Welles dominated policy formulation in the State Department, often putting him at odds with Pasvolsky.

By all rights Welles should have triumphed. He was close to Roosevelt, who had little time for Hull or the advice coming from the State Department. In addition, the relationship between Welles and Roosevelt went back some way. In the fall of 1905, the twelve-year-old Sumner was page boy at the wedding of Eleanor and Franklin, where he carried the bride's train as she walked down the aisle. He was chosen because his mother was a good friend of Eleanor's mother, a connection further strengthened when he shared a room at Groton School with Eleanor's brother. Coming from a wealthy family, Welles, like Roosevelt, was part of the east coast aristocracy, and they shared similar liberal values.

After graduating from Harvard, where he studied economics, Iberian literature and culture, Welles asked Roosevelt, who was then assistant secretary of the navy, to lend him a hand with his career. On 15 March 1915, Roosevelt wrote to Secretary of State William Jennings Bryan to put in a good word for Welles: 'I have known [Welles] since he was a small boy and have seen him go through school and college, and I should be most glad to see him successful in entering the Diplomatic Corps.'[11]

Welles may have depended on contacts to ease his way into the State Department, but once in, his ability saw him move up quickly.

His career came to a sudden stop, however, when he made the mistake of having an affair with Mathilde Scott Townsend, the wife of Senator Peter Gerry, who happened to be a good friend of President Coolidge. After a messy divorce, Welles married Mathilde in 1925, prompting the president to end his diplomatic career. Independently wealthy, Welles retired to his forty-nine room 'country cottage' known as Oxon Hill Manor in Maryland, where he devoted himself to writing a two-volume history of the Dominican Republic, *Naboth's Vineyard*, which appeared in 1928. He also provided Roosevelt with foreign policy advice in the run-up to the 1932 presidential election, as well as allowing him to use Oxon Hill for weekend escapades with one of his mistresses.

Welles returned to the State Department in 1933 after Roosevelt was elected president, and on 20 May 1937, FDR appointed Welles undersecretary of state, which made him Hull's deputy.

It did not take Hull long to develop a strong dislike for his ambitious deputy, and they often clashed, with Welles railing against Hull's conservatism, while Hull despised Welles's habit of bypassing him and briefing the president directly. The result was a house divided against itself, with cliques coalescing around the two rivals within the State Department. Dean Acheson, who worked at the State Department at the time and would eventually become secretary of state under

President Truman, described the toxic atmosphere that descended on the State Department:

> Suspicious by nature, he [Hull] brooded over what he thought were slights and grievances, which more forthright handling might have set straight. His brooding led, in accordance with Tennessee-mountain tradition, to feuds. His hatreds were implacable – not hot hatreds, but long cold ones. In no hurry to 'get' his enemy, 'get' him he usually did.[12]

While Hull and Welles often clashed, Hull's bouts of illness put him at a disadvantage. He often took time off to recuperate from sarcoidosis (a respiratory infection similar to tuberculosis) and had no choice but to leave Welles in charge, which gave his deputy ample opportunities to run his own show.

Within this poisonous environment, Pasvolsky and Welles battled to shape the successor to the League of Nations, with Hull and Roosevelt playing cameo roles.

Unlike Pasvolsky, Sumner Welles was anything but invisible. At six foot three inches, ramrod straight and slim, he cut a regal figure, possessing 'such irreproachable punctilio that he is rumoured to have been christened in a top hat'.[13] Fastidiously groomed, he was described as a 'powerfully-built, beautifully tailored man with the glacial manner, and an expression which suggests that a morsel of bad fish has somehow or other lodged itself in his moustache'.[14] *Time* magazine compared him to a 'tall glass of distilled ice water,' while a fellow diplomat observed that 'even his blond mustache looks cold'.[15] Despite his lack of human warmth, even his detractors recognised that Welles had a first-class brain, the courage to pursue bold ideas and excelled at his job. But when he was crossed, his adversary would find himself stealthily 'stabbed to the heart with an icicle'.[16]

One area of conflict was over the shape of the United Nations, where Hull relied heavily on the advice of Pasvolsky. While Pasvolsky may not have possessed the silky-smooth skills or political connections of Welles, intellectually, he could more than hold his own and, as an accomplished chess player, could turn most situations around to his advantage.

Pasvolsky felt particularly unhappy with Welles's model, in which the new international body would be structured around a number of regional bodies: the Americas, East Asia, Europe, the British Commonwealth and the Near East. Instead, Pasvolsky advocated a universalist model, with all countries belonging to a single body. Structuring global security around regional groups, Pasvolsky warned, would give license to 'large states with their spheres of influence surrounded by groups of smaller states', and friction between these blocs, he feared, could trigger the next war.[17]

Pasvolsky pointed to other problems with the regional model. With the US closely linked to the western hemisphere, it might encourage isolationists to oppose its engagement with the wider world. Pasvolsky was also concerned that within the European region, the Soviet Union would dominate, with neither Great Britain nor France able to challenge its hegemony. Finally, the regional structure would see the rise of local trading blocs, which would soon be at war with one another.

This debate was not settled quickly, with Hull taking Pasvolsky's side in the debate, while Roosevelt vacillated between the two models. Its outcome, however, would play a major role in the future successes and failures of the United Nations.

Constructing the peace

The first step to creating the United Nations, although at this stage the new organisation had no name, occurred in Argentia Bay off Newfoundland where Roosevelt met Winston Churchill in the summer of 1941. Although the US was neutral, it was providing war materials to Great Britain, whose back was up against the wall. Roosevelt wanted the meeting to lock in the aims of the war and start discussions on what the postwar world might look like.

Hull was infuriated when the president chose to take Welles rather than him, but for Roosevelt the choice was not difficult. 'One, I trust him [Welles] ... Two, he doesn't argue with me. Three, he gets things done.'[18] His faith was rewarded when Welles was able to navigate some difficult issues to come up with words that satisfied all parties.

On 14 August, both leaders committed to the Atlantic Charter, which presented a liberal vision of the postwar world based on global economic cooperation, lower trade barriers, improved labour standards and disarmament. One clause of the Charter called for a 'permanent system of general security',[19] a deliberately vague euphemism for some future world body. In earlier drafts, Welles had wanted a more specific commitment to an 'effective international organization', but Roosevelt removed this phrase because he did not want to show his hand quite yet, knowing it would provoke isolationists and raise the hackles of his enemies in Congress.[20]

On 7 December 1941, the Japanese attacked Pearl Harbor, ending US neutrality. For Great Britain this was a godsend, coming at a time when the Nazis were getting on top, and it desperately needed the support of its new ally. On 22 December, Churchill arrived in Washington together with his military chiefs to discuss grand strategy, command structure and armaments production.

During their private meetings, the two leaders agreed to create an international body, which would secure the peace once the war was won. Churchill preferred to keep the name League of Nations, but Roosevelt felt it was unwise because the new organisation would then be associated with its predecessor's failures. But could he come up with a better name? According to an entry from his personal secretary Margaret 'Daisy' Suckley's diary, Roosevelt showed that he was up to the challenge:

> 'FDR got into his bed, his mind working & working,' she recorded. 'Suddenly he got it – United Nations! The next morning, the minute he had finished his breakfast, he got onto his chair & was wheeled up the hall to W.S.C.'s [Churchill's] room. He knocked on the door, no answer, so he opened the door & went in and sat on a chair & the man went out & closed the door. He called to W.S.C. & in the door leading to the bathroom appeared W.S.C., "a pink cherub" (FDR said), drying himself with a towel & without a stitch on! FDR pointed at him & exploded: "The United Nations!" "*Good*!" said W.S.C.'.[21]

On New Year's Day 1942, the Soviet Union and twenty-two allied nations endorsed the Atlantic Charter in a 'Declaration by the United Nations', marking the first public airing of the new name. However, this name was freely used to refer collectively to the allied powers, although internally it was also to be the name of the new international organisation.

During 1942, planning for the UN progressed steadily. On 29 May 1942, Roosevelt floated the idea of a two-tier structure with the Soviet foreign minister, Vyacheslav Molotov. Acting as the 'four policemen', the US, USSR, Great Britain and possibly China would maintain sufficient armed force to curb aggression. Three days later, Stalin approved the proposal, which became, with some modifications, the basis of the Security Council.[22]

Having handed the task of planning the new international organisation to the State Department, Roosevelt was not happy with reports that Hull and Welles did not get on. This affected work within the State Department, as these two men competed to shape the UN.

Their relationship reached a new low when Hull read a flattering profile of Welles that appeared in *Time* magazine on 11 August 1942. It reported that 'in the War of Brains, he [Welles] is a field marshal', while a passing mention of Hull referred to him as being 'rich in guile'. It concluded that Welles was the obvious choice to take over from the ailing Hull as secretary of state.[23] What remaining civility that existed between the two men quickly disappeared, with Hull barely on speaking terms with 'that polecat in the next room'.[24]

For Hull, 1942 was not a good year. His periods away from Washington convalescing grew longer, and he missed almost six months, leaving the field open to Welles, who had used this opportunity to stamp his ideas on the United Nations. Work had advanced to the point that on 19 June, Welles was able to present the 'Draft Constitution of the International Organization' to Roosevelt.

Soon after, Hull returned to the State Department and asked Pasvolsky to revise the draft. The most significant amendment to Welles's draft was the removal of regionalism, but otherwise Pasvolsky's changes were cosmetic. This win did not satisfy Hull. He was determined to get rid of his troublesome deputy, and he believed he knew just how to accomplish it.

Hull's chance to nail Welles came when, in late 1942, he heard of a scandal involving his deputy. It was an old rumour, but if true, would destroy Welles. On 18 September 1940, during a train ride from Alabama, Welles had been drinking heavily. At 4 a.m. he left the dining car for his sleeping quarters and, according to historian Irwin Gellman, Welles began 'to ring his service bell. When a Negro porter answered, the drunken Under Secretary offered him money to commit homosexual acts. The shaken attendant rejected this proposition, but his rebuff did not stop Welles from repeating his call several times. Only when none of the porters would accept his advances, did the buzzing finally stop.'[25] Welles had breached two taboos: homosexuality and sex that crossed racial lines, with the latter being the more unforgiveable in America at that time.

Hull approached FBI director, J. Edgar Hoover, on 24 October 1942, who confirmed that he had damning evidence on Welles. With the file in his possession, true to form, Hull procrastinated. What tipped him over the edge was a front-page article that appeared in the *New York Times* on 4 August 1943, blaming the State Department's 'sluggishness' on Hull's administrative failings and inability to deliver a 'cohesive policy'. Evidently based on a leak (Hull suspected Welles was the source), the article further suggested that such was the contempt for Hull that subordinates referred to him by an 'odious epithet'.[26]

On 10 August 1943, Hull confronted Roosevelt and demanded that he sack Welles, leaving the president in a quandary. He had to make a choice between Welles, who was quick-witted, energetic, bold and in tune with the president's thinking, or his secretary of state, who was elderly, conservative and constantly frustrating his plans. Moreover, Welles was a friend, and Roosevelt believed (being a fellow Groton old-boy) that drunkenness could excuse the most disgraceful behaviour. But Hull, Roosevelt knew, was extraordinarily popular with the public, and he needed Hull's influence over southern Democrats to smooth the way for his policy agenda. The next day Roosevelt told Welles of his conversation with Hull and suggested he become a special envoy for the president, but did not demand his resignation. On 14 August, Welles suffered a heart attack and two days later decided that his position was untenable and resigned. While

Welles was recuperating, Hull 'called James Reston, the rising star of the *New York Times*, and offered to leak him the Southern Railway affidavits about Welles, but Reston walked out, disgusted'.[27]

Ed Stettinius replaced Welles as undersecretary. A businessman who had done a good job administering the Lend-Lease programme, he claimed little background in international affairs. Unlike Welles, Stettinius possessed neither the knowledge nor the inclination to become involved in shaping the UN. As a result, Pasvolsky had the field to himself, and it was his draft of the UN's constitution that provided the basis for future negotiations between the Great Powers.[28] It is a moot point of how much of this draft owes its authorship to Welles, to whom history has been unkind, giving all the credit to Pasvolsky.

On the domestic front, Roosevelt's willingness to stand by Hull, despite his unhappiness with Hull's performance as secretary of state, was about to pay off. Using his credibility with senators, Hull convinced leading Republicans and Democrats, whose support would prove essential if the treaty was to sail through the Senate, to join the Administration's negotiating team. Hull astutely picked out legislators who were well-regarded on Capitol Hill. Senators Tom Connally (D-Texas) and Arthur Vandenberg (R-Michigan), in particular, were key players.

During a summit held in Moscow in October 1943, Great Britain, the USSR and the US made a commitment to 'the necessity of establishing at the earliest practicable date a general international organisation, based on the principle of the sovereign equality of all peace-loving states'.[29]

This was followed up by a meeting at Dumbarton Oaks, an estate just outside Washington, between 21 August and 7 October 1944, which negotiated the main components of the postwar collective security system. This time, China was included.[30] Unfortunately, Hull's health was still poor, and after opening the conference, he let Stettinius take over under the watchful eye of Pasvolsky. At this meeting, all parties agreed that the UN would consist of a General Assembly, with universal membership, which would serve as a forum for debate, and a smaller Security Council, with the Great Powers providing the military muscle to enforce the peace.

One of the more contentious issues was whether the Great Powers could veto decisions of the UN. Britain argued strongly that if the new system was to attract the adherence of the other countries, the veto should only be used in restricted circumstances and not, for example, in situations to which a Security Council member was a party. The Soviet Union, on the other hand, maintained that right to veto should apply to all activity in the Security Council. The US, although initially undecided, eventually yielded to an unrestrained veto because

Roosevelt knew that the Senate would not support a measure that allowed US troops to be called out by an external body. To Roosevelt's credit, he had originally floated the proposal that the Great Powers should refrain from voting on disputes to which they were a party. This would counter accusations that the Great Powers would be treated differently. Stalin, however, insisted that all permanent members of the Security Council would have an unqualified veto, and Roosevelt caved in. In the end, the conference decided that all decisions of the Security Council would need unanimity by the Great Powers, effectively providing them with a veto.

Other important parts of the package were the creation of an Economic and Social Council and an International Court of Justice.

With most of the issues ironed out, Churchill, Roosevelt and Stalin decided to invite the other allied powers to San Francisco, where the final Charter would be approved.

In the fall of 1944, Hull's health took a turn for the worse and he was bedridden. Told by his doctors that he was unlikely to recover, on 30 November 1944, Hull resigned and Stettinius took his place. According to one State Department insider, Joe Johnston, 'Ed Stettinius made up his mind that he was going down in history as the guy who established the United Nations. He did not then, and never till the day of his death, fully understood the United Nations. He was not an intellectual.'[31]

As Stettinius prepared to take centre stage in the greatest role of his career, he would have been well advised to take heed of an aphorism quoted by Churchill as a warning of the challenges ahead in San Francisco: 'The eagle should permit the small birds to sing and care not wherefore they sang.'[32]

The small birds sing

The final act in the creation of the UN in San Francisco was to put flesh on the Dumbarton Oaks' skeleton. True to Churchill's prediction, the small to medium countries (referred to as the Lesser Powers) cooed, chirped, twittered and squawked, excited by the package the Great Powers put before them. But they also saw room for improvement.

Even before proceedings commenced, plans were thrown into disarray when Roosevelt died suddenly of a massive cerebral haemorrhage. Just thirteen days before the conference was to open, the US found that it had a new president. Although Harry Truman had not played any role in the negotiations and knew little of the issues to be debated, he decided to allow the conference to go ahead, making no changes to the plans made by his predecessor.

The US delegation was led by Stettinius, who leaned heavily on Pasvolsky to manage the policy and technical issues thrown up during the conference.

As the conference progressed, the spirits of participants were buoyed by news of successive German defeats as the Allies sped towards Berlin. Midway through the conference, peace was declared in Europe. These victories made the task of fashioning the postwar world more pressing, and delegates took to the task with gusto.

Whenever a difficult problem arose at the conference, the heads of the Great Powers would meet privately in Stettinius's penthouse suite on the fourth floor of the Fairmont Hotel, where they decided whether an amendment was acceptable. They seldom, however, accepted any change that substantially varied from the agreement they had reached at Dumbarton Oaks.

The most serious challenge was to the veto the Great Powers could exercise. A sizeable number of smaller nations, led by Herbert 'Doc' Evatt, the irascible foreign minister from Australia, argued that this privilege breached the principle of sovereign equality between members of the UN. In a tense confrontation, Senator Connally explained that if the UN intended to depend on the Great Powers, the US in particular, to keep the peace, then they should have the right to veto the use of their troops against their will. This was a deal-breaker, Connally explained in no uncertain terms. '[H]ere we are, come together in this beautiful city of San Francisco to reach an agreement on the United Nations Charter and wouldn't it be a damn shame if we had to go home without one.'[33] Connally's threat worked, and the Australian amendment was defeated 20 to 10, with fifteen abstentions and five countries absent.

While the Great Powers presented a united front, when it came to matters they had agreed to at Dumbarton Oaks, some in the US delegation still had misgivings. Vandenberg, for example, noted in his diary: 'The veto bizzness [sic] is making it very difficult to maintain any semblance of a fiction of "sovereign equality" among the nations here at Frisco.'[34]

Another challenge came from a powerful bloc of Latin American countries. They wanted to incorporate a strong regional structure into the UN, which would consolidate the authority of the Pan-American Union. This represented a rehash of the scheme promoted by Welles. Opposed by Pasvolsky, it nevertheless enjoyed support from some members of the US delegation, led by Nelson Rockefeller, assistant secretary for Latin America in the State Department, and Senator Vandenberg. Pasvolsky held firm, attacking regionalism, which he claimed would mean that 'the world organization is finished' because it 'will convert the world into armed camps and end up with a world war unlike any we have yet seen'.[35]

The conference was rescued from disaster by a face-saving compromise drafted by Pasvolsky that allowed regional pacts, provided they were solely devoted to self-defence and their activities were consistent with the purposes of the UN itself. Pasvolsky appeared to have walked away with a major victory, but history suggests that the laurels should have gone to Welles.[36]

This compromise opened a loophole that saw the creation of a number of regional military alliances, which went against the spirit of the UN, as it was originally conceived. By 1955, the North Atlantic Treaty Organization (NATO), Warsaw Pact, Organization of American States (OAS), and South East Asia Treaty Organization (SEATO) populated the security terrain. Ironically, Pasvolsky's own amendment helped undermine his universalist model. An argument could be made that Sumner Welles's regional model prevailed and, as Pasvolsky predicted, divided the world into spheres of influence.

Once the dust had cleared from the battles fought on the conference floor, participants believed that the final Charter offered a real chance for durable peace. On 26 June, fifty countries signed the Charter, with a space left for Poland, which had no government at the time and would sign later. While the Axis powers were not initially included, once they signed peace treaties they were admitted to the UN.

After the closing ceremony, the conference's secretary general, Alger Hiss, escorted the new UN Charter back to Washington for safekeeping until the UN acquired its own building where the Charter would be permanently housed. On the flight, Hiss realised his own importance, as he wryly remarked later: '[S]ince the Charter was so valuable it had a parachute attached to it – and I didn't!'[37]

The next major hurdle involved ratification by the US Senate, whose opposition had sunk the League of Nations in 1919. This time around, the Roosevelt Administration had consulted widely, and former isolationists had been included in the US delegation to San Francisco, notably Vandenberg, Connally and Thomas Dewey.

On 28 July 1945, the UN treaty sailed through the Senate, 89 to 2, and by the first meeting of the General Assembly, held in London on 10 January 1946, fifty-one countries had ratified the Charter.

The ass that went to Mecca

The creation of the UN came at a unique juncture in human history. After the Second World War, the US was the undisputed superpower, as the war had crippled its potential rivals. Rather than impose its own order on the world, as victors had done since time immemorial, the US gifted the world with the rule of law as the keystone of a new liberal order. Harry Truman hammered the point home, informing delegates at the opening session of the San Francisco conference:

> While ... [the] great states have a special responsibility to enforce the peace, their responsibility is based upon the obligations resting upon all states, large and small, not to use force in international relations except in the defense of law. The responsibility of the great states is to serve and not to dominate the world.[38]

Returning to this theme at the closing session, Truman said, 'no matter how great our strength – that we must deny ourselves the license to do as we please'.[39]

The hope vested in the UN was that it would resolve disputes by mediation. Should war break out, then the community of nations would act collectively to restore peace through diplomacy and, if that failed, by using sanctions before resorting to armed force, as a last resort.

In its early years, there was reason for optimism that the UN might fulfil its promise. In 1946, the UN persuaded the Soviet Union to withdraw its troops from northern Iran, and France yielded to pressure and removed its military forces from Syria and Lebanon. The UN also played a part in decolonisation, helping Indonesia, Somalia and Libya achieve independence in the late 1940s. In addition, it helped create the State of Israel in 1949.

Sadly, such success stories give a false picture of the overall performance of the General Assembly, which has been dismal. Analysing the problem, Dean Acheson, who was US secretary of state between 1949 and 1953, reasoned that countries had not put aside their national interests to pursue some higher good.

> They are still nations, and no more can be expected of this forum for political adjustment than the sum total of the contributions. In the Arab proverb, the ass that went to Mecca remains an ass and a policy has little added to it by its place of utterance.[40]

The Security Council fared even worse. Outnumbered, the USSR used its veto to undermine the effectiveness of the organisation. During the first ten years of the UN, the Soviet minister for foreign affairs, Vyacheslav Molotov, cast seventy-nine vetoes, earning him the nickname 'Mr Nyet'. So rather than acting as the world's police, enforcing the decisions of the UN by force if necessary, the Security Council fell victim to Cold War politics. While Acheson was quick to cast the USSR as the main villain, by the 1970s, the US and other permanent members of the Security Council were also ready to wield their veto to protect their geopolitical interests. Consequently, the UN was only able to act in those parts of the world that none of the permanent members of the Security Council had an interest.

The UN has enjoyed more success dispensing the rule of law through international treaties. These addressed global problems, particularly those that protect human rights and the environment. As most lacked sanctions, they relied on moral authority to sustain them and have become norms of international behaviour. Many even gained legal standing when governments incorporated their provisions into national laws.

Within two generations, the fall of the Berlin Wall and the collapse of the USSR allowed the US, once again, to assume the position as the world's only superpower. There was some hope that the US might renew its gift, when, on 16 January 1991, George H.W. Bush gave a speech that addressed the future role of the UN.

> We have before us the opportunity to forge for ourselves and for future generations a 'new world order'. A world where the rule of law, not the law of the jungle, governs the conduct of nations. When we are successful, and we will be, we have a real chance at this 'new world order', an order in which a credible United Nations can use its peacekeeping role to fulfill the promise and vision of the U.N.s' founders.[41]

As much as Bush seemed to be echoing the same sentiments as Truman, 9/11 ended hopes of reviving the rule of law. President George W. Bush tapped into a deep vein of American mythology, which he weaved into his new doctrine of international relations. In his State of the Union address in January 2002, he warned the world about the 'axis of evil', adding:

> Americans are a free people who know that freedom is the right of every person and the future of every nation. The liberty we prize is not America's gift to the world, it is God's gift to humanity. We Americans have faith in ourselves – but not in ourselves alone. We do not claim to know all the ways of Providence, yet we can trust in them, placing our confidence in the loving God behind all of life, and all of history.[42]

This address presents an aggressive reaffirmation of 'American exceptionalism', which is the belief that the US has a divine destiny to act as a force on history, not be subject to historical forces. Historian Margaret MacMillan of the University of Cambridge sees a link between American exceptionalism and US difficulties with the international rule of law. While Americans are 'eager to set the world to rights', they also have 'a tendency to preach at other nations rather than listen to them, a tendency as well to assume that American motives are pure where those of others are not', concludes MacMillan.[43]

During the Bush Administration, as if ordering from an à la carte menu, the US became very particular on which treaties to sign and which to ignore. Even those agreements it had no intention of signing, the US would still join negotiations, weakening provisions before turning its back on it. Worse still, it used methods fair and foul to undermine existing treaties that it disliked.

There is no better example of American mendacity than how it responded to the Rome Statute. This accord established the International Criminal Court, a judicial tribunal with the power to prosecute individuals for genocide, crimes against humanity and war crimes.

The US worried that the new court would hold its military and political leaders to a global standard of justice, bypassing its national courts. Realising that it had little chance of sinking the treaty, US negotiators fought to include a provision for the Security Council to sign off each case before it could be taken to the court. This would have allowed the US to veto any dockets it opposed. When this failed, the US campaigned to weaken and undermine the court in other ways.

At the end of December 2000, just as he was about to vacate the White House, President Bill Clinton signed the treaty, but advised his successor not to put it to the Senate for ratification due to its 'flawed' nature.[44] On 6 May 2002, President George W. Bush 'unsigned' the treaty.[45] Going further, Washington negotiated Bilateral Impunity Agreements with other countries, exempting its nationals from prosecution by the Court. When faced with a recalcitrant government, the Bush Administration threatened to withdraw economic aid and military assistance or harm the country in some other way.[46] This campaign has been largely successful, resulting in two sets of rules: one for the United States and the other for the rest of the world. Furthermore, by imposing Bilateral Impunity Agreements on signatories to the Rome Statute, the US was forcing them to breach their obligations under the treaty to extradite alleged war criminals, regardless of their nationality.

This is not the only instance of Washington refusing to allow the international rule of law to apply to the United States. Under President George W. Bush, America's distain for the rule of law reached new heights, as members of his administration seemed to take perverse delight in rebuffing international treaties. For example, the US failed to ratify the Land Mines Treaty, opted out of the Kyoto Protocol on global warming and the 1972 Anti-Ballistic Missile Treaty, and sabotaged reform of the Biological and Toxin Weapons Convention. His administration also opposed the Law of the Sea Treaty because it permits an international body to wield control over US extraterritorial mining interests.

With the US no longer willing to champion the international rule of law, it is being sustained by other liberal countries, mainly from Europe. As a result, it is increasingly vulnerable to illiberal states like China and a resurgent Russia, which are expected to play a greater role in shaping the global order into the twenty-first century.

Notes

1. Interview with Stephen Schlesinger on CNN's Diplomatic License, 24 December 2004.
2. T.T. Connally and A. Steinberg, *My Name Is Thomas Connally* (New York: T.Y. Crowell, 1954), p. 279.
3. Interview with Joseph E. Johnson conducted by Richard D. McKinzie in Princeton, NJ on June 29, 1973 (Independence Missouri: Truman Library, 1973).
4. C.E. Rothwell, *From Mines to Minds: An Oral History Conducted 1984 by Malca Chall* (Berkeley: Regional Oral History Office, The Bancroft Library, University of California, 1985), pp. 94 and 95.
5. Hull received the Nobel Peace Prize in 1945 for his role in establishing the United Nations. It was undeserved, as his role was incidental, other than his work to cultivate support in the Senate, ensuring its ratification in the US.
6. S.C. Schlesinger, *Act of Creation* (Boulder: Westview Press, 2003), p. 33.
7. Quoted by Kenneth Weisbrode in 'The Master, the Maverick, and the Machine: Three Wartime Promoters of Peace', *Journal of Policy History*, 21:4 (2009), 375.
8. Interview with Joseph E. Johnson.
9. S.C. Schlesinger, *Act of Creation*, p. 35.
10. Interview with Donald C. Blaisdell conducted by Richard D. McKinzie in Princeton, NJ on 29 June 1973 (Independence Missouri: Truman Library, 1973).
11. Quoted by Christopher O'Sullivan in *Sumner Welles, Postwar Planning, and the Quest for a New World Order, 1937–1943* (New York: Columbia University Press, 2007), p. 3, based on letter from Welles to Roosevelt, dated 1 March 1915; Roosevelt to Welles, dated 15 March 1915; Roosevelt to William Jennings Bryan, dated 15 March 1915.
12. D.G. Acheson, *Present at the Creation* (New York: W.W. Norton, 1969), pp. 9 and 11.
13. C. Fisher, *The Columnists* (New York: Howell, Soskin, 1944), p. 240.
14. Quoted by Benjamin Sumner Welles IV in *Sumner Welles: FDR's Global Strategist* (New York: St Martin's Press, 1997), p. 209.
15. Anon., 'Diplomat's Diplomat', *Time* magazine (11 August 1941), pp. 10–13.
16. Anon., 'Diplomat's Diplomat', pp. 10–13.
17. Quoted by Stephen C. Schlesinger in *Act of Creation*, p. 179.
18. Quoted by Benjamin Sumner Welles IV in *Sumner Welles: FDR's Global Strategist*, p. 301.
19. The Atlantic Charter, Official Statement on Meeting between the President and Prime Minister Churchill (14 August 1941).
20. R.C. Hilderbrand, *Dumbarton Oaks: The Origins of the United Nations and the Search for Postwar Security* (Chapel Hill, NC: University of North Carolina Press Books, 2001), p. 13.
21. G.C. Ward, *Closet Companion* (Boston: Houghton Mifflin, 1995), pp. 384–5.
22. P.J. Hearden, *Architects of Globalism* (Fayetteville: University of Arkansas Press, 2002), p. 149.
23. Anon., 'Diplomat's Diplomat', pp. 10–13.

24 I.F. Gellman, *Secret Affairs: Franklin Roosevelt, Cordell Hull and Sumner Welles* (Baltimore: Johns Hopkins University Press, 1995), p. 308.
25 I.F. Gellman, *Secret Affairs*, pp. 236–7.
26 J.H. Crider, 'Conflicts Impair State Department, President is Told', *New York Times* (4 August 1943), p. 1.
27 B.S. Welles IV, *Sumner Welles: FDR's Global Strategist*, p. 349.
28 While Pasvolsky did the lion share of the drafting, he was supported by James Dunn and Isaiah Bowman in the US and Gladwyn Jebb and Charles Webster on the British side. The USSR was represented by Arkadi Sobolev.
29 L.M. Goodrich, E. Hambro and A.P. Simons, *Charter of the United Nations* (Third and Revised Edition, New York and London: Columbia University Press, 1969), p. 3.
30 The negotiations were divided into two parts. In the first China was excluded because Stalin did not want to provoke the Japanese into attacking the USSR. After Stalin left, China sat in on a second round of negotiations, which was mainly symbolic and the nationalist government contributed little.
31 Interview with Joseph E. Johnson.
32 Quoted by Charles E. Bohlen in *Witness to History* (New York: Norton, 1973), p. 181.
33 Quote provided by Lawrence Finkelstein on 23 November 1990 in his interview as part of the United Nations Oral History Project.
34 A.H. Vandenberg Jr. (ed.), *The Private Papers of Senator Vandenberg* (Boston: Houghton Mifflin, 1952), p. 200.
35 Quoted by S.C. Schlesinger in *Act of Creation*, pp. 178–9.
36 B.S. Welles, *Where Are We Going?* (London: Hamish Hamilton, 1947), p. 36.
37 Interview with Alger Hiss on 13 February 1990, United Nations Oral History Project.
38 Address by President Harry S. Truman, wired and read to the UN General Assembly on 25 April 1945.
39 Address by President Harry S. Truman at the Closing Session of the United Nations Conference, delivered in San Francisco on 26 June 1945.
40 Speech delivered by Dean Acheson at West Point in 1962, quoted by James Chace in *Acheson: The Secretary of State Who Created the American World* (New York: Simon and Schuster, 1998), p. 107.
41 Transcript of the 'Comments by Bush on the Air Strikes Against the Iraqis', *New York Times* (7 January 1991), p. A14.
42 State of the Union Address by President George W. Bush, delivered on 28 January 2003.
43 M. Macmillan, *Peacemakers: The Paris Peace Conference of 1919 and its Attempt to End War* (London: John Murray, 2001), p. 22.
44 Statement by US President Bill Clinton, authorising the US signing of the Rome Statute of the International Criminal Court, dated 31 December 2000 and issued at Camp David, Maryland, United States.
45 Remarks made by Marc Grossman, undersecretary for political affairs, 'American Foreign Policy and the International Criminal Court', Center for Strategic and International Studies, Washington, DC (6 May 2002).

46 S. Eberhardt, *Countries Opposed to Signing a US Bilateral Immunity Agreement (BIA): US Aid Lost In FY04 &FY05 and Threatened In FY06* (Washington DC: Coalition for the International Criminal Court, 2006).

3
Dawn over Bretton Woods

> From this place and from this day forth commences a new era in the world's history and you can all say that you were present at its birth. (Goethe, *Campaign in France in the Year 1792*)

Betwixt and between

In late 1940, the British Ministry of Information asked John Maynard Keynes to broadcast a rebuttal on the BBC to a blueprint for a new economic order, announced by Hitler's finance minister, Walter Funk. To everyone's surprise, Keynes was ambivalent. 'If Funk's plan is taken at its face value, it is excellent and just what we ourselves ought to be thinking of doing.' Keynes was attracted to the plan's commitments to free trade, fixed exchange rates and strict capital controls. 'If it is to be attacked, the way to do it would be to cast doubt and suspicion on its *bona fides*.'[1]

Over the next four years, Keynes would work with his American counterpart, Harry Dexter White, to design an international economic order that was liberal in nature and would be one of the foundation stones of economic globalisation.

Maynard, as he preferred to be called, was born in Cambridge on 5 June 1883 to an upper middle-class family. His father, John Neville, lectured Moral Sciences at Cambridge University. His mother, Florence Ada Brown, was a lifelong activist for liberal causes, which gained prominence when she became the first woman to serve as Mayor of Cambridge.

In 1902, Maynard was admitted to Cambridge University where he acquired a taste for philosophy, 'higher sodomy' and golf, which he played badly.

Through one of his lovers, he fell in with the Bloomsbury Group, a collection of artists, aesthetes, writers and intellectuals. The group included novelists Virginia Woolf and E.M. Forster, biographer Lytton Strachey, art critic Clive Bell, and painters Duncan Grant, Vanessa Bell and Roger Fry.

Within the highly talented Bloomsbury Group, Keynes dazzled with his intellect and erudition, as he did with politicians, economists, artists and intellectuals outside his immediate circle. One of the greatest philosophers of the twentieth century wrote in his autobiography of the awe Keynes commanded. 'Keynes's intellect was the sharpest and clearest that I have ever known', confessed Bertrand Russell. 'When I argued with him, I felt that I took my life in my hands, and I seldom emerged without feeling something of a fool.'[2] Keynes clearly revelled in dominating, whether in a sitting room or in the corridors of power and he was seldom bested.

Keynes had an imposing physical presence, and at six foot six inches, he towered over others. His mouth featured full, sensual lips topped with a thick moustache, while his grey-blue eyes have been described as 'soft as bees' bottoms in blue flowers',[3] that could instantly turn icy if he was crossed. He did not like to lose an argument. Possessing a velvet-soft voice, Keynes's conversation sparkled with impish wit, while his argument displayed 'ingenuity which turns commonplaces into paradoxes and paradoxes into truisms, which discovers – or invents – similarities and differences, and associates disparate ideas – that gift of amusing and surprising with which very clever people, and only very clever, can', observed Clive Bell.[4]

With the encouragement of family friend and eminent scholar Alfred Marshall, Keynes turned his attention from philosophy to economics in 1905, for which he quickly exhibited a prodigious talent. Writing to Strachey, he joked, 'I find Economics increasingly satisfactory, and I think I am rather good at it. I want to manage a railway or organise a Trust, or at least swindle the investing public.'[5]

Having embarked in a career in the civil service in 1906, by the time the First World War broke out, the top brass at the Treasury recognised Keynes's extraordinary talent, and he soon found himself advising the chancellor of the exchequer, David Lloyd George. Willing to offer fearless advice, on one occasion, when asked by Lloyd George to comment on remarks he had just made on the state of affairs in France, Keynes replied, 'With the utmost respect, I must, if asked for my opinion, tell you that I regard your account as rubbish.'[6] To Chancellor Lloyd George's credit, Keynes's bluntness only served to bolster the young man's stocks. Over the next four years, Keynes, although he was a pacifist, found himself in the uncomfortable position of advising the government on how to mobilise its financial resources to support the war effort.

In 1919, Keynes travelled to Paris to help the British delegation negotiate peace by advising on financial matters. He quickly realised that the terms the victors had in mind were 'outrageous and impossible and can bring nothing but misfortune'.[7] Having concluded that he could do no good, on 5 June Keynes quit, confiding in Lloyd George that the 'battle was lost' and that he was 'slipping away from this scene of nightmare'.[8]

On his return to Cambridge, where he had accepted a teaching position, he set about writing *The Economic Consequences of the Peace*. In this pamphlet, he attacked the Treaty of Versailles, accusing leaders of the victorious powers for being preoccupied with 'frontiers and nationalities, to the balance of power, to imperial aggrandisements, to the future enfeeblement of a strong and dangerous enemy, to revenge, and to the shifting by the victors of their unbearable financial burdens on to the shoulders of the defeated'.[9]

Appearing in bookshops in December 1919, his pamphlet sold over 100,000 copies, was translated into eleven languages and was widely reported in the newspapers. A bestseller, it marked Keynes's arrival as a public intellectual of rare courage, prepared to speak out against prevailing passions and prejudices. But it came at a personal cost. One critic called him 'Herr Johann von Keynes', while another suggested that he should be awarded the Iron Cross, Germany's highest medal for valour. Not easily ruffled, Keynes remarked, 'I woke up like Byron, famous and disreputable.'[10]

For Keynes, the peace treaty was a lost opportunity to not only 'return to the comforts of 1914, but to an immense broadening and intensification of them', referring to the first phase of globalisation or, in his words, 'an extraordinary episode in the economic progress of man'.[11] He would have to put this dream on hold until the Second World War, when conditions were more favourable.

In November 1921, to everyone's surprise, not least to Keynes, he fell in love with Russian ballerina, Lydia Lopokova. She danced the role of the Lilac Fairy in *The Sleeping Princess*, which was playing at the Alhambra Theatre in London. While the ballet was a flop, love-struck Keynes sat, night after night, in the half-empty stalls, captivated by this exotic sprite. Soon after, they were living together in Bloomsbury and married in 1925 after Lydia divorced her previous husband. Keynes enjoyed her unconscious daffiness, ribald sense of humour and sensuality, so refreshingly different from the refined milieu in which he lived. 'I am not like you talented in idea put into words', she once told him in her fractured English. 'I express myself in impulses.'[12]

Keynes had been a promiscuous homosexual since the age of sixteen, with many affairs, which he did little to keep secret, turning up at one champagne supper fetchingly attired in gown of chiffon, with a headdress of pink ribbons. So this unexpected turn of events came as a shock to his friends, many of whom did not take to Lydia, who endured petty snubs and wounding rudeness from the likes of Strachey, who called her 'a half-witted canary',[13] while Virginia Woolf said she 'has the soul of a squirrel'.[14] Predictably, a rumour started that their marriage was a sham. It was wrong, and their letters reveal that Keynes clearly enjoyed a busy and inventive sex life with Lydia. He even entertained the idea that they might have children, and after he was elevated to the peerage he was want to refer to himself as 'Lord Barren'.[15]

Lydia proved her devotion to Keynes when his health deteriorated. In early 1931, her husband began to experience episodes of severe chest pains and shortness of breath. Later diagnosed as bacterial endocarditis, an infection of the heart valve, Keynes was warned that his condition was untreatable and life-threatening. For the rest of his life, Lydia assiduously managed his diet and valiantly tried to curb his predilection to work himself into the ground. Without her tender ministrations, Keynes may not have lived to reach the crowning achievements of his career: the publication of *The General Theory of Employment, Interest and Money* in 1936, which changed the face of economics in the twentieth century, or the introduction of a liberal economic order in the wake of the Second World War.

Keynes's ideas matured during the interwar years, particularly in response to the Great Depression. During the 1930s, countries waged economic warfare by raising tariffs and artificially devaluing their currencies to gain an unfair advantage over others. Keynes's believed that 'if nations can learn to provide themselves with full employment by their domestic policy ... there need be no important economic forces calculated to set the interest of one country against that of its neighbours'.[16] To provide governments with the freedom to pursue full employment and social welfare, Keynes understood that these objectives needed a stable international economic environment built on predictable exchange rates, an equilibrium between each country's terms of trade and regulations to stop speculators creating havoc with interest rates.

Such reforms were not pursued during the 1930s, as governments stubbornly refused to budge from their beggar-thy-neighbour policies. The results were unemployment, social dislocation and the rise of political extremism, all factors that paved the way to the Second World War.

Liberal economic order

After Great Britain declared war on Nazi Germany in September 1939, Keynes returned to London, where he became an economic advisor to the chancellor of the exchequer in what he breezily described as a 'demi-semi-official' position.[17] Independently wealthy from his investments, Keynes did not ask to be paid for his services; for him, it was a case of old-fashioned noblesse oblige. His health had improved by this time under Lydia's tender care, and he threw himself into his war work while juggling his commitments at Cambridge University and continuing to edit the *Economic Journal*.

In the early years of the war, Keynes devoted most of his time struggling to keep funds flowing into the war effort. However, after reading Funk's plan, he started to turn his attention to coming up with an alternative. Having seen President Woodrow Wilson's quixotic campaign for an international order run aground because of lack of preparation, Keynes was determined to work up a plan that was practical and in which all the details were worked out.

Keynes had a head start, as he could mine many of the economic theories he had developed in the 1930s. These addressed three features that he believed were essential to the new order: 'Economic Efficiency, Social Justice and Individual Liberty.'[18] Moreover, he decided the new order would eschew laissez-faire policies, which had led to 'chaos' during the 1930s. Instead, he believed that 'Any new system would involve regulation of currency exchange',[19] admitting that he had 'taken the line that what we offer is the same as Dr Funk offers, except that we shall do it better and more honestly'.[20] He started work on his plan in September 1941.

By happy coincidence, a high-ranking official in the US Treasury was thinking along the same lines. His name was Harry Dexter White. On 30 December 1941, he sketched his ideas on a new economic order in a twelve-page memorandum, which Secretary of Treasury Henry Morgenthau endorsed.

When Keynes and White discovered that they were working on the same problems, they swapped plans in April 1942. Keynes's reaction to White's proposal was mixed. 'Seldom have I been simultaneously so much bored and so much interested.'[21] While Keynes believed that many of the technical solutions White offered were impractical, he saw that they shared many of the same objectives.

On 23 October 1942, Keynes and White met in London to explore how they might reconcile their plans. The next two years saw a series of tough negotiations between the two men to thrash out their differences.

Outside the corridors of the US Treasury, White was largely unknown. Certainly his resume was not a patch on that of Keynes. White was the son of a Lithuanian Jewish father and Catholic mother, who owned a crockery and hardware store in Boston. The family anglicised its name from Weit upon arriving in the US. Going one step further, young Harry invented the middle name 'Dexter' in his first year at high school to obscure his foreign roots. A clever student, he obtained a PhD from Harvard University in 1930 and then taught for four years.

During this time at university he learned Russian in the hope of obtaining a fellowship to research Soviet central planning. This interest in the USSR would later come to haunt him. In November 1945, a self-confessed Soviet agent and FBI informant named Elizabeth Bentley denounced White as a Soviet spy. The case against him was circumstantial, but it has retrospectively tarnished his reputation and achievements.[22]

After failing to secure the fellowship, in 1934 White joined the Roosevelt Administration. He quickly came to the attention of Morgenthau, and by the time the war broke out White had become Morgenthau's most trusted assistant secretary, and he allowed White total freedom to negotiate with Keynes.

The physical contrast between the two men could not have been greater. Stooping to shake hands, Keynes towered over White, who was a good twelve inches shorter. The American possessed a round face, fleshy lips, and behind his rimless spectacles, his bright blue eyes sparkled with native intelligence.

Nevertheless, it soon became clear that they were far from being mismatched, and Keynes found White a formidable negotiator. For once in his life, Keynes found that he could not dominate and it rankled. Frustrated, he described White as an 'over-bearing, a bad colleague, always trying to bounce you, aesthetically oppressive in mind and manner; he has not the faintest conception of how to behave or observe the rules of civilized intercourse'.[23] Keynes opinion of White was not unearned, as the American took perverse enjoyment in needling Keynes, such as addressing the great economist as 'Your Royal Highness'.[24] On another occasion, in a backhanded compliment, the down-to-earth White told a member of the British negotiating team, 'Your Baron Keynes sure pees perfume.'[25]

With quite different personalities, their negotiations turned into an epic struggle, as a first-hand account of their battles reveals.

> Their modes of debate were diametrically opposed. White was full of vigour and manful thrust. He could be wrathful and rude. His earnestness carried him forward in a torrent of words, which sometimes outstripped his grammatical powers. Keynes, we know, was different; he was always ready with his beautifully polished sentences; he detected any inconsistency in the opposition, even in the most abstruse matter, with lightning celerity, and pointed it out with seeming gentleness in barbed and sometimes offensive sentences.[26]

It must have been extraordinarily uncomfortable for Keynes, who quickly realised he was being bested by White. It was not so much that White's arguments were superior to those of Keynes; they weren't. Keynes's difficulty was that Great Britain was heavily in debt to the US, which left him in a weak negotiating position: 'May it never fall to my lot again to have to *persuade* anyone to do what I want, with so few cards in my hand.'[27] To his credit, Keynes fought the good fight, wining some important concessions, but in the end, he knew he had little choice but to come to an accommodation with White 'The alternative simply is not thinkable; therefore, we must be of good courage', he conceded.[28]

In one sense, Keynes prevailed as his economic theories permeated the final agreement, but on specific issues White often came out on top.[29] Keynes's greatest defeat was when White rejected his proposal to include an automatic mechanism that would penalise the excess reserves of creditor nations. This would have kept the global economy on an even keel and prevented imbalances that lead to instability. With significant surpluses, the US was not interested in limiting its exports or increasing imports. They would only agree to provide loans to debtor nations with balance of payment problems. The US never imagined that one day it would be the world's largest debtor nation, a circumstance it faced in the decades following the late 1960s.

As negotiations approached their conclusion, Keynes developed a grudging respect and even warmed to White, admitting that he was a 'very able and devoted public servant, carrying an immense burden of responsibility and initiative, of high integrity and of clear-sighted idealistic international purpose, genuinely intending to do his best for the world'.[30] Perhaps even more extraordinary, as time went on an unlikely friendship sprang up between the two men, as Keynes saw another side to White, which was generous, warm and even playful. And while in the US, White even inducted the erudite Keynes into the mysteries of baseball, which must have been quite a sight to behold.

By the fall of 1943, Keynes and White agreed on a framework they could both live with, and in April 1944, they submitted a 'Joint Statement by Experts' to their respective governments. This plan favoured an open world economy, in which its stability would be supported by the rule of law.

Now committed to a single vision, Keynes and White forgot their disagreements and worked as a close-knit team to create the foundations of a new economic order. The next step was to convene a conference that would allow the Keynes/White scheme to be put before the international community for approval. Originally planned to be held in the US capital during the summer of 1944, Keynes pleaded with White not to 'take us to Washington in July, which should surely be a most unfriendly act'.[31] Taking pity on the ailing Englishman, White changed the venue to Bretton Woods, New Hampshire, where the mild alpine climate would reduce the stress on Keynes's heart.

The organisers settled on the Mount Washington Hotel, which was large enough to contain several hundred delegates. Unlike others, this hotel accepted Jews as guests, which was an important criteria as not only was White Jewish, but so was the conference host, Morgenthau. This choice did, however, come with other difficulties. The hotel had only been opened after being mothballed for two years. So, when delegates arrived, they found the plumbing unreliable, the staff inexperienced and the rooms poky. As complaints flooded in, the hotel manager locked himself in his room with a case of whiskey.

Keynes approached the conference with trepidation. Referring to it as the 'biggest monkey house yet', he wondered whether it would be possible to wring an agreement out of the 730 delegates on such a complex and far-reaching package before 'acute alcoholic poisoning set in'.[32]

Certainly there were enough dramas and scandals off the main stage to keep chins wagging, some fuelled by alcohol, some not. The Chinese delegates, out for a stroll in the countryside, encountered 'a trigger-happy hermit who mistook them for Japanese bent on subverting the conference'.[33] The Russians, while less than cooperative during formal proceedings, put on some of the best cocktail parties in which vodka and caviar were lavished on guests, who they entertained with lusty renditions of folk songs. And Lydia scandalised those venturing out for an early morning walk, when they found that she enjoyed a refreshing dip in a natural pool fed by the nearby Ammonoosuc River, just behind the hotel, au naturale.

Inside the conference halls, however, the mood was business-like, as delegates participated in punishing rounds of negotiations. These frequently ran as late as 3:30 a.m. and started again the next morning with a working breakfast at 7:30 a.m..

While Keynes and White worked as a tight team, the American shouldered the heavier burden, often having to survive on just five hours sleep. Keynes attended as many sessions as he could, but, because of his bad heart, Lydia insisted he retire after supper. On 19 July, needing to thrash out some critical issues, Keynes broke curfew and paid the price when he collapsed on the hotel stairs while returning to his suite. He had suffered a mild heart attack. Word of his demise quickly spread, as Keynes later recalled. 'By the time it had reached Germany, the rumour said I was dead and I am told I received most satisfactory obituaries.'[34] After a good night's rest, Keynes was back at the negotiating table and saw the conference through to the end.

Despite Soviet intransigence, a futile effort by Latin American countries and China to incorporate silver into the new monetary system, a last minute threat by Australia to withdraw because the final agreement failed to include a commitment to full employment and the consumption of prodigious quantities of hard liquor, after three weeks the conference concluded; its success mainly owed to the Herculean efforts of White and Keynes.

On Saturday 22 July, delegates from forty-four countries trooped into the Gold Room of the hotel to sign the 'Final Act', a mere ninety-six pages.

The most important part of the Bretton Woods package is the International Stabilization Fund, later known as the International Monetary Fund. It created a stable exchange rates system with the US dollar as the reserve currency; lent money to countries that ran into temporary financial difficulties through no fault of their own; and sanctioned governments to use capital controls to regulate 'the ebb and flow of international capital movements or flights of hot money',[35] allowing them to manage their national economies.

In these ways, the IMF aimed to 'make finance the servant, not the master of human desires', concluded Richard Gardner in *Sterling-Dollar Diplomacy*, his authoritative history of the Bretton Woods negotiations.[36]

The second body forged at Bretton Woods was the Bank for Reconstruction and Development, which became known as the World Bank. According to Keynes, the bank's immediate task, although not its most important, was to provide loans to finance the 'permanent reconstruction and the restoration of industry and agriculture' in war-devastated countries, including former enemies.[37] The bank's long-term work, however, would be 'the development of the less-developed areas of the world in the general interests of the standard of life, of conditions of labour, and the expanse of trade everywhere', explained Keynes.[38]

Seen as a whole, the most revolutionary feature of the Bretton Woods package is its formal construction around international institutions and commitment to the rule of law. This innovation, its architects insisted, would discourage the return of economic nationalism. To achieve this end, Keynes argued that the new order required governments to accept a 'measure of financial disarmament',[39] with limits on their ability to make monetary policy, which in future would have to take into account its impact on the overall health of the global economy. Remarkably, all the governments that signed the Bretton Woods agreement accepted some diminution of their sovereignty as the price they had to pay to create a stable monetary system. With the introduction of the rule of law, political scientist, Professor John Ikenberry, suggested that the new liberal order is 'an unprecedented experiment in international economic constitution building'.[40]

Malicious fairies

Soon after the war ended, all eyes were on the inaugural meetings of the World Bank and the IMF, which would flesh out how they would operate. Keen to protect his legacies, in March 1946, Keynes travelled to Savannah, Georgia, to attend these joint meetings.

After arriving in the US on the *Queen Mary*, Keynes travelled to Washington, DC, where he had a preliminary meeting with the US treasury secretary, Fred Vinson, who had replaced Morgenthau. When Vinson told him that the IMF and World Bank would be located in the nation's capital, Keynes exploded: '[I]n that case these bodies could not be regarded as international institutions but were being treated as an appendage of the American Administration.'[41] It was the early days of the Cold War and Keynes suspected that the US might use these international organisations to support its political objectives.

Not willing to give up easily, Keynes used his opening speech in Savannah to dissuade the US from its plans. Keynes was in top form as he opened with an analogy from the christening-party in *The Sleeping Princess*. This ballet held sentimental value for Keynes, for it was where he first saw Lydia dance back in 1921. He related his hope that the Bretton Woods twins – 'Master Fund and Miss Bank' – would receive the gift of a many-coloured coat 'as a perpetual reminder that they belong to the whole world'. In a pointed attack on Vinson, he referred to another character in the ballet: Carabose, a 'malicious fairy' who lays a curse on Princess Aurora, putting her to sleep. He went on to describe what such a curse might mean for the Bretton Woods twins:

> You two brats shall grow up politicians; your every thought and act shall have an arrière-pensée; everything you determine shall not be for its own sake or on its own merits but because of something else.

By this stage he was becoming maudlin and predicted that should the meeting make the wrong decisions, then 'the children will fall into an eternal slumber, never to waken or be heard again in the courts and markets of Mankind'.[42] Rather than winning over the Americans, Keynes's speech irritated Vinson, who muttered, 'I don't mind being called malicious, but I do mind being called a fairy.'[43] Keynes's warning went unheeded as Vinson won the day.

A month later, now back in England, Keynes died of a heart attack on Easter Sunday; and so he never saw that his prediction was proved right, although Washington did not overly pervert the Bretton Woods institutions to serve its political ends, and when they did they often faced resistance from the heads of these institutions.

Despite heroic efforts in 1944, White failed to convince the USSR to join the IMF and World Bank. Instead, the USSR set up its own Council for Economic Assistance. However, rather than creating a realistic alternative to the Bretton Woods institutions, and thereby fragmenting the liberal economic order, the Soviet Union used this body to dominate the economies of its client states in Eastern Europe.

In the absence of a credible rival, the Bretton Woods institutions achieved some modest successes. War-torn countries quickly rebuilt their economies with the help of the World Bank. Stability within the monetary system helped expand the global economy at an average annual rate of 4.91 per cent between 1950 and 1973.[44]

Many industrial countries invested this new-found prosperity in social security and insurance schemes, as well as pursuing policies to keep unemployment levels low. Once people felt sheltered against the turbulence of international markets, they were willing to embrace the liberal order. John Ruggie from Harvard University termed this system 'embedded liberalism', which involved 'a grand social bargain whereby all sectors of society agreed to open markets, which in many places had become almost autarchic, but also to share the social adjustment costs that open markets inevitable produce'. International institutions created at Bretton Woods played their role by moderating 'the volatility of transactional flows across borders and providing social investments, safety nets and adjustment assistance – but all the while pushing liberalisation', explained Ruggie.[45]

Despite all that Bretton Woods achieved, Keynes did not believe that it was the end of the job, as he told the Bretton Woods conference on the last day. In his closing speech, he urged governments to 'continue in a larger task as we have begun in this limited task', concluding that, should they succeed, '[t]he brotherhood of man will have become more than a phrase'.[46]

One of the main reasons for creating a stable monetary system was that it was expected to help multilateral trade flourish. However, this would require rules, and, in a separate process, negotiations were underway to finish the job by adding the 'third leg of Bretton Woods stool'.[47]

Crippled third leg

The main drive for an international trading regime came from the US secretary of state, Cordell Hull, whose passion for free trade was long-standing. Having witnessed first-hand the outbreak of economic warfare during the 1930s, he concluded that 'unhampered trade dovetail[s] with peace; high tariffs, trade barriers and unfair economic competition, with war'.[48] However, between the wars, his pleas for an international trading regime fell on deaf ears, as the isolationists were in the ascent.

When the Second World War broke out, Hull decided that with internationalism on the rise, it was time to try again, and so he commissioned a report that he hoped would see the creation of an international trade agency. At about the same time, economist James Meade had worked up a proposal for a Commercial Union for the British Department of Commerce. Comparison between the two plans revealed they had much in common, and formal talks between British and American officials commenced in September 1943.

Leading the negotiations for the US was Will Clayton, undersecretary of state for Economic Affairs. The British chief negotiator was Sir Stafford Cripps, who was the president of the Board of Trade.

Like Hull, Clayton was a fervent believer in free trade. After a successful career in business, on 1 August 1944 he joined the State Department. After going to Washington, he said, 'I went without any political ambitions and having acquired none ... I can look these fellows in the eye and tell them where to go.'[49] A fine figure of a man, tall and ruggedly handsome, he was an effective operator who quickly earned a reputation for his frankness, which as times caused problems during the trade talks.

Cripps was a welter of contradictions. In 1930, before entering politics, he was a high-priced lawyer earning £30,000 (£2.2 million in 2015 currency), defending rich corporations by day and denouncing the evils of capitalism by night. A self-declared Marxist, he was raised in an aristocratic household and was knighted in his own right 1930, after which he was known as the 'Red Squire'. He was an imperialist who railed against the royal family. While possessing an analytical mind and quick intelligence, Cripps was ill-suited to engage in sensitive negotiations: his style was didactic, his demeanour frigid and in the heat of argument he was 'likely to hurl the heaviest of bricks'.[50] And his self-righteousness earned him an epithet from Churchill: 'There but for the grace of God goes God.'[51]

The first phase of negotiations was held between the US and Great Britain, with the intention of presenting a united front before multilateral talks began at a later date. Negotiations went badly from the start, as misunderstandings and growing enmity poisoned the relationship between Clayton and Cripps; soon neither trusted the other.

There were a number of issues over which the two men clashed.[52] America demanded that the UK abolish its imperial preferences, in which it applied lower tariffs for trade with Commonwealth countries. Before it was willing the wind back this arrangement, Great Britain demanded that the US substantially reduce its tariffs, arguing that otherwise it could not afford to sacrifice imperial preferences. Britain's problem was that after the war, its economy was in dire straits, leaving Cripps with little room to manoeuvre. Clayton showed little sympathy for Britain's predicament, and when he tried to exert further pressure, an embittered member of the British negotiating team accused Clayton of 'blackmail[ing] ... Cripps into dropping imperial preferences under threat of no help for Britain under the Marshall Plan'.[53]

When multilateral talks began in Havana on 21 November 1947, Cripps and Clayton were not able to present a united front, and the conference became a new battleground for the two men. To get the deal through and isolate Great Britain, Clayton bent over backwards to make concessions to the other nations.

This strategy served another purpose. With the Cold War starting to heat up, he was keen to get an agreement because he believed that increased trade within the non-Communist bloc would intensify interdependence and nurture solidarity within the free world.

As the conference came to an end, Cripps threatened to walk away. However, he was outmanoeuvred by Clayton, who had made sufficient concessions to have won the support of European, Commonwealth and developing countries. Feeling isolated, on 24 March 1948 the British government signed the Havana Charter, together with fifty-two other countries, creating a set of trading rules that would be managed by the newly created International Trade Organization.

Other than reducing tariffs, the Havana Charter reflected the liberal idea that trade needed to serve broader social objectives. One was to 'maintain full employment'.[54] Another addressed labour rights, recognising 'that measures relating to employment must take fully into account the rights of workers … [and] that unfair labour conditions, particularly in production for export, create difficulties in international trade, and … [each country should] eliminate such conditions within its territory'.[55]

The Charter also addressed the behaviour of transnational corporations by attacking restrictive business practices. ITO members were required to:

> prevent, on the part of private or public commercial enterprises, business practices affecting international trade which restrain competition, limit access to markets, or foster monopolistic control, whenever such practices have harmful effects on the expansion of production or trade.[56]

Finally, developing countries were allowed additional time to reduce their levels of protection so that their domestic industries had a chance to grow before they were subject to the cold winds of international competition.

After negotiations concluded, the Havana Charter needed to be ratified by legislatures before it could come into force. Unfortunately, the most vocal opposition came from within the US. As the largest trading country in the world, the Havana Charter would be dead in the water if the US failed to ratify it. Its prospects, however, were not good. The business sector felt that the trade treaty was weak, complicated and exception-ridden, the result of too many concessions made by Clayton. One commentator even suggested that the ITO 'will be as toothless as a hen and reduced to clucking admonitively'.[57] US politicians had a different concern; they worried that the ITO power might usurp their country's sovereignty.

Faced with widespread opposition, the newly appointed secretary of state, Dean Acheson, made a brave effort to sell the Havana Charter, heralding it as 'the beginning of law in the realm of world commerce and the vehicle for the growth of a spirit of mutuality and interdependence in trade relations'.[58] When it looked like he had failed to win over the opposition, the Truman Administration quietly withdrew the Havana Charter from Congress in 1950.

What had started as a grand project to free world trade ended in a whimper, and in the interim the General Agreement on Tariffs and Trade (GATT) was signed in Geneva by 23 countries on 30 October 1947. Originally intended to operate until the ITO was up and running, when the Havana Charter failed, GATT became a permanent feature of the liberal order, although its remit was limited to negotiating voluntary tariff reductions. GATT was replaced by the World Trade Organization (WTO) in 1995, finally adding the third leg to the Bretton Woods stool. However, the ITO and WTO were quite different beasts. The latter was heavily shaped by neoliberal ideas and lacked the integrated approach taken by the liberal ITO, which accepted that trade should meet social objectives and its rules were fairer to less developed countries, allowing them to build up their industries before reducing tariff levels to match their more developed trading partners.

Notes

1 D.E. Moggridge (ed.), *The Collected Writings of John Maynard Keynes* (Cambridge: Macmillan/Cambridge University Press, 1980), Vol. XXV, p. 2.
2 B. Russell, *Autobiography* (London: Routledge, 2009), pp. 61–2.
3 R.L. Heilbroner, *The Worldly Philosophers: The Lives, Times and Ideas of the Great Economic Thinkers* (New York: Touchstone, seventh edition, 1999), p. 261.
4 A.C.H. Bell, *Old Friends* (Chicago: University of Chicago Press, 1973), pp. 52 and 60.
5 R.F. Harrod, *The Life of John Maynard Keynes* (London: Macmillan & Co., 1951), p. 111.
6 John Maynard Keynes quoted by Henry William Spiegel in *The Growth of Economic Thought* (Durham, NC: Duke University Press, third edition, 1991), p. 602.
7 Letter from John Maynard Keynes to Florence Keynes, dated 14 May 1919, quoted by F. Roy Harrod in *The Life of John Maynard Keynes* (London: Macmillan & Co, 1951), p. 249.
8 E. Johnson (ed.), *The Collected Writings of John Maynard Keynes* (Cambridge: Macmillan/Cambridge University Press, 1971), Vol. XVI, p. 469.
9 J.M. Keynes, *The Economic Consequences of the Peace* (New York: Harcourt, Brace and Howe, 1920), p. 56.
10 John Maynard Keynes quoted by Justyn Walsh in *Keynes and the Market* (Hoboken, NJ: John Wiley & Sons, 2008), p. 13.
11 J.M. Keynes, *The Economic Consequences of the Peace*, p. 10.

12 Lydia Lopokova quoted by Judith Mackerell in *Bloomsbury Ballerina* (New York: Weidenfeld & Nicolson, 2008), p. 198.
13 Lytton Strachey quoted by Noel Annan in 'Keynes and the Bloomsbury Group', *Biography*, 22:1 (1999), 16–31.
14 Virginia Woolf quoted by Judith Mackerell in *Bloomsbury Ballerina*, p. 257.
15 L. Menand, 'Buried Treasure: The Impish Brilliance of John Maynard Keynes', *New Yorker* (28 January 2002), pp. 82–8.
16 E. Johnson and D.E. Moggridge (eds), *The Collected Writings of John Maynard Keynes* (London and Basingstoke: St Martin's Press, 1973), Vol. VII, p. 382.
17 D.E. Moggridge, *Maynard Keynes: An Economist's Biography* (London: Routledge, 1992), p. 118.
18 J.M. Keynes, *Essays in Persuasion* (New York: Harcourt Brace & Co, 1932), p. 344
19 E. Johnson and D.E. Moggridge (eds), *The Collected Writings of John Maynard Keynes*, Vol. VII, p. 8.
20 John Maynard Keynes quoted by Armand van Dormael in *Bretton Woods: Birth of a Monetary System* (London: Macmillan, 1977), p 7.
21 John Maynard Keynes quoted by Donald Moggridge in *Maynard Keynes*, p. 687.
22 R.B. Craig, *Treasonable Doubt: The Harry Dexter White Spy Case* (Lawrence, KA: University Press of Kansas, 2004) and J.M. Boughton, 'The Case Against Harry Dexter White: Still Not Proven', *History of Political Economy*, 33:2 (2001), 219–39.
23 R.J.A. Skidelsky, *John Maynard Keynes, Volume 3: Fighting for Britain 1937–1946* (London: Macmillan, 2000), pp. 323–4.
24 Anon., 'One Man's Greed', *Time* magazine (23 November 1953).
25 R.J.A. Skidelsky, *Keynes: A Very Short Introduction* (Oxford: Oxford University Press, 2010), p. 115.
26 R.F. Harrod, *The Life of John Maynard Keynes*, pp. 557–8.
27 Letter from John Maynard Keynes to Florence Keynes, dated November 21 1945, quoted by Robert Skidelsky in *John Maynard Keynes, Volume 3*, p. 438. Emphasis in the original.
28 D.E. Moggridge (ed.), *The Collected Writings of John Maynard Keynes*, Vol. XXV, p. 447.
29 J.M. Boughton, *Why White, Not Keynes? Inventing the Post-War International Monetary System*, IMF Work Paper WP/02/52 (Washington, DC: IMF, 2002).
30 R.J.A. Skidelsky, *John Maynard Keynes, Volume 3*, pp. 323–4.
31 R.J.A. Skidelsky, *John Maynard Keynes, Volume 3*, p. 339.
32 D.E. Moggridge (ed.), *The Collected Writings of John Maynard Keynes* (Cambridge: Macmillan/Cambridge University Press, 1980), Vol. XXVI, p. 41.
33 A.E. Eckes Jr., *A Search for Solvency: Bretton Woods and the International Monetary System, 1941–1971* (Austin: University of Texas Press, 1975), p. 139.
34 John Maynard Keynes quoted by Ed Conway in *The Summit* (London: Little, Brown and Company, 2014), p. 272.
35 D.E. Moggridge (ed.), *The Collected Writings of John Maynard Keynes*, Vol. XXVI, p. 16.
36 R.N. Gardner, *Sterling-Dollar Diplomacy: Anglo-American Collaboration in the Reconstruction of Multilateral Trade* (Oxford: Clarendon, 1956), p. 76.

37 Statement by Lord Keynes on the proposed Bank for Reconstruction and Development released at Bretton Woods (London: United Nations Information Organisation – Press Division).
38 Statement by Lord Keynes on the proposed Bank for Reconstruction and Development released at Bretton Woods (London: United Nations Information Organisation – Press Division).
39 D.E. Moggridge (ed.), *The Collected Writings of John Maynard Keynes*, Vol. XXV, p. 89.
40 G.J. Ikenberry, 'The Political Origins of Bretton Woods', in Michael D. Bordo and Barry Eichengreen (eds), *A Retrospective on the Bretton Woods System* (Chicago: University of Chicago Press, 1993), pp. 155–98, quote on p. 155.
41 D.E. Moggridge (ed.), *The Collected Writings of John Maynard Keynes*, Vol. XXVI, p. 211.
42 D.E. Moggridge (ed.), *The Collected Writings of John Maynard Keynes*, Vol. XXVI, pp. 215–16.
43 B. Steil, *The Battle of Bretton Woods: John Maynard Keynes, Harry Dexter White, and the Making of a New World Order* (Princeton and Oxford: Princeton University Press, 2013), p. 300.
44 A. Maddison, *The World Economy: A Millennial Perspective* (Paris: Development Centre of the Organization for Economic Co-operation and Development, OECD, 2001), pp. 126–7.
45 J.G. Ruggie, 'Creating Public Value: Everybody's Business', Address to Deutsche Bank/Herrhausen Society, delivered in Frankfurt, Germany on 15 March 2004.
46 D.E. Moggridge (ed.), *The Collected Writings of John Maynard Keynes*, Vol. XXVI, pp. 102–3.
47 W. Diebold Jr., 'Reflections on the International Trade Organization', *Northern Illinois University Law Review*, 14 (Spring 1994), p. 335.
48 Cordell Hull quoted by Daniel T. Griswold in *Mad about Trade: Why Main Street America Should Embrace Globalization* (Washington, DC: Cato Institute, 2009), p. 141.
49 Will Clayton quoted by Gregory A. Fossedal in *Our Finest Hour: Will Clayton, the Marshall Plan, and the Triumph of Democracy* (Stanford, CA: Hoover Institution Press Publication No. 412, 1993), p. 82.
50 S. O'Leary, 'Stafford Cripps: Lord of Austerity', *Sydney Morning Herald* (28 February 1948), p. 5.
51 Winston Churchill quoted by Daniel Yergin and Joseph Stanislaw in *The Commanding Heights: The Battle between Government and the Marketplace* (New York: Free Press, 1998), p. 8.
52 J.N. Miller, 'Personality, Ideology, and Interest in the Origins of the Modern World Trading System: The Case of Stafford Cripps and Will Clayton', paper presented to the Historical Society at its Annual Conference in Atlanta, Georgia in May 2002.
53 A. Bullock, *Ernest Bevin: Foreign Secretary 1945–1951* (London: W.W. Norton and Company, 1983), p. 462.
54 Final Act of the United Nations Conference on Trade and Employment: Havana Charter for an International Trade Organization, 24 March, 1948, Article 2(a), preamble.
55 Final Act of the United Nations Conference on Trade and Employment: Havana

Charter for an International Trade Organization, 24 March, 1948, Chapter II, Article 7.
56 Final Act of the United Nations Conference on Trade and Employment: Havana Charter for an International Trade Organization, 24 March, 1948, Article 46.1, preamble.
57 Anon., 'Postponed: Freer Trade', *Time* magazine (5 April, 1948).
58 D.G. Acheson, 'Economic Policy and the ITO Charter', *Department of State Bulletin*, 20:575 (1949), 623–7.

4
The European experiment

> I have the map! I have the map! And the day after tomorrow ... The world!
> (*Time Bandits* film, 1981)

Birth of *Méthode Monnet*

On 16 March 1979, all flags on European Community buildings flew at half-mast in honour of Jean Monnet, the undisputed architect of European unity, who had just died. The supranational governance system he put in place was not only revolutionary, but Monnet hoped would act as an exemplar to others. 'The Community we have created is not an end in itself', he explained in his *Memoirs*, but 'a stage on the way to the organized world of tomorrow'.[1]

Jean Omer Marie Gabriel Monnet was born on 9 November 1888, in Cognac, located in south-west France along its Atlantic coast. Although brought up in haute bourgeoisie comfort, Jean comported himself like 'a refined peasant',[2] having assimilated the values and native wiles of his grandparents, who came from solid rural stock.

His mother, Maria Demella, played an important part in shaping his character. 'I may have my father's imagination', he wrote in his *Memoirs*, 'but my mother taught me that nothing can be achieved unless it is built on reality'.[3]

His father, Jean-Gabriel, was a successful brandy merchant who had a burning ambition for Monnet Cognac to conquer the world. Always on the lookout for ways to expand, Jean-Gabriel often invited home guests from Great Britain, Germany, Scandinavia, America and other countries where he did business. Over good food and fine wines, he would barrage them with questions on their local politics, as well as delve into the tastes, habits and prejudices of local consumers. During these meals, Jean watched his father cultivate useful relationships, which helped his business grow.

Jean ended his formal schooling at sixteen. The French system of rote learning bored him and he struggled with his studies. In 1904, Jean-Gabriel lost no time bringing his son into the family business. As the Anglo-Saxon world represented a promising market, Jean-Gabriel shipped his son off to his London agent, Mr Chaplin, for a two-year apprenticeship. Attired in a bowler hat and made-to-measure nailed boots, a dapper Jean Monnet started to learn the ropes of the family business and improve his English.

In 1907, his father sent Jean to North America to open up new markets. Before he left, his father advised him, 'Don't take any books. No one can do your thinking for you. Look out the window, talk to people. Pay attention to your neighbors.'[4] The experience profoundly affected the young man. As he moved around Canada and the US, he spoke to people from all walks of life. In the process, he fell in love with the New World. 'With few boundaries, change was accepted, expansion was assured', remarked Monnet.[5] 'Here, I encountered a new way of looking at things: individual initiative could be accepted as a contribution to the general good.'[6] His father rounded off Jean's education by sending him on business trips to Egypt, Sweden, Russia, China and Greece.

Short and stocky, Monnet sported a neatly clipped moustache and his habit of enjoying brisk walks every morning gave his complexion a ruddy appearance. His private secretary, René Foch, observed that 'his circumspect manner of inspecting a problem from every angle [was] ... like a peasant buying a cow'.[78] Monnet, however, did not hold the attitudes of a conventional peasant, wedded to tradition; instead, he possessed the restless ambition of a homesteader on the American frontier, constantly searching for opportunities to innovate and expand.

Monnet first made his mark on the world during the First World War. Exempt from military service because he suffered from chronic lung disease, in 1914 he started work at the Ministry of Commerce. True to his father's advice, he did not rely on reading reports of how the war was progressing. Instead, he marched down to the docks and wandered around train stations to see what was really going on. He also spoke to those engaged in moving war materiels to the front. The system he saw was in shambles, as British ships arrived in France with the holds filled and left with them empty, while French cargo boats heading for England returned with empty holds. There were other problems. Charged with securing raw materials, Monnet watched prices soar as France competed with Britain on the world market. With a measure of coordination, the solution to these problems, he believed, was within reach.

Once Monnet had worked up a proposal to coordinate logistics between the allies, he decided that he needed to go to the very top for his plans to have any chance of being adopted. For a junior official, acquiring the ear of the prime minister was no easy task. 'Like Americans, I was trained to think if something needs to be changed, every man has the right to point this out.'[9] When he asked his father to use his contacts, Jean was told, in no uncertain terms, that he was 'big-headed to want to bypass everyone and go straight to the top'.[10] Eventually, Jean-Gabriel relented, and in September 1914, Jean met the French prime minister, René Viviani. Impressed by Monnet's plan, Viviani asked him to collaborate with Étienne Clémentel, the minister of trade. In November 1917, the informal arrangements Monnet had put in place gave way to the Inter-Allied Maritime Transport Council, which included France, Great Britain and Italy. Monnet also helped form the Wheat Executive, which coordinated the purchase and distribution of food supplies from scarce reserves to Britain, France and Italy.

One lesson Monnet took from these experiences was that each crisis also presented a window of opportunity to exploit, as his good friend George Ball described in his introduction to Monnet's *Memoirs*.

> Monnet understood instinctively the supreme importance of timing, recognizing that, at moments of crisis, political leaders could be induced to make far braver decisions than they would ever consider in conditions of less stress.[11]

This strategy became an important element of what has been called the '*Méthode Monnet*',[12] and during his public career Monnet would exploit each new crisis to further the cause of European unity.

Statesman of interdependence

Having cut his teeth fostering cooperation between allies during war, Monnet's natural gift for personal diplomacy was tested during peacetime. In 1919, Georges Clemenceau and Arthur Balfour, prime ministers of France and Great Britain, asked him to become the League of Nations' first deputy secretary general. At the time, Monnet thought, 'the dangers of international anarchy were so great that any opportunity for common discipline and fair arbitration had to be seized'.[13] Thus, he found his way to the League's temporary home, Hôtel National (later renamed Palais Wilson) in Geneva.

Throwing himself into global hotspots, Monnet put his considerable diplomatic and creative skills to good effect to resolve the dispute between Germany and Poland over control of Upper Silesia. He faltered, however, when faced with competing claims over the Saar region, occupied by France after the war, but claimed by Germany. He enjoyed more success helping Austria grapple with hyperinflation by arranging a loan of $130 million, which stabilised its currency.

While Monnet was totally committed to the objectives of the League, he also recognised its weaknesses. 'Goodwill between men, between nations, is not enough', he concluded. 'One must also have international laws and institutions.'[14] Without sanctions to enforce its rules, Monnet realised that little had changed from the old order in which the strong dominated the weak.

In 1923, his sister, Marie-Louise, told him that the postwar slump was killing the family business. Disappointed with the League, Monnet had no qualms resigning. Finding the company in dire straits, Monnet decided to take advantage of opportunities in North America by establishing an outlet on Saint-Pierre-et-Miquelon, a French territory just twelve miles from the Newfoundland coast. Sales into Canada soon skyrocketed, but rather than solely meeting the demand from thirsty Canadians, most of the crates of Monnet brandy were smuggled across the Great Lakes into the warehouses operated by Al Capone, whose trade thrived during Prohibition.

After getting the family business back on its feet, Monnet became an investment banker, building up his personal fortune, and by the 1930s Monnet was a multimillionaire. Spending considerable time in New York, he befriended a number of businessmen who would later become key figures in future Republican and Democrat administrations and important allies in his campaign to unite Europe.

In the late 1930s, Monnet was distracted by the news coming out of Germany. 'The whole of my attention was directed at the dangers that were piling up in Europe and threatening world peace.'[15]

On 3 October 1938, French Prime Minister Éduoard Daladier asked Monnet to undertake a secret mission to persuade President Roosevelt to sell warplanes to France. With excellent contacts in Washington, Monnet was the perfect choice. His mission became even more urgent once war broke out. As a frequent visitor to the US, Monnet was distressed to see that America was not doing enough to build up its stock of armaments. George Ball, then a junior official in the Roosevelt Administration, describes what Monnet did next.

> He never ceased putting pressure on Roosevelt's entourage. During the Spring of 1941, indeed, he was probably the key factor in pushing for the American war mobilization before Pearl Harbor.[16]

His influence resulted in a major escalation in production, which John Maynard Keynes judged 'may well have shortened the war by a whole year'.[17]

On 6 December 1939, Monnet was asked to establish the Franco-British Coordinating Committee, a planning role similar to the one he had occupied in the previous war. Independently wealthy, Monnet sought no payments, even covering his own travel expenses.

As the Nazis advanced across France, Monnet saw how he could take advantage of this crisis to further the cause of European unity. On 6 June 1940, he convinced Prime Minister Churchill to ask Paul Reynaud, his French counterpart, whether France was willing to enter into a federal union with Great Britain.[18] This, Monnet believed, 'would seize the imagination and sweep aside the material and psychological obstacles that were delaying joint action by Allies'.[19] At the time, the French cabinet was holed up in Bordeaux, having fled the advancing German army. After debating the proposal, the ministers decided that France was in a hopeless position and that their only option was an armistice with Germany, which they signed on 22 June. At this point, Winston Churchill did not see much point in merging with a corpse and dropped the proposal. Monnet, however, regarded this as a missed opportunity:

> [T]hink what it would have meant if the political offer of union had succeeded. There would have been no way of going back on it. The course of the war, the course of the world might have been different. We should have had the true beginnings of a union of Europe.[20]

In 1943, Monnet spotted another opening to champion a European confederation. In February, Monnet flew to Algiers to join the *Comité français de Libération nationale*, a government-in-exile led by Charles de Gaulle. On 5 August, Monnet sent a note to the committee, arguing that a durable peace required a new economic and political order.

> There will be no peace in Europe if States are reconstructed on the foundation of national sovereignty, with all that implies in terms of prestige politics and economic protectionism. The countries of Europe are too small ... To enjoy the prosperity and social progress that are essential, the States of Europe must form a federation or a 'European entity' that will draw them together into a single economic unit.[21]

Monnet believed that Europe would be condemned to repeat the mistakes of its unhappy past if the peace was simply based on a new balance of power. On 17 October, Monnet provided more details to de Gaulle on the first step towards the single European entity in which a supranational authority would manage the Rhine coal and iron fields for the benefit of participating countries. Unfortunately, de Gaulle was preoccupied with organising the Resistance and paid little attention to Monnet's ideas.

Not easily discouraged, over the next few years Monnet started to flesh out his proposal with the help of what he called his 'overworked amanuenses'.[22] They included George Ball, an American lawyer whom he befriended in London during 1940, Paul Reuter, the professor of international law at Université d'Aix, along with other experts he roped in, as needed. He wanted to be armed with a practical plan when the next opportunity cropped up.

In a 1944 interview with *Fortune* magazine, the Frenchman reflected on another important element of the *Méthode Monnet*: 'The great thing about brandy is that it teaches you to wait. Man proposes – but time and God have to be on your side. I can wait a long time for the right moment.'[23] By 'right moment,' Monnet was patiently looking forward to the next crisis, which he might be able to exploit to promote European unity.

The right moment

For Monnet, the stars aligned in the spring of 1949. Tensions on the French-German border threatened stability on the Continent. France worried that Germany would once more dominate Europe's economy if allowed to regain control over the Ruhr industrial basin, run by the International Ruhr Authority, and reclaim the Saar region, a French Protectorate. As a result, France was unwilling to normalise relations with Germany. In September, Secretary of State Dean Acheson, unhappy with the impasse, insisted that French Foreign Minister Robert Schuman reach an accommodation with the West Germans before their next scheduled meeting held in London on 10 May 1950.

When Monnet heard that Schuman had no idea how to respond, he tried to get his proposal[24] to the French foreign minister through formal channels, with no success. When he heard that the foreign minister spent every weekend in Metz, to be with his family, Monnet lay in wait for him at Gare de l'Est on the morning of Saturday 29 April. As Schuman sat waiting for the train to leave, Monnet handed the startled foreign minister his well-developed plan for a European Coal and Steel Community. Not noted for a particularly creative mind, Schuman was nevertheless an astute politician who immediately saw how Monnet's proposal would solve several problems. For one, France would gain equal access to Germany's rich coal reserve and steelmaking capacity. Second, closer cooperation would eliminate France's reason to continue its policy of undermining Germany's economic recovery. Next, it would satisfy Acheson by drawing France, Germany and other European countries closer together, providing the US with effective Continental allies in the Cold War, which was in its early stages. Finally, it provided a practical expression of Schuman's long-held desired to see Europe united.[25] On Monday morning, after getting off the train in Paris, he told his *chef de cabinet* Bernard Clappier, who was there to take him back to the Foreign Ministry at the Quai d'Orsay: 'Well, I have read the Monnet paper; it is a revolution. My answer is yes.'[26]

With just ten days to Acheson's deadline, Schuman sprang into action. According to Monnet's confidant, François Fontaine, what followed was a 'conspiracy' to disarm any opposition to the plan, by keeping it completely secret until the last moment.

> Had it been publicly debated, conservative forces would have torn it to pieces. The diplomats would have 'negotiated'. There had been more than enough talk. Another criticism rested on a more solid base: that fusing two huge systems of production, eliminating economic frontiers and ancient protectionist practices, would need months of consultations and technical study. However, the case had to be settled in a week, without experts. On this point, Monnet and Schuman had the same ideas and the same clear conscience: experts would come later. It was an essentially political proposal.[27]

A few days later, Acheson was briefed on the plan, but only after he was sworn to secrecy. 'Schuman began to expound what later became known as the "Schuman plan," so breath-taking a step towards the unification of Europe that at first I did not grasp it', Acheson recalled years later.[28]

Schuman next put Monnet's proposal to his ministerial colleagues, deliberately waiting until the last moment before seeking their approval. On the morning of 8 May, rather than circulating the draft or reading the text, he 'recounted' it, keeping everything deliberately vague. Without fully understanding what they were approving, the Council of Ministers gave Schuman carte blanche to table the plan at the London meeting, in two days' time. At about the same time, a handwritten letter describing the proposal was handed to the German Chancellor Konrad Adenauer. Although Adenauer had no forewarning, he saw that it resolved a number of problems between France and West Germany, and so he immediately answered: 'I approve wholeheartedly.' Everyone was now on board.

At 4 p.m. on 9 May, in the gilded Salon de l'Horloge at Quai d'Orsay, Schuman announced 'his' plan to create a European Coal and Steel Community. The press conference attracted around 200 journalists, who heard the minister promise: 'Out of all this will come forth Europe, a solid and united Europe.'[29] While his short speech was rich in optimistic generalities, he was unable to answer simple questions on how this new entity would work, admitting his proposal was 'a leap into the unknown'.[30]

As Schuman had hoped, by acting quickly, he gave the opposition little time to organise. One of the few objections came from de Gaulle, who at the time was trying to resurrect his political career. Entering the debate, he ridiculed the plan as 'a kind of hodgepodge of coal and steel, which nobody knows who runs it or who definitely profits from it'.[31] However, he made little impact.

For Monnet, the launch of the Schuman Plan vindicated his long-held view that 'when ideas are lacking, they [politicians] accept yours with gratitude – provided they can present them as their own'.[32] By 3 June, Belgium, Netherlands, Luxembourg and Italy confirmed their interest in joining the new Community. On the other hand, Great Britain worried that the proposal would compromise its ties with Commonwealth countries. Prime Minister Clement Attlee, unlike his European counterparts, balked at taking a leap into the dark by transferring British resources to 'an irresponsible body that is appointed by no-one and responsible to no-one'.[33]

The hub of Monnet's Coal and Steel Community was a supranational 'High Authority', which possessed the power to override national policies, regulations and rules that limited free trade and fair access to resources. Importantly, it could back its decisions with sanctions. It even had direct taxing powers so that politicians could not use their budgetary control to manipulate its policies and decisions. A European Court of Justice arbitrated disputes, acting as the main check on the High Authority. To complete the package, a Council of Ministers provided oversight, but Monnet tried his best to limit its power. According to political scientist Ernst Haas, 'Monnet considered the High Authority as the repository of European General Will, with evil governments merely spokesmen for the selfish political wills.'[34]

With in-principle support, Monnet threw himself into negotiating the details. When roadblocks appeared, he would pull aside delegates for one-to-one sessions, in which his persuasive skills came to the fore. When matters got out of hand, Schuman would cajole delegates to focus on their historic mission of creating a united Europe. On the other side of the Atlantic, George Ball kept key players, particularly Acheson, fully briefed in the hope that the US would be favourably disposed towards European integration.

On 18 April 1951, after six months of intense negotiations, representatives of France, German, Italy, Belgium, Netherlands and Luxembourg signed the Treaty of Paris, creating the European Coal and Steel Community. Monnet understood the value of symbolism, so the final treaty was printed by Imprimerie Nationale de Paris on Dutch vellum with German ink using Louis XIV type, then bound in Belgian parchment using Luxembourg paste and adorned with a marker of Italian silk.

Appointed its president on 10 August 1952, Monnet convened the first meeting of the High Authority in Luxembourg. From day one, he insisted members swear never to accept instructions from their governments; their first loyalty was to the European project. The beating heart of the Community would become the powerful bureaucrats who ran its day-to-day affairs from Luxembourg (later Brussels). Their authority hinged on the conceit that the Community's administration was a technical, not a political exercise.

In the first few years, Monnet dismantled national cartels; ordered the removal of customs barriers; outlawed discriminatory taxes, hidden subsidies and quotas; and forced governments to repeal anti-competitive regulations. As a result, the relative prices of steel and coal dropped, while Italian steel-making and Belgian coalmines expanded. In addition, industry attracted substantial investment now that it had access to a large market. While many hailed these achievements as a triumph, Monnet confided in his vice president, Albert Coppé, 'I do not care for Coal and Steel; it is Europe I want to create.'[35] Nevertheless, for Monnet, this experiment in supranational governance allowed the Community to establish an important precedent: the 'abnegation of sovereignty in a limited but decisive field'.[36] It represented an innovation that also excited internationalists, providing an alternative model to the weak institutions created in Bretton Woods and San Francisco. What the two projects shared, however, is a commitment to embedded liberalism in which internal free markets are complemented by national labour law and social welfare systems. As the Community expanded, ordinary Europeans warmed to the social element of the project.

Monnet's long-term plan was to create an archipelago of communities that would eventually merge. His next targets included transport, oil, gas, atomic energy and a single European army.

In August 1954, Monnet's strategy faltered when the French Parliament rejected a proposal for an integrated European Defence Community. Concerned that the European project might stall, on 23 June 1955 Monnet resigned from the High Authority so that he could lobby without the restrictions of being a civil servant. This allowed Monnet to operate behind the scenes, where he did his best work.

Esprit de corps

On 13 October 1955, Monnet announced the formation of the *Comité d'action pour les Etat-Unis d'Europe* (Action Committee for the United States of Europe), which he hoped would encourage member governments to 'transfer more and more of their powers to common institutions'.[37]

Tapping into his extensive networks, Monnet managed to recruit influential trade unionists and politicians to his committee. Italian socialists and French Gaullists, on the other hand, refused his invitations, while the communists, whom Monnet described as 'extreme conservatives',[38] were not asked. Monnet also excluded business executives, whom he believed would pursue a narrow commercial agenda that could be at odds with his vision of a united Europe.

Within the Action Committee, Monnet cleverly created a non-partisan atmosphere, guarding against the intrusion of ideology. With membership dominated by strong personalities, Monnet went about 'converting their egocentric strength into a common resolution'.[39] To succeed, Monnet decided that the committee's deliberations should be kept secret, which allowed participants 'complete and total freedom, including the privilege of contradicting yourselves'. That meant they could confide their true beliefs in private, even when they might differ from their public utterances to supporters. However, once the committee agreed on a course of action, Monnet insisted that its members 'must make sure that the motions you pass are voted on in the parliaments'.[40] This strategy permitted Monnet to mould this disparate collection of powerful men and women into an effective lobby group.

To draw attention to the committee's resolutions, Monnet would hop on a plane or train to Bonn, Paris, London, Brussels or any place he could best apply his unique personal diplomacy. It was not uncommon to receive a phone call from Monnet, who would burble, 'I absolutely must come and see you. Don't move. I'll come to you. Just tell me what day suits you.'[41] He had no difficulty getting access to prime ministers and high officials, but he would also seek out an obscure civil servant whom he had discovered was an important cog in shaping a government's policy and explain to him or her the latest scheme being promoted by the Committee.

Another strategy used by the Action Committee was to co-opt support from global policy clubs. The Bilderberg Group, which George Ball joined in 1954, was an early advocate for Europe unity. Monnet was directly involved in the Pesenti Group, initiated by Italian industrialist Carlo Pesenti, which included political leaders like Robert Schuman, Konrad Adenauer, Antoine Pinay and Giulio Andreotti. Later, members of the Action Committee would assume positions in the Trilateral Commission and World Economic Forum.

In 1957, the Action Committee enjoyed an early success. Its lobbying for an Atomic Energy Community succeeded, and Euratom drew together expertise and resources to develop nuclear power, with costs and technology shared among European countries.

The Committee also helped rally support for the Treaty of Rome, which, in 1958, created the European Economic Community. This agreement reduced trade restrictions; instituted common external tariffs; reduced barriers to the free movement of people, services and capital; and developed common agricultural and industrial policies. Unfortunately, individual governments often played to populist passions, erecting bureaucratic barriers to the common market.

After he became president of the Fifth Republic in 1962, de Gaulle was determined to curb the influence of the Action Committee and its head. 'We are not in the era where Monsieur Monnet could command', the new president declared.[42] De Gaulle did not oppose the European project, but he strongly objected to what he called Monnet's 'supranational monstrosity'.[43] Instead, the French president wanted a *Europe des patries* – an association of nations – in which governments would make all decisions by consensus, not Eurocrats in Brussels. As long as the process remained under the strict political control of democratically elected leaders, de Gaulle was quite content to see closer economic cooperation between European countries.

Matters came to a head in July 1965, when the Council of Ministers looked like they would allow their decisions to be settled by a majority vote. De Gaulle was horrified, as this proposal would strip France of its veto. To kill it off, he withdrew the French representative from the Council of Ministers so no decision could be made on this or anything else, for that matter. This tactic has been termed the 'empty chair' protest. Monnet hit back, arguing that de Gaulle's insistence that decisions be unanimous 'will produce paralysis', as it had 'at the Security Council of the United Nations'.[44] During the December 1965 elections, Monnet very publicly supported pro-European François Mitterrand, who forced de Gaulle into a second ballot that the General only narrowly won. Once back in the Élysée Palace, de Gaulle stuck to his guns.

The stalemate lasted six month before ministers caved in, and on 29 January 1966 they signed the 'Luxembourg compromise' that reinstated the veto on decisions that governments deemed 'very important to national interests'.[45] This deal would contribute to growing paralysis within the European Commission over the next twenty years, as bold reforms were unable to attract unanimous support.

In 1975, now age eighty-seven, Monnet dissolved the Action Committee and began writing his *Memoirs*. Despite the Action Committee being wound up, its former members, sustained by the *esprit de corps* Monnet had nurtured, kept the dream alive and continued the fight.

On 16 March 1979, Jean Monnet died in his home at Houjarray at the grand age of ninety-one. His funeral was held in the Montfort-l'Amaury Church, and he was buried in the cemetery at Bazoches-sur-Guyvonne. In 1988, his ashes were moved to the Panthéon mausoleum of Paris where French greats are laid to rest.

His *Memoir*, completed three years earlier, contained a fitting epithet that, even at this low point in the European project, reflected his optimism for the future. It stated: '[W]e are going towards our goal, the United States of Europe, on a journey with no return.'[46]

Stop, start

In 1982, the president of the European Parliament, Pieter Dankert, fretted that the 'infant which held so much promise 25 years ago has changed into a feeble cardiac patient'. Rather than moving towards greater integration, Dankert complained that de Gaulle's model of *Europe des patries* was gaining the upper hand, with member governments often pursuing their national interests at the expense of the European project. The result: 'Mobility and dynamism have given way to stagnation and passivity.'[47]

On 20 March 1982, *The Economist* proclaimed that Europe was 'in a coma'.[48] While this diagnosis was not new, the article stung the business sector into action. In a report that appeared in *Newsweek* on 28 March 1983, Wisse Dekker, CEO of Philips, declared:

> If we wait for our governments to do anything, we will be waiting for a long time. ... You can't get all tied up with politics. Industry has to take the initiative. There is no other way.[49]

On 6–7 April 1983, seventeen CEOs gathered in Paris to announce the formation of the European Round Table of Industrialists, and over the next decade, this group helped build support within the private sector for a single European market. As part of its campaign, on 10 January 1985, Dekker unveiled the Round Table's plan: *Europe 1990*. Warning that the 'survival of a united Europe is, in fact, at stake', it outlined a series of reforms to eliminate internal barriers to trade and commerce.[50]

Jacques Delors, president of the European Commission, could not have timed his entrance better, taking up the post on 1 January 1985. Keen to put an end to 'Eurosclerosis', over the next decade Delors would use his formidable political and diplomatic skills to aggressively pursue further integration. To help him, Delors enlisted support from the business sector, whom he astutely judged had the most to gain from further integration.

On 14 January 1985, Delors told the European Parliament that he intended to fully unify Europe's internal markets within seven years, by pushing through the Single European Act. Up to that point, the Act had met with stiff resistance, as national governments saw it as a threat to cosy arrangements they had to protect their local industries from competition. Once the 'Luxembourg Compromise' had gone, countries found their sovereignty curtailed so they were no longer able to frustrate the spread of a single market. Delors was determined to revive the fortunes of this legislation, and while he faced opposition from vested interests and some governments, he found that major European corporations were willing to support his campaign.

Delors received strong support from the European Round Table of Industrialists, which worried that should Europe remain a group of separated national markets, it would not reach 'the scale necessary to resist pressure from non-European competitors'.[51] As Delors was gearing up his campaign, Dekker released a report, 'European Community Home Market', which called for the unified market to be in place by 1990, which was two years earlier than Delors was aiming for. To support his case of such urgency, Dekker was reported in the *Financial Times* warning that European multinationals would relocate overseas 'if Europe does not unite'.[52]

According to the European Commissioner for Competition, Peter Sutherland, pressure by the business sector paid off.

> In fact, one can argue that the whole completion of the internal market project was initiated not by governments but by the Round Table, and by members of it, Dekker in particular, and Philips playing a significant role ... And I think it played a fairly consistent role subsequently in dialoguing with the Commission on practical steps to implement market liberalisation.[53]

With the strong support of the leaders of major European powers – Margaret Thatcher in the UK, François Mitterrand in France and Helmut Kohl in West Germany – the Single European Act was signed on 17 February 1986 by the nine member states and on 28 February 1986 by Denmark, Italy and Greece. It entered into force on 1 July 1987, and included a deadline of 1992 to achieve a single market.

While the issue for the business sector and neoliberal leaders like Thatcher and Kohl was the elimination of market barriers, Delors's agenda went further. He believed that the prosperity created by the single market should be used to satisfy social ends. Soon after its passage, Delors sponsored a package that delivered higher levels of welfare protection and transferred wealth from Europe's rich heartland to its poorer fringes. In essence, this package was designed to strengthen the embedded liberal compromise within the borders of Europe, as he explained in his 1988 book, *La France par L'Europe*:

> There is no sense in competition developing to the detriment of the standards of social protection and the working conditions upon which the European economic model is founded. Europe will not be built if the workers do not feel involved, if social progress is not part of its final objectives.[54]

Another important element of the corporate agenda was the creation of a monetary union, which would significantly reduce costs of doing business within the European market. The idea of a monetary union was not new, and had been floating around since the 1970s, possibly earlier. The European Round Table of Industrialists breathed new life into it by publishing *Reshaping Europe* in September 1991.[55] This report was timely, providing welcomed support for Delors's campaign for a single currency, which was part of a new reform package[56] that would be incorporated into the Maastricht Treaty. Signed on 7 February 1992, the eighteen members of the Eurozone put the euro into circulation in 2002.

Slouching towards a more perfect union

The steady progress of the European project was rudely interrupted by the global financial crisis, which created doubt about the viability of the Eurozone. The stakes could not be higher. 'If the euro fails, then Europe fails', Angela Merkel grimly warned in her speech to the Bundestag, delivered on 19 May 2010.[57]

As easy as it is to blame the problems of the Eurozone on the US subprime crisis, it only served to expose deep cracks within the architecture of the currency union, making it an accident waiting to happen. Without effective fiscal controls in place,[58] a number of member countries, particularly those to the south, had gone on a spending spree, with little prospect of ever repaying their debts.

The Eurozone was not the only European institution that was flawed, and it follows a pattern first established by Monnet, according to political economist John Gillingham, who observed, 'The institutions he [Monnet] created (or tried to create) in order to advance the political and economic union of Europe did not operate properly, were unstable, or did not work at all.'[59] Rather than being a failure, it was an important element of the *Méthode Monnet*, according to George Ball. Until a perfect union was in place, Monnet understood the architecture would be inherently unstable, which, in turn, presented new opportunities to complete the job, as Ball explained:

> [W]ith his usual perspicacity, Monnet recognized that the very irrationality of the scheme would compel progress and might then start a chain reaction. The awkwardness and complexity resulting from the singling-out of coal and steel would compel member governments to pool other production as well.[60]

The formation of the currency union was no exception, riddled as it was with logical inconsistencies, as pointed out by Wolfgang Schäube, German finance minister:

We introduced the common currency within a community of nation states that still retain their full budgetary sovereignty. With that, we had a common currency but no fiscal union, no supra-national control over national budgets, and no European regulation of banks. No wonder a serious financial crisis stretched the systems to breaking point.

Taking a page out of the *Méthode Monnet*, Schäube argued, '[W]e need more integration in order to overcome existing problems', concluding that 'the crisis has been helping to advance it [the European project]'.[61]

Schäube is in good company and there is significant support among the European elites for reforming the union by extending it. Mario Draghi, president of the European Central Bank, has proposed 'a banking union' that would be complemented by 'more effective rules in the fiscal domain'.[62] In his state of the union address in 2012, European Commission President José Manuel Barroso urged member countries to 'create a banking union and a fiscal union and ... We need to take concrete steps now, with a political union as a horizon.'[63] Without economic and political union, Barroso argued that the Eurozone would continue to limp along like 'a man with one leg'.[64]

Under normal circumstances, once the solutions were identified, the elites would push ahead with reform in the knowledge that they could secure popular support, or at least acquiescence for their plan. What they discovered, in the wake of the euro crisis, was that the rules of the game had changed.

Once the public understood that the monetary union was badly flawed, they became resistant to any fix that involved expanding the powers of the European Union. This opposition is not unexpected, for those advocating further reform were the same members of the European elite who had turned Europe into 'a joyless union of penalties, punishments, disciplines and seething resentments', as Ian Traynor described the impact of austerity programmes in *The Guardian*.[65] Many people were hurt by high unemployment, cuts in social security benefits and increases in the pension age. They understandably took these assaults on their welfare as a betrayal of the embedded liberal compromise, which struck at the very *raison d'être* of the European Union.

In this environment, Eurosceptic populists have been particularly adroit in whipping up anti-European sentiment, led by extremist parties on the left and right, and winning surprising support during the 2014 European elections.[66] Even mainstream politicians have been willing to rattle the sabre, with no better example than Prime Minister David Cameron, who has promised a referendum that could see the United Kingdom commence divorce proceedings in 2017.

Perhaps most worrisome is that on the fringes of politics, xenophobic fanatics and violent anti-immigrant groups have thrived, echoing the rise of fascism in Europe in the 1930s.

So, for the first time since Monnet started Europe on its path to integration, it may unravel, which has implications beyond the borders of the Union. Thinking about the unthinkable, Martin Wolf has warned that the current crisis not only threatens Europe with an 'existential challenge', but also has wider implications for the course of globalisation:

> If everything is not resolved, the collapse of the European model of integration would permanently shatter the credibility of what was, for all its faults, the most promising system of peaceful international integration there has ever been.[67]

Notes

1 J.O.M.G. Monnet, *Memoirs* (London: Collins, 1978), p. 524.
2 F. Duchêne, *Jean Monnet: The First Statesman of Interdependence* (New York: Norton, 1994), p. 27.
3 J.O.M.G. Monnet, *Memoirs*, p. 37.
4 J.O.M.G. Monnet, *Memoirs*, p. 44.
5 J.O.M.G. Monnet, *Memoirs*, p. 46.
6 J.O.M.G. Monnet, *Memoirs*, p. 45.
7 F. Duchêne, *Jean Monnet*, p. 27.
8 F. Duchêne, *Jean Monnet*, p. 27.
9 Jean Monnet quoted by Merry and Serge Bromberger in *Jean Monnet and the United States of Europe* (New York: Coward-McCann, 1969), p. 13.
10 J.O.M.G. Monnet, *Memoirs*, p. 50.
11 G.W. Ball, 'Introduction', in Jean Monnet's *Memoirs*, p. 13.
12 W. Wessels and A. Faber, 'Vom Verfassungskonvent zurück zur "Methode Monnet"? Die Entstehung der "Road map" zum EU-Reformvertrag unter deutscher Ratspräsidentschaft', *Integration*, 4 (2007), 370–81.
13 J.O.M.G. Monnet, *Memoirs*, p. 84.
14 Jean Monnet quoted by Merry and Serge Bromberger *Jean Monnet and the United States of Europe*, p. 19.
15 Quoted by François Duchêne in *Jean Monnet*, p. 65.
16 George Ball quoted by Emmanuel Monick in *Pour mémoire* (Paris: Mensil, impr. Firmin-Didot, 1970), p. 64.
17 John Maynard Keynes quoted by Emmanuel Monick in *Pour mémoire*, p. 64.
18 Jean Monnet was not the first to make this suggestion. A union of France and Great Britain had been raised by others, including Chatham House in Great Britain and the *Centre d'études de politique étrangère* in France.
19 J.O.M.G. Monnet, *Memoirs*, p. 19.

20 J. Davenport, 'M. Jean Monnet of Cognac', *Fortune* magazine (August 1944), pp. 121–6, 214, 216, quote on p. 214.
21 J.O.M.G. Monnet, 'Note de réflexion de Jean Monnet', Alger, 5 August 1943. Translated by the author.
22 F. Duchêne, *Jean Monnet*, p. 13.
23 J. Davenport, 'M. Jean Monnet of Cognac', p. 122.
24 In August 1944, Monnet's ideas appeared in an interview conducted by John Davenport ('M. Jean Monnet of Cognac', pp. 121–6, 214, 216). He relied heavily from input from Pierre Uri, Etienne Hirsh and, in particular, Paul Reuter who worked out many of the details.
25 Robert Schuman gave a series of speeches from 1947 to 1951 calling for a European union that included a post-Nazi Germany so that war would become both unthinkable and 'materially impossible'.
26 J. Cheminade, 'FDR and Jean Monnet: The Battle vs. British Imperial Methods Can Be Won', *Executive Intelligence Review*, 27: 24 (2000), 44–55.
27 F. Fontaine, 'May 1950: A Behind-the-Scene Account of What Happened', *European Community*, No. 134 (May 1970), 4–5.
28 Dean Acheson quoted by David S. McClellan in *Dean Acheson: The State Department Years* (New York: Dodd, Mead, 1976), p. 251.
29 P. Fontaine, *A New Idea for Europe: The Schuman Declaration – 1950–2000*, Series: European Documentation (Luxembourg: Office for Official Publications of the European Communities, 2000), p. 14.
30 F. Fontaine, 'May 1950: A Behind-the-Scene Account of What Happened', 4–5.
31 F. Duchêne, *Jean Monnet*, p. 205.
32 F. Duchêne, *Jean Monnet*, p. 347.
33 Speech by Clement Attlee made in the House of Commons on 7 June 1950, quoted by Edmund Dell in *The British Abdication of Leadership in Europe* (Oxford: Oxford University Press, 1995), p. 176.
34 E.B. Haas, *The Uniting of Europe: Political, Social and Economic Forces 1950–57* (Stanford, CA: Stanford University Press, 1958), p. 456.
35 Quoted by Roch Hannecart in 'Albert Coppé, le bon élève ?', in G. Duchenne, M. Dumoulin and V. Dujardin, *Rey, Snoy, Spaak: Fondateurs belges de l'Europe. Actes du colloque organisé par la Fondation Paul-Henri Spaak et l'Institut historique belge de Rome/ Belgisch Historisch Instituut te Rome, en collaboration avec le Groupe d'études d'histoire de l'Europe contemporaine, les 10 et 11 mai 2007 à Rome*, (Brussels: Bruylant, 2007), pp. 213–32, quote on p. 216.
36 J.O.M.G. Monnet, *Memoirs*, p. 316.
37 J.O.M.G. Monnet, *Memoirs*, p. 408.
38 Jean Monnet quoted by François Fontaine in 'Forward with Jean Monnet', in Douglas Brinkley and Clifford Hackett (eds), *Jean Monnet: The Path to European Unity* (New York: St Martin's Press, 1991), pp. 1–66, quote on p. 58.
39 Jean Monnet quoted by François Fontaine in 'Forward with Jean Monnet', in D. Brinkley and C. Hackett (eds), *Jean Monnet*, p. 46.

40 Jean Monnet quoted by Merry and Serge Bromberger in *Jean Monnet and the United States of Europe*, p. 156.
41 Jean Monnet quoted by François Fontaine in 'Forward with Jean Monnet', in D. Brinkley and C. Hackett (eds), *Jean Monnet*, p. 47.
42 F. Duchêne, *Jean Monnet*, p. 315.
43 Charles De Gaulle quoted by Richard Mayne in 'Gray Eminence', in D. Brinkley and C. Hackett (eds), *Jean Monnet*, pp. 114–28, quote on p. 117.
44 Jean Monnet quoted by Merry and Serge Bromberger in *Jean Monnet and the United States of Europe*, p. 278.
45 A.L. Teasdale, 'The Life and Death of the Luxembourg Compromise', *Journal of Common Market Studies*, 31:4 (1993), 567–79.
46 J.O.M.G. Monnet, *Memoirs*, p. 794.
47 P. Dankert, 'The European Community: Past, Present and Future', *Journal of Common Market Studies*, 21:1 (1982), 1–18, quote on p. 8.
48 Anon., 'Alas, Poor Europe', *The Economist* (20 March 1982), pp. 11–12.
49 Anon., 'European Round Table (ERT): Agenda Setting for the EU', *Newsweek* (28 March 1983).
50 European Round Table of Industrialists, *Europe 1990* (Paris: ERT, 1985).
51 European Roundtable of Industrialist, *Foundations for the Future of European Industry*, Memorandum to EC Commissioner Davignon, dated 10 June 1983.
52 Anon., 'Multinationals May Leave "If Europe Does Not Unite"', *Financial Times* (27 April 1985), p. 1.
53 B. Van Apeldoorn, 'Transnational Class Agency and European Governance: The Case of the European Round Table of Industrialists', *New Political Economy*, 5:2 (2000), 157–81, quote on p. 168.
54 Quoted and translated by Mark Gilbert in *European Integration: A Concise History* (Plymouth: Rowman & Littlefield Publishers, 2012), p. 148.
55 J. Monod, P. Gyllenhammar and W. Dekker, *Reshaping Europe* (Brussels: European Round Table of Industrialists, 1991).
56 *Report on Economic and Monetary Union in the European Community*, Committee for the Study of Economic and Monetary Union (Luxembourg: Office for Official Publications of the EC, 1989).
57 J. Coman, 'Eurozone Crisis: European Union Prepares for the "Great Leap Forward"', *The Observer* (20 November 2011).
58 Fiscal controls did exist, embodied in the 1997 Stability and Growth Pact. It was designed to prevent any country pursuing fiscal policy that would endanger financial and economic stability of the other members of the Eurozone. It was deeply flawed because it was not policed and was riddled with loopholes.
59 J. Gillingham, *European Integration, 1950–2003: Superstate or New Market Economy?* (Cambridge: Cambridge University Press, 2003) p. 4.
60 G.W. Ball, 'Introduction', in D. Brinkley and C. Hackett (eds), *Jean Monnet*, p. xiii.
61 The 2012/2013 ESC Annual Lecture, delivered by Wolfgang Schäube, German

Federal Minister of Finance on 29 October 2012 at St Anthony's European Studies at Oxford University.

62 M. Draghi, 'Europe's Pursuit of "A More Perfect Union"', lecture by Mario Draghi, president of the ECB, delivered at Harvard Kennedy School, Cambridge (USA), on 9 October 2013.

63 José Manuel Durão Barroso, president of the European Commission State of the Union 2012 address, delivered during the plenary session of the European Parliament in Strasbourg on 12 September 2012.

64 J. Coman, 'Eurozone Crisis', p. 20.

65 I. Traynor, 'As the Dust Settles, a Cold New Europe with Germany in Charge Will Emerge', *The Guardian* (9 December 2011), p. 12.

66 O. Treib, 'The Voter Says No, But Nobody Listens: Causes and Consequences of the Eurosceptic Vote in the 2014 European Elections', *Journal of European Public Policy*, 21:10 (2014), 1541–4.

67 M. Wolf, 'Afterword: How the Financial Crises Have Change the World', in Robert C. Feenstra and Alan M. Taylor (eds), *Globalization in an Age of Crisis: Multilateral Economic Cooperation in the Twenty-First Century* (Chicago and London: University of Chicago Press, 2013), pp. 401–8, quote on p. 407.

Part II

Sovereignty of global markets

Richard Nixon, even once he became president, was never convinced that he was held in affection by the American people. He was probably right. So when his advisors urged him to make an economic statement to the nation by interrupting the top-rated western *Bonanza*, beloved by millions of Americans, he hesitated, seeing this as yet another reason for people to dislike him. Eventually, he relented once he was told that his announcement had to be made before the end of the weekend so as not to spook financial markets. So, *Bonanza* it had to be.

At 9 p.m. on 15 August 1971, a dour Nixon appeared on primetime TV to announce that his administration was floating the US dollar.[1]

This decision had been made at Camp David that weekend and it was designed to stop the run that threatened to empty Fort Knox of gold. So large were its debts to its trading partners that America's gold stock would soon prove insufficient to meet the swelling demand for gold, which was convertible at $35 per ounce. The threat was real, as America's trading partners were convinced that the US did not possess the will to manage its growing trade deficit and runaway budgets, and so, a number of countries decided to convert their dollars to gold.

By 9:20 p.m., viewers were relieved to get back to the adventures of Ben, Hoss and the rest of the Cartwright family, with few grasping the full import of Nixon's announcement.

This decision, referred to as the 'Nixon Shock', was not simply a domestic matter, but ripped the heart out of the Bretton Woods agreement, which had made the US dollar the world's reserve currency, being the only currency directly convertible to gold at a fixed rate.

Nixon's Sunday night announcement also came as a complete surprise to the international community. Such was Nixon's disregard for the IMF that the Treasury summoned the IMF's managing director, Dr Pierre-Paul Schweitzer, to a meeting where he watched Nixon's address on television and was then handed a letter informing him that the US was unilaterally leaving the IMF's fixed exchange system. Political leaders from America's main trading partners were treated with equal disdain and had to read about the decision in the next day's newspapers.

After Nixon had crippled the international rule of law created at Bretton Woods, Paul Volcker wryly remarked that now '[n]obody's in charge'.[2]

Nixon was never much interested in economic policy, and the package was sold to him as a way to magically fix the country's ballooning debt and trade deficit without having to make any hard decisions to rein in America's profligacy. Even his treasury secretary, John Connelly, admitted that it was a cynical exercise, famously quipping that 'foreigners are out to screw us, our job is to screw them first'.[3]

One of the people present at Camp David, however, viewed the floating of the dollar as a matter of high principle. He was George Shultz, head of the Office of Management and Budget at the White House. A friend and disciple of monetarist economist Milton Friedman, together, they were key figures in the decision to float the dollar. Their success represented an important beachhead for freeing capital markets.

The Nixon Shock ended the dominance of liberal economic order and marked the rise of a new phase in which globalisation would be built around neoliberal policies. This turning point represented an important victory in the 'war of ideas', which neoliberals had been waging against Keynesian economic planning since the 1930s, spreading from academe to the political and business elites. Attacks on Bretton Woods from free market zealots undoubtedly accelerated its descent, but it was already in trouble, burdened by its inherent flaws.

The Bretton Woods monetary policies were run by the IMF, largely as a technical operation. According to Robert Leeson, an associate professor in economics at Murdoch University, hubris infected the technocrats who managed the system:

> In their defence of civilisation, the IMF played the role of policeman, prosecutor, judge, jury and executioner. Heretics were examined through a procedure that resembled an Inquisition.[4]

The problem was that only smaller nations were brought to heel by the IMF, while the major economies – the US, Japan, United Kingdom and Germany – were never subjected to any discipline. As a result, the IMF failed to deal with global imbalances caused by the US, which had become a chief debtor because its government was unwilling to fund the Vietnam War or its generous welfare system through taxes. The rise of Germany and Japan, which were building large surpluses, exacerbated the situation. As a result, US dollars accumulated in overseas accounts. Called Eurodollars, they were traded in an uncontrolled global market, making the task of maintaining stable exchange rates difficult and ultimately impossible.

When stagflation, which was rife during the 1970s, was added to the mix, politicians understandably lost faith in the liberal economic order.

In 1982, George Shultz became the secretary of state in the Reagan Administration, where he found a government that was even more sympathetic to his neoliberal ideas than he had encountered working for Nixon. Outside the US, market-based policies were also implemented by Margaret Thatcher in the United Kingdom, Joe Clark in Canada, Helmut Kohl in West Germany, David Lange and Roger Douglas in New Zealand, Bob Hawke and Paul Keating in Australia and Augusto Pinochet in Chile. Developing countries also adopted the neoliberal agenda, often imposed on them by the World Bank and IMF, which had redefined their mission now that they were no longer custodians of the Bretton Woods system. And so, the 1980s became the breakthrough decade for the neoliberal global order.

These governments wound back social security and policies to reduce unemployment, unravelling the 'embedded liberal' compromise on which Bretton Woods had been based. These policies understandably left the public more exposed to the vagaries of the global marketplace. While many prospered, a significant number of people were left behind.

Milton Friedman, who was on the frontline of the war of ideas, congratulated Nixon, whom he claimed 'broke an ice jam and jarred exchange rates loose'. But this only marked a start, and he looked forward to the creation of a truly free market economy with the elimination of 'exchange controls and barriers to the movement of goods and capital'.[5]

With the tide turning, Friedman was pleased to see the neoliberal agenda was starting to have an impact, with the 1990s seeing major treaties negotiated that protected free trade and foreign investment, as well as removing barriers on the free movement of capital.

In place of the liberal order, globalisation entered a new phase in which the sovereignty of global markets replaced the principle that finance should be the 'servant, not the master of human desires'.[6] According to neoliberals, the free market is a benevolent sovereign, pulling many millions out of poverty and creating unprecedented prosperity. In support of this argument, James Wolfensohn, president of the World Bank, explained: 'Over the past 20 years, the number of people living on less than $1 a day has fallen by 200 million, after rising steadily for 200 years.'[7]

On the other hand, global markets have become so powerful that governments live in fear of the judgment of bond traders, and desperately compete against one another to attract transnational corporations to their shores, offering low corporate tax rates and reduced burden of business regulations.

Dismantling Bretton Woods also eliminated controls on the movement of capital and freed exchange rates. These changes led to increased market volatility, as 'hot money' moved from one country to another. Speculators thrived in this casino economy, exposing the world's economy to escalating episodes of debilitating instability.

Despite growing dissatisfaction with the neoliberal order, it was sufficiently resilient to avoid the crisis experienced by the Bretton Woods system in the 1970s. Nevertheless, by the turn of the century, it was under siege and looking for a way to answer its critics.

Notes

1. The package announced by Nixon contained other elements. They included increased tariffs, and wage and price controls. All the measures were meant to be temporary, but the floating of the dollar became the only permanent feature of the package.
2. R. Lowenstein, 'The Nixon Shock', *Bloomberg Businessweek* (4 August 2011).
3. J.S. Odell, *US International Monetary Policy: Markets, Power, and Ideas as Sources of Change* (Princeton: Princeton University Press, 1982), p. 263.
4. R. Leeson, *Ideology and the International Economy: The Decline and Fall of Bretton Woods* (New York: Palgrave Macmillan, 2003), p. 32.
5. M. Friedman, 'Keep the Dollar Free', *Newsweek* (29 December 1971), p. 83.
6. R.N. Gardner, *Sterling-Dollar Diplomacy: Anglo-American Collaboration in the Reconstruction of Multilateral Trade* (Oxford: Clarendon, 1956), p. 76.
7. *World Bank Global Economic Prospects and the Developing Countries 2002: Making Trade Work for the World's Poor* (Washington, DC: World Bank, 2002).

5
The war of ideas

Praise the Lord and pass the ammunition. (Lieutenant Howell M. Forgy)

Herr Professor

In an odd quirk of history, the two economists whose ideas fought a fierce contest to determine the shape of globalisation shared the job of fire warden at Cambridge University during the Second World War, taking turns watching out for bombs dropped by the Luftwaffe.

During his weekend visits to the university, John Maynard Keynes's lanky frame could be found perched on the Gothic roof of King's College Chapel. He undoubtedly used this quiet time to mull over the practical problems that stood in the way of the liberal international order, which would be launched at Bretton Woods in the summer of 1944. The other figure, younger and a virtual unknown, was Friedrich August Hayek, whose thoughts were dominated by how he could lead a rebellion against what he believed were the misguided economic policies of Keynes. To this end, Hayek used the solitude to plan a new war, where ideas – not bombs – would be the main munitions.

Cambridge was not a high-value target, so both men were left to ponder the future with mercifully few interruptions.

At the time, it looked like Keynes's theories were unassailable, as most economists in academia and government service embraced his prescriptions. This rankled Hayek, who believed that Keynes was wrong. For Hayek, a new global order would be created spontaneously by free markets, not government planners.

Hayek was a scholar of considerable talent, originality and intellectual courage, but that was no guarantee that he was the best person to prosecute the war of ideas he had in mind. Fortunately, a young RAF pilot with fire in his belly rescued Hayek's theories from obscurity. His name was Antony Fisher, and in the mid-1950s he escalated the war of ideas through his think tank, the Institute of Economic Affairs (IEA). It was later to serve as a model for others and through their efforts the international liberal order established by Keynes and Harry Dexter White in Bretton Woods found itself under siege.

Friedrich August Hayek, or 'Fritz' to his parents and friends, was born in Vienna on 8 May 1899. Hayek describes his childhood as one of unclouded happiness. 'We probably had an ideal family', he recalled. 'Three meals together every day, talking about every subject under the sun, always left free by our parents to roam, to think, even to commit minor peccadilloes.'[1] His parents encouraged Fritz to read serious books. As a teenager, he ploughed his way through tomes by Hugo de Vries, a Dutch geneticist, the philosophical works of Ludwig Feuerbach, Aristotle's *Ethics*, poetry of Schiller and the literary works of Goethe. He even harboured literary aspirations of his own, and the unworldly Fritz wrote tragedies 'on rather violent and more or less erotic themes'.[2] Lacking literary talent, he compounding this inadequacy by writing about subjects in which he lacked intimate experience.

When the First World War broke out, Fritz was just fifteen years old, and he had to wait until he turned eighteen before he joined the Austro-Hungarian Army. As part of an artillery regiment, he fought in northern Italy, where he was decorated for bravery. Physically brave but lacking practicality, as a radio operator he was almost killed trying to parachute out of an observation balloon without first disconnecting his earphones.

After the war, Hayek decided to concentrate his studies on economics, with the intention of following the 'family tradition'. Both his grandfathers, whom he knew as a child, were scholars; one an eminent economist and the other a natural scientist. His father also aspired to an academic career. 'You see, my determination to become a scholar was certainly affected by the unsatisfied ambition of my father to become a university professor.' His father achieved this ambition near the end of his life, lecturing botany at the University of Vienna, but for 'the greater part of my childhood', recalled Hayek, 'the hope for a professorship was the dominating feature' of his father's ambition.[3] In 1919, he enrolled at the University of Vienna, where he received doctorates in law (which included subjects on economics) and political science in 1921 and 1923, respectively.

Initially, Hayek leaned towards socialism, but this changed after he met Ludwig von Mises in October 1921. A prominent member of the Austrian School of economics, Mises supported classical liberalism (what today is commonly referred to as 'neoliberalism'),[4] with its emphasis on limited government and the free market. Hayek's lucky break came when Lionel Robbins, professor at the London School of Economics (LSE), wanted to recruit Mises to counterbalance Keynes's growing influence. When Mises declined the offer, Robbins appointed Hayek, who found himself, much to his own astonishment, a professor at the tender age of thirty-two.

His colleagues at the LSE, when they first ran into Hayek, encountered a lean, distinguished looking man with a neatly clipped moustache. Old-fashioned in dress, he embodied the perfect Viennese gentleman, right down to a fob watch, an affectation he wore across his vest, though when he needed to tell the time he consulted his wrist watch. A tall man of six feet two inches, Hayek was surprisingly athletic, which came from years of serious mountain climbing and skiing. Referred to as 'Herr Professor' by students, his courses were not popular because he possessed a ponderous style and spoke with a thick accent. But those who persisted were rewarded with economic lectures rich in references to history, philosophy, politics and law.

Even before Hayek started at the LSE, Robbins asked him to critique Keynes's *Treatise on Money*. Hayek's highly critical two-part review appeared in *Economica* in August 1931 and February 1932. By attacking Keynes, Hayek quickly made his name as a fearless – some would say foolhardy – scholar, willing to stand up to the dazzling Keynes, whose was recognised as the greatest economist of his generation.

Not accustomed to being challenged, Keynes quickly fired back a scathing rebuttal. Rather than answering Hayek's criticisms, Keynes launched a blistering assault on Hayek's *Prices and Production*, which appeared in 1929. He wrote: 'The book, as it stands, seems to me to be one of the most frightful muddles I have ever read, with scarcely a sound proposition … It is an extraordinary example of how, starting with a mistake, a remorseless logician can end up in Bedlam.'[5] The attack did not cause Hayek to blink. Instead, he revelled in academic battle, and this opening skirmish represented the first shot fired in what Hayek would come to call the 'war of ideas'.

What followed surprised everyone, as an unlikely friendship blossomed between Keynes and Hayek in the wake of this scrap. Keynes 'had a habit of going like a steamroller over a young man who opposed him', recalled Hayek of their first meeting. 'But if you stood up against him, he respected you for the rest of your life.'[6] During the war, Keynes arranged for Hayek and his family to relocate to Cambridge, even helping them with accommodation. Though charmed by Keynes, Hayek's candid opinion was that he was 'a man with a great many ideas who knew very little economics'. But he could not help admiring Keynes for being 'one of the most intelligent and most original thinkers I have known'.[7]

While his colleagues savoured the intellectual jousting between the two men, Hayek was painfully aware that most of his peers dismissed the substance of his neoliberal ideas. To illustrate the dominance of Keynesianism, during one tutorial, Herr Professor removed from his wallet a crumpled piece of paper on which he had jotted down the names of liberal economists, with Keynes topping his list. He looked at it, sighed theatrically, distressed at the length of list, and returned it to his wallet, much to the amusement of his students.

The road to war

Unhappy with the ascendency of Keynesian economics, during the 1930s Hayek started to sketch out a grand strategy to support the war of ideas.

As much as Hayek disagreed with their socialist ideology, he modelled his strategy on the British Fabian Society. Playing the long game, the Fabians had employed intellectuals to convince the public and left-leaning politicians to embrace the welfare state and state ownership of strategic industries. They reached the apogee in 1945 when many Fabian proposals were implemented by the Attlee Labour government.

Taking this example as inspiration, Hayek conceived a grand strategy in which neoliberals could overwhelm their opponents by engaging in a 'war of ideas'. The secret of success, according to Hayek, was to have the 'courage to be Utopian', and construct uncompromising proposals that were not limited by what is politically possible today, but present a compelling vision of the future. Hayek had enormous faith in the power ideas to transform society, and he believed that 'intellectuals are the organs which modern society has developed for spreading knowledge and ideas'.[8]

By 'intellectuals' Hayek did not mean ivory-tower academics like himself, but 'professional second-hand dealers in ideas'. They included 'journalists, teachers, ministers, lecturers, publicists, radio commentators, writers of fiction, cartoonists, and artists, all of whom may be masters of the technique of conveying ideas, but are usually amateurs so far as the substance of what they convey is concerned'.[9] These opinion leaders, Hayek predicted, would spread the good news about free markets to political leaders, the media and the wider community. In this way, he hoped that neoliberalism could overcome the Keynesian orthodoxy.

Having called for a war of ideas and seeing few willing to engage the enemy, in March 1944, Hayek reluctantly ventured outside the safe confines of academia to publish *The Road to Serfdom*. First in Great Britain and six months later in the US, Hayek hoped it would be read widely, although he had little confidence that he would sell many copies.

Explaining the title of his book, Hayek coupled socialism with fascism, arguing that both depended on government planning, which invariably led to a condition 'scarcely distinguishable from slavery'.[10] He also attacked Keynes's middle way, in which capitalism coexisted with state planning, claiming that it would still lead down the road to serfdom, just at a more leisurely pace.[11]

One of the main themes running through *The Road to Serfdom* is that individual liberty is not possible without economic liberty. Government planning, Hayek contends, deprives people of the freedom to decide their own destiny. Only free markets provide individuals with a full range of choices to meet their needs, and the main role of governments, beyond keeping the peace, is to defend the rule of law, private property and free markets.

The timing of its publication was crucial. In 1944, it was clear that the allies would win the war, and politicians had started talking about postwar reconstruction, which under the influence of the Fabians and social democrats meant a highly managed economy. *The Road to Serfdom* allowed Hayek to offer an alternative model for the postwar order, based on small government, economic liberty, protection of property rights and the rule of law.

Much to Hayek's surprise, his book was a runaway success. Despite paper rationing, the book went through a number of reprints, after its initial print run of 2,000 copies sold out within days in Great Britain.

Hayek had trouble finding an American publisher, because the book was mainly written for an English audience. Eventually the University of Chicago Press agreed to publish *The Road to Serfdom*, although it expected modest sales of less than 1,000. The publisher invited Hayek to undertake a book tour, and he agreed to give lectures at five universities. To everyone's surprise, 17,000 copies flew off the shelves in the US in the 20 days after the book's release. It gained an even wider readership after it was condensed and republished in April 1945 by *Reader's Digest*, which enjoyed a worldwide circulation of well over 8 million.

When Hayek arrived in the US the same month for his lecture tour, he was no longer an obscure economist but a best-selling author. Anticipating strong interest in his book tour, his publisher handed over the organisation of the tour to the National Concerts and Artists Corporation, which had experience promoting celebrities. On arriving in New York, the organisers told donnish Hayek that his first lecture was arranged for the next day, and that over 3,000 people were expected. 'My God,' he exclaimed, 'I have never done this. I can't possibly do it. I have no experience in public speaking.'[12] Despite his discomfort at addressing non-academic audiences, Hayek's talks were enthusiastically received, which gave him hope that he may not be a lone voice in the wilderness after all.

The attacks on *The Road to Serfdom* by socialists in Europe, New Dealers in the US and Labour Party MPs in Great Britain showed Hayek that even his opponents, who had once ignored his ideas, were now taking neoliberalism seriously. One of the more viperous attacks came from well-known Fabian, Herman Finer, who denounced Hayek's book as 'the most sinister offensive against democracy to emerge from a democratic country for many years', accusing the author of promoting the dictatorship of markets over the will of the people.[13]

Such controversies helped sales, not just in English-speaking countries but around the world. By the end of the war, *The Road to Serfdom* had been reprinted five times and in early 1945, translations were commissioned into French, Swedish, Italian, Portuguese and Dutch. The book was also circulated clandestinely among dissidents in the Soviet Union, in a typescript version known as *Samizdat*.

Perhaps the most unexpected response to *The Road to Serfdom* came from Keynes, who everyone expected to attack the book. He read the book while sailing across the Atlantic on his way to Bretton Woods, and then wrote Hayek a letter in which he confided that 'morally and philosophically I find myself in agreement with virtually the whole of it; and not only in agreement with it, but in a deeply moved agreement'.[14] From this correspondence, it is clear that the two men were not diametrically opposed, but then again they also were not in total accord. Later in his letter, Keynes made clear that 'what we want is not no planning, or even less planning ... I should certainly say that we almost certainly want more.'[15] Keynes's point is that limited government intervention is acceptable on those occasions when markets became unbalanced or even failed, and that Hayek was wrong to suggest that any planning will eventually lead to a Soviet-type command economy.

Band of brothers (and one sister)

After the success of *The Road to Serfdom*, Hayek decided to establish 'a kind of International Academy of Political Philosophy', which would comprise a 'closed society, whose members would be bound together by common convictions and try both to develop this common philosophy and to spread its understanding'.[16]

Hayek decided to hold an exploratory meeting to gauge the interest in creating a new neoliberal society. But two things stood in his way: shortage of money and good organisational skills. According to British economist Ralph Harris, who knew Hayek well: 'I don't think Hayek was a very practical man. ... I can't imagine, if I may say so, Hayek running a picnic.'[17] It is unlikely that this meeting would have even taken place had not Hayek had the good fortune to meet Albert Hunold, a Swiss industrialist who possessed the skills that Hayek lacked. Hunold was an inveterate networker and highly competent organiser. In November 1945, Hunold introduced Hayek to a group of Swiss industrialists and bankers, who provided 18,000 Swiss francs to cover the costs of organising the meeting. Fares and expenses of US delegates were covered by the William Volker Charities Fund, a conservative philanthropic foundation.

Hunold also took on the organisation of the meeting. Hayek, however, chose the location, which was Mont Pèlerin in the Swiss Alps, an area where he had spent many happy hours hiking and skiing. The setting is picturesque, overlooking Lac Léman and the alpine Dents du Midi.

The meeting was held between 1 and 10 April 1947, and of the fifty-eight invitations issued, thirty-nine scholars from ten countries accepted. They included such eminent academics as Karl Popper, Wilhelm Röpke, Ludwig von Mises, Milton Friedman, and Lionel Robbins, along with a handful of journalists and corporate executives. The participants were all men, with the exception of Veronica Wedgwood, a British historian.

Tempers soon flared, and for a while it looked like the project would go no further. To calm everyone down Hayek lead his band of economists on brisk walks in the hills surrounding Mont Pèlerin, which offered panoramic views of the French Alps, Lake Geneva and the Jura mountains.

Before the meeting, Hayek held out hope that he was recruiting fighters in his war of ideas.[18] His expectations took a dive when he found that his band of brothers (and one sister) behaved more like a fractious family, dwelling on what divided them rather than concentrating on what united them. Nevertheless, at the conclusion of the gathering, everyone agreed to continue meeting annually and adopted the name the Mont Pèlerin Society. Hayek was elected its president and Hunold its secretary.

In the years that followed, its proceedings were dominated by fierce intellectual disputes, and the Society quickly became a debating club. It also became a place to network with fellow true believers, but came nowhere close to becoming a training ground for fighters in the war of ideas. Like Hayek, all its members were passionate about free market economics, but few had the fire in the belly that was needed to take the fight outside the ivory towers of academe. Rather it became a refuge, providing 'a spiritual fountain of youth', observed Milton Friedman, 'to which we could all repair once a year or so to renew our spirits and faith among a growing company of fellow believers'.[19]

Nevertheless, the Mont Pèlerin Society was important, keeping the flame alight for neoliberal intellectuals during the fallow years, which stretched from its formation until the late 1970s. The invitation list also included more practical men and women, many from the business world, who would go on to occupy the trenches in the war of ideas.

Marshalling true believers

A true believer who was spoiling for a fight was decorated fighter pilot, Antony Fisher, who had seen action in the Battle of Britain and was ready to take up arms again in the war of ideas.

Fisher was born in London on 28 July 1915 into a prosperous family, and enjoyed a carefree youth, sailing through Eton and Cambridge University where he studied engineering. Often in the company of his brother, Basil, who he loved dearly, Antony enjoyed nothing more than speeding through the country lanes of Cambridgeshire in his Speed 20 Avis sports car or taking a joy flight in his Vega Gull aeroplane to Paris. With his good looks and sense of fun, Antony's pre-war life was full of parties, dancing and pretty girls. He also dabbled in business, with mixed success.

As the war approached, Antony and Basil enlisted in the RAF, and were in the thick of fighting during the Battle of Britain. On 15 August 1940, a crack Luftwaffe squadron launched a surprise attack on their airbase. Flying Hurricanes, the British squadron replied with a daring ambush, forcing the enemy to flee across the channel, but not before engaging them in a fierce dogfight over the Sussex countryside. Antony watched in horror as a Messerschmitt peppered Basil's plane with machinegun fire. His brother successfully bailed out, but then Antony saw Basil's parachute catch fire. Basil's death devastated Antony, leading to bouts of depression. It also resulted in deep soul searching. When he left the RAF, he was no longer a playboy but a man determined to make Britain a better place after the war, otherwise the sacrifices would, he reasoned, be for nothing. But how?

He found the answer to his question when he read *The Road to Serfdom*. Determined to meet the author, in late 1945 Fisher knocked on Hayek's door at LSE. Before him, a bemused Hayek encountered a passionate young man who 'had this bee in his bonnet that the war had been fought ... over freedom and individual self-expression, and increasingly the state seemed to be closing in on people from all parties'. Explaining why he wanted to meet Hayek, Fisher told him, 'I share all your worries and concerns as expressed in *The Road to Serfdom* and I'm going to go into politics and put it all right.' With his good looks, gift for public speaking and impressive war record, Fisher was confident he could win a seat in Parliament. Hayek's response came as a surprise. 'No, you're not!' he told Fisher. 'Society's course will be changed only by a change in ideas. First, you must reach the intellectuals, the teachers, and writers with reasoned argument. It will be their influence on society which will prevail, and the politicians will follow.'[20] Hayek further suggested that Fisher would make better use of his talent by engaging in the 'great battle of ideas and policy' and joining 'with others in forming a scholarly research organisation to supply intellectuals in universities, schools, journalism, and broadcasting with authoritative studies of the economic theory of markets and its application to practical affairs'.[21] What Hayek had in mind was a think tank that could take on the Fabian Society 'who had tilted the political debate in favour of growing government intervention'.[22]

While impressed by what Hayek had told him, Fisher was not quite ready to act. He had a young family to support, and he first needed to shore up his own financial position. Deciding to factory farm chickens, Fisher was frustrated by regulations that made little sense to him. None of the breeds of chicken available in the UK were suitable, and Fisher wanted to import White Rock chickens from the US, which matured quickly and produced high quality meat. But regulations banned the importation of chickens and eggs from the US. Unwilling to let a few rules stand in his way, Fisher wrapped twenty-four fertilised eggs in silver foil, telling Customs they were Easter eggs when they inspected his hand luggage.

His enterprise was a runaway success, and in 1956, Fisher decided he had the time and funds to establish a neoliberal think tank in Great Britain, along the lines suggested by Hayek. With £500 donated by Sir Robert Renwick, a British industrialist, and £500 of his own money, Fisher founded the Institute of Economic Affairs, which opened its doors for business on New Year's Day 1957.

Fisher left the day-to-day running of the IEA in the hands of Ralph Harris. Possessing a strong academic background in political economy, as well as being a leader writer for the *Glasgow Herald*, Harris had a combination of talents that Fisher believed would be the key to the IEA's success.

The institute mainly relied on like-minded economists and experts to write papers, which it would publish as pamphlets and books. Harris made sure that such reports and articles avoided stodgy language, much loved by academics, and IEA publications were written in clear English so their ideas could be easily understood by the public, politicians and newspaper reporters.

Harris saw the IEA as the 'high command'[23] in the war of ideas, and in the early years it waged a guerrilla war which was 'deliberately intended to affront [the establishment] and wake them up'.[24] Harris's deputy was Arthur Seldon, who also kept the IEA on a permanent war footing.

> The IEA would be the artillery firing the shells (ideas). Some would land on target (the intellectuals), while others might miss. But the Institute would never be the infantry engaged in short-term, face-to-face grappling with the enemy. Rather, its artillery barrage would clear the way for others to do the work of the infantry later on. The IEA would show why matters had gone wrong and set out broad principles, while others would argue precisely how matters should be put right.[25]

The IEA was not the first neoliberal think tank, although earlier ones lacked its belligerent proclivity. In 1939, the American Economic Foundation was started by Fred G. Clark. The American Enterprise Institute and Institute for Public Affairs in Australia were both founded in 1943, while the Foundation for Economic Education opened its doors for business in 1946. Nevertheless, IEA's remarkable success attracted imitators.

In keeping with Hayek's grand strategy, which called for 'a liberal Utopia', IEA papers and policy recommendations paid scant attention to the current political climate and pursued policies, no matter how unpopular, that promoted the free market, the sanctity of private property, the value of limited government and the rule of the law.

Early on, Harris set boundaries on how the IEA would deal with politicians. 'You don't want to get drawn behind the chariot wheels of politicians, who will use you and misuse you if you're not very careful.'[26] That did not mean that politicians were not targeted. In fact, the IEA showered politicians on the left and right with its reports and studies, as well as providing face-to-face briefings to members of parliament and ministers. They also ran informal lunches to court the press. Sir Alistair Burnet, editor of *The Economist*, describes how easy it was to come under the spell of Harris and his colleague. 'They were polite, even courteous, plainly intelligent fellows who enjoyed an argument. Only after a bit did it become apparent that they usually won their arguments. The well-drilled ranks of us Keynesians began to suffer uncomfortable casualties.'[27]

Another important element of the IEA model was to draw in financial support from the private sector. They were not only the engine room of the free market, and a natural ally, but they had the most to gain from deregulation and low taxes, which were issues vigorously pursued by neoliberal think tanks. At first, corporate funding in the United Kingdom was hard to access, but this changed as the IEA began to show that it could exercise political influence. In the US, corporations and conservative charitable foundations were more receptive and had a long history of contributing to political causes and think tanks.

For its first twenty years, the IEA swam against a strong current. The tide started to turn in 1974 when Hayek received the Nobel Prize for economics, followed by Milton Friedman in 1976 and IEA author George Stigler in 1982.[28] This coincided with a crisis in Keynesian economics, which failed to solve the stagflation that plagued the 1970s. In addition, key elements of the Bretton Woods system had broken down following the Nixon Shock. This lead policymakers and politicians, particularly on the right, to look to the neoliberal alternative for answers.

This upwelling of interest saw Fisher in demand, as neoliberal activists asked for his advice on how to create think tanks along the IEA model. Answering his critics, who worried that he was spreading himself too thinly, Fisher replied: 'Proliferation is required because it is vitally necessary that common sense should be made available from as many directions as possible.'[29] During the 1970s, Fisher spent considerable time outside Great Britain assisting others neoliberals set up think tanks, along the lines pioneered by the IEA.

In 1974, he headed to Canada to help establish the Fraser Institute. In 1976, Fisher travelled to Australia where he met Greg Lindsay, who later founded the Centre for Independent Studies. In 1977, now in New York, he helped set up the Manhattan Institute. That same year he collaborated with Edwin Feulner, who had interned at the IEA in 1964, to launch the Heritage Foundation. He then journeyed to Scotland, where he lent his assistance to brothers Pirie and Eamonn Butler in setting up the Adam Smith Institute. In 1979 in San Francisco, he helped found the Pacific Institute for Public Policy, while in Peru he supported Hernando de Soto, who in 1984 would create the *Instituto Libertad y Democracia* (Institute for Liberty and Democracy).

Back in the UK, the IEA played a key role in introducing the newly elected opposition leader, Margaret Thatcher to Hayek. According to Harris, who arranged the meeting, 'Although she is known as being a rather overpowering lady she sat down like a meek schoolgirl and, for about ten minutes, said nothing while Hayek deployed his arguments.' After thirty minutes, she left, and the IEA people gathered around Hayek to hear his reaction. After an unusually long pause, looking quite overawed, he said, 'She's so beautiful.'[30]

Over the next four years, Thatcher and her senior ministers absorbed many of the policy prescriptions the IEA had to offer. Many of these ideas came together in November 1977 when the Conservative Party produced a report, *Stepping Stones*, which set out its blueprint for changing the face of Britain.[31] This report formed the basis of Thatcher's 1979 election platform, which she won; as she did three more times off the back of unashamedly pro-market policies.

Even at the height of the neoliberal ascendancy in the UK, few people appreciated the pivotal role that Antony Fisher had played. Not so Margaret Thatcher, who, in the summer of 1979, wrote to Fisher, thanking him: 'You created the atmosphere which made our victory possible.' And she was no less fulsome in public. In a speech Thatcher gave in 1987 to celebrate the thirtieth anniversary of the IEA, she gushed that 'what we have achieved could never have been done without the leadership of the Institute of Economic Affairs'.[32]

In the US, the neoliberal think tank, the Heritage Foundation, published *Mandate for Leadership* in 1980, which became the 'bible of the Reagan Administration',[33] when the new president sent a copy to each of his cabinet members and directed them to read it. During the 1980s, thousands of its recommendations for tax, welfare and health reform were adopted. In October

1983, in a speech to the Heritage Foundation, Reagan acknowledged that its 'frequent publications, timely research, policy papers, seminars, and conferences account for your enormous influence on Capitol Hill and, believe me, I know, at the White House'.[34] Hayek's influence was again on display in the 1994 *Contract with America*, in which Republicans pledged to shrink big government and deregulate the economy.

Littering the world

Seeing the tide turn so decisively, Fisher wanted to open up even more fronts in the battle of ideas. As economic globalisation took hold during the 1970s, Fisher became excited by the thought that the free market did not have to be confined by borders and that the pro-market philosophy he had nurtured in the UK could be taken to the world.

In 1980, Hayek again affected the trajectory of Antony Fisher's career. In a letter to Fisher on New Year's Day, his mentor advised that:

> the time has come when it has become desirable and almost a duty to extend the network of institutes of the kind of the London Institute of Economic Affairs. Though it took some time for its influence to become noticeable, it has by now far exceeded my most optimistic hopes ... And I am more convinced than ever that the method practiced by the IEA is the only one which promises any real results ... This ought to be used to create similar institutes all over the world and you have now acquired the special skill of doing it.[35]

Always the innovator, Fisher was convinced that there had to be a way to mass produce new think tanks along the IEA model.

By 1981, he was ready to act. At that time, Fisher was living in San Francisco, and thus based his new enterprise in the US. Called the Atlas Economic Research Foundation (now called the Atlas Network), its mission was 'to litter the world with free-market think tanks'.[36] Fisher took the name from Greek mythology and it alludes to one of the Titans, Atlas, who supports the world on his shoulders.

Located in a two-room suite in the elegant Mills Building in Montgomery Street, Fisher worked with a small staff, who provided resources to help 'intellectual entrepreneurs' create new think tanks. According to Atlas, the typical intellectual entrepreneur combines a good grasp of free market economics with the ability to run a business. One of its early publications was a fifty-page manual on the do's and don'ts for setting up a think tank, while another addressed fundraising. It also provided seed money to help new think tanks get going and sponsored intellectual entrepreneurs who do not come from the business sector, enrolling them in its 'think tank MBA', which was designed to help recruits build economically sustainable businesses.

In 1983, Hayek acknowledged Fisher's genius, praising him for setting up Atlas, which had succeeded in creating 'institutions scattered around the entire western half of the globe, from which sound ideas emanate'.[37]

Although its total budget is only around $6 million, Atlas conquered new territories in Eastern Europe after the fall of communism. It also took the battle deep into South America and even helped lodge think tanks through the length and breadth of Africa. As well as networking over 478 market-oriented think tanks in 85 countries, in 2013 Atlas trained 622 personnel and distributed over $4 million to its partners.[38]

Others have imitated Atlas's pioneering work. The Economic Freedom Network links think tanks around its annual *Freedom of the World* reports, the Stockholm Network is centred in Western Europe, and the International Policy Network brings together think tanks working on global issues.

In 1985, three years before he died, Fisher, in a letter to Hayek, acknowledged that 'your inspired idea imparted to me in 1945 is still growing and having much more important consequences'.[39]

Fisher was always happy to blend into the background, and only a few intimates fully understood the significance of his contributions. One was Margaret Thatcher, who, in 1988, recommended he be included on the Queen's birthday honours list. Cited for his contributions to 'public and political services', Harris later teased him by suggesting he should have been knighted for 'private and anti-political services'. While Fisher saw his point, he decided that he would keep the knighthood anyway.[40] Another tribute to his contribution came from the publishing tycoon Steve Forbes Jr., who said of Fisher, 'You are an extraordinary fellow who is having an enormous impact on much of the civilized world. It must be heartening to you how much your institutes are influencing public debates!'[41] *The Times* obituary also acknowledged his remarkable contributions: 'The change in public opinion that has taken place in many countries in the last two decades is undoubted due to Fisher's vision.'[42]

Hayek's ideas and those of other neoliberal economists have undoubtedly shaped the architecture of globalisation, particularly since the 1980s. However, they may well have remained voices in the wilderness without think tanks to promote their ideas and help transform abstract theories into policies that could be implemented by governments. This was Fisher's legacy.

The result, as observed by political scientist Eric Helleiner, is that the pro-market think tanks have helped overturn large parts of 'the restrictive Bretton Woods financial order'.[43] Capital markets have been liberated; national regulations and tariffs, which had hindered trade, have been reduced; and international agencies now look to market-based solutions to solve global environmental, social, and health problems.

Notes

1. Anon., 'Obituary: Prof Friedrich von Hayek', *Daily Telegraph* (25 March 1992), p. 21.
2. Friedrich Hayek quoted by Alan Ebenstein in *Friedrich Hayek: A Biography* (New York: Palgrave, 2001), p. 13.
3. Interview between Friedrich Hayek and Bob Chitester on video retrieved from: http://hayek.ufm.edu/index.php/Bob_Chitester_part_II (accessed 5 January 2015).
4. The term neoliberalism was coined by Alexander Rüstow at the 'Colloque Walter Lippmann', held in Paris in 1938.
5. Hayek's review essay of Keynes's *Treatise on Money* as well as Keynes's reply are reprinted in Bruce Caldwell (ed.), *The Collected Works of F.A. Hayek*, Vol. 9 (Chicago: University of Chicago Press, 1995).
6. 'Friedrich A. von Hayek', Oral History Program (Los Angeles: University of California, 1983), pp. 114–15.
7. 'Friedrich A. von Hayek', Oral History Program, pp. 118–20.
8. F.A. Hayek, 'The Intellectuals and Socialism', *University of Chicago Law Review*, 16:3 (1949), 417–33, quote on p. 420.
9. F.A. Hayek, 'The Intellectuals and Socialism', 417.
10. F.A. Hayek, *The Road to Serfdom* (London and Henley: Routledge & Kegan Paul, 1944 and reprinted 1979), p. 150.
11. F.A. Hayek, *The Road to Serfdom*, p. 150.
12. 'Friedrich A. von Hayek', Oral History Program, pp. 464–5.
13. H. Finer, *The Road to Reaction* (Chicago: Quadrangle Books, 1945), p. v.
14. D.E. Moggridge (ed.), *The Collected Writings of John Maynard Keynes* (Cambridge: Macmillan/Cambridge University Press, 1980), Vol. XXVII, pp. 387. Letter to Friedrich Hayek dated 28 June 1944.
15. D.E. Moggridge (ed.), *The Collected Writings of John Maynard Keynes*, Vol. XXVII, pp. 387.
16. Friedrich Hayek quoted by Angus Burgin in *Great Persuasion: Reinventing Free Markets since the Depression* (Cumberland, RI: Harvard University Press, 2012), p. 95.
17. Interview conducted with Lord Ralph Harris on 17 July 2000 and part of the PBS programme *Commanding Heights*.
18. Before the meeting, Friedrich Hayek wrote a memo to himself that captured his hopes for the meeting: 'We must raise and train an army of fighters for freedom ... to shape and guide that opinion.' See Alan Ebenstein in *Friedrich Hayek: A Biography* (New York: Palgrave, 2001), p. 143.

19 M. Friedman, 'Foreword', in *Essays on Hayek*, ed. Fritz Machlup (Hillsdale, MI: Hillsdale College Press, 1976), pp. xxi–xxiv.
20 Friedrich Hayek quoted by John Blundell in 'Hayek, Fisher and *The Road to Serfdom*' in the 'Introduction' of the condensed version of *The Road to Serfdom* as it appeared in the April 1945 edition of *Reader's Digest* and republished by the Institute of Economic Affairs in 2001, p. 20.
21 A.G.A. Fisher, *Must History Repeat Itself?* (Enfield: Churchill Press 1974), p. 103.
22 A.G.A. Fisher, *Must History Repeat Itself?*, p. 103.
23 Interview conducted with Lord Ralph Harris on 17 July 2000 and part of the PBS programme *Commanding Heights*.
24 Anon., 'Obituary: Lord Harris of High Cross', *Daily Telegraph* (20 October 2006).
25 J. Blundell, *Waging the War of Ideas* (London: Institute of Economic Affairs, 2007), p. 21.
26 Ralph Harris is quoted in Dorian D. Fisher (ed.), *Manual: Some Do's and Don'ts for Public Policy Institutes* (San Francisco: Atlas Economic Research Foundation, 1983), p. 14.
27 Sir Alistair Burnet quoted by Gerald Frost in *Antony Fisher: Champion of Liberty* (London: Profile Books, 2002), p. 94.
28 Its proper name is the Sveriges Riksbank Prize in Economic Sciences in Memory of Alfred Nobel.
29 Antony Fisher quoted by Gerald Frost in *Antony Fisher*, p. 137.
30 Ralph Harris quoted by Richard Crockett in *Thinking the Unthinkable* (London: HarperCollins, 1994), p. 197.
31 J. Hoskyns and N. Strauss, *Stepping Stones* (14 November 1977), 2/6/1/248, Thatcher MSS, CC. Retrieved from: www.margaretthatcher.org/document/111771 (accessed 25 March 2015).
32 Margaret Thatcher is quoted by Daniel Stedman Jones in *Masters of the Universe* (Princeton: Princeton University Press, 2012), p. 162.
33 D.E. Abelson, *Capitol Idea* (Montreal: McGill-Queen's University Press, 2006), p. 34.
34 Remarks made by President Ronald Reagan at a dinner marking the tenth anniversary of the Heritage Foundation, delivered on 3 October 1983 in the International Ballroom at the Washington Hilton Hotel.
35 Richard Freeman and Jeffrey Steinberg in 'The Legacy of Friedrich von Hayek: Fascism Didn't Die with Hitler', *Executive Intelligence Review*, 22:8 (1995), 46–9, quote on p. 49.
36 Quote taken from the newsletter of Atlas Consulting, *Highlights*, Winter 2006/7, p. 15.
37 W.W. Bartley (ed.), *The Collected Works of F.A. Hayek* (Chicago: University of Chicago Press, 1988), p. 193.
38 Atlas Network, *Year in Review 2013* (Washington, DC: Atlas Network, 2014), pp. 4 and 29.
39 Friedrich Hayek quoted by Daniel Stedman Jones in *Masters of the Universe*, p. 157.
40 R. Harris, 'Review: "Antony Fisher"', *United Press International* (11 November 2002).

41 Alejandro Chafuen, private communication. The quote comes from an article that Steve Forbes submitted to *Forbes* magazine but was never published.
42 Quoted by J. Stanley Marshall in 'Antony Fisher, Margaret Thatcher, and the James Madison Institute', *Journal of the James Madison Institute*, Number 44 (Spring/Summer 2009), 59–65, quote on p. 64.
43 E. Helleiner, *States and the Reemergence of Global Finance: From Bretton Woods to the 1990s* (Ithaca, NY: Cornell University Press, 1994), p. 3.

6

The new globalists

For God's sake let us sit upon the ground
And tell sad stories of the death of kings ... (William Shakespeare, *Richard II*)

Masters of their own destiny

During the late 1960s, a group of prominent CEOs began a public campaign to reform the international order so that it was no longer built solely around the nation-state but around global markets. None were more prominent than George Ball.

After working with Jean Monnet on European integration, Ball was appointed undersecretary of state in the Kennedy Administration in 1961. Known as the 'champion of lost causes',[1] his greatest defeat was when the president ignored his advice on the deployment of 16,000 military trainers to Vietnam. Ball bluntly told JFK: 'Within five years we'll have 300,000 men in the paddies and jungles and never find them again.' Kennedy just shrugged and replied: 'Well, George, you're supposed to be one of the smartest guys in town, but you're crazier than hell. That will never happen.'[2]

After leaving Washington in September 1966, other than a brief stint as ambassador to the United Nations, Ball spent the rest of his career as a banker with Lehman Brothers' Kuhn Loeb. At about this time, Monnet, who had long been his mentor, counselled: 'George, you should stop diffusing your energies. You should select a single, great objective and concentrate on it until it is accomplished.'[3]

While at Lehman Brothers, Ball found a cause that he could make his own. Keen to expand the bank's operations overseas, Ball was frustrated by national regulations that introduced unnecessary 'rigidities and obstructions', often serving no other purpose than to protect local enterprises from foreign competition.[4]

Ball fired the opening salvo of his campaign in October 1967, during an address to the British National Committee of the International Chamber of Commerce, when he launched into a full-blooded attack on the nation-state.

Ball complained that transnational corporations were unable to pursue 'the true logic of the global economy' by the 'ceaseless interference from its puzzled parent, the sovereign state'. The problem was that while 'the world corporation ... is a modern concept evolved to meet the requirements of the modern age, ... the nation-state ... is still rooted in archaic concepts unsympathetic to the needs of our complex world'.[5] Business, in particular, needed to be liberated from the 'political boundaries of nation-states [which] are too narrow and constricted'.[6] No business executive of his stature had engaged in such a frontal, let alone public, assault on the nation-state.

This was a step too far for many in his audience, and Ball wryly observed that his speech was not greeted by 'dancing in Threadneedle Street'.[7] This was not surprising as most were from the very companies that enjoyed the political protection that Ball was intent on exorcising.

As it turned out, Ball was not quite alone. In subsequent years, high-profile executives came out of the woodwork to publicly support this position. They included Orville Freeman and Eldridge Hayes from Business International Corporation, Aurelio Peccei and Giovanni Agnelli from Fiat, Sol Linowitz from Xerox, IBM executives Jacques Maisonrouge and Tom Watson Jr., Walter Wriston, chairman and CEO of CitiBank, David Rockefeller of Chase Manhattan Bank, and A.W. (Tom) Clausen of Bank of America. In 1972, CitiBank president, William Spencer, described this growing band of businesspeople as the 'new globalists'.[8]

Like Ball, the new globalists questioned the relevance of the nation-state, which they argued hindered the globalisation of markets. For example, Aurelio Peccei wrote in his book, *Before it is Too Late*: 'If we want to move ahead into the future with a sporting chance of success and survival, we must purge and purify our minds of the myth of sovereignty, which is a political and philosophical leftover from a dead past.'[9] Walter Wriston contrasted the 'politically neutral' business sector, which exists 'only to satisfy the economic desires of the world's people', to politicians, who stick to the 'older idea that business is – or should be – the chosen instrument of the state'. He went on to criticise politicians for 'fragmenting the world, while the multinational corporations have been viewing the planet as one marketplace'.[10] David Rockefeller, intent on exposing the contradictions, maintained that 'complete national sovereignty' denies the general populace the 'real benefits' of global markets by restricting the ability of multinational corporations to move 'goods and capital and technology across borders freely'.[11]

Having identified the source of the malaise, how did the new globalists suggest transnational corporations cut loose from the stultifying grip of national supervision? Ball proposed 'the establishment by treaty of an international company's law, administrated by a supranational body'. This would denationalise corporations so that they would 'become quite literally citizens of the world', subject to international rules.[12] Neil Jacoby, a consultant to Rand Corporation, picked up the idea five years later, calling on the United Nations to create a 'World Corporation Authority' that would take on 'supranational chartering of multinational corporations'.[13]

Other solutions proposed by new globalists ranged from finding loopholes to skirt around government rules to suggesting that transnational corporations use their mobility to dissuade governments from pursuing onerous regulations. As Wriston explained: '[C]apital, both human and material, will leave countries where it is not welcome.'[14]

There were also more fanciful solutions, and while they had little hope of seeing the light of day, they reflected the frustration building among CEOs in the 1970s. Peccei, for example, proposed that 'to give the multinational corporation an international charter, it may be located in a real or symbolic territory'. This would grant them equivalent status to nation-states, and Peccei went so far as to suggest that the United Nations recognise their de facto sovereignty.[15] Carl Gerstacker ran with the idea: 'I have long dreamed of buying an island owned by no nation and of establishing the World Headquarters of the Dow Company on the truly neutral ground of such an island, beholden to no nation or society.' He even offered to 'pay any natives handsomely to move elsewhere'.[16]

Rather than pursuing madcap schemes to colonise unclaimed islands, the conversation turned to how the corporate sector could become master of its own destiny.

Eldridge Hayes, founder of Business International, suggested 'that the multinational can influence the course of history toward peace, international cooperation and a finer quality of life than we have ever known'.[17] Tom Clausen was more specific, proposing that business should be at the table when decisions are made on globalisation. For him, corporations should be able to 'deal with governments on a basis other than a sovereign-subject relationship'. He went on to predict that '[t]here now is reason to believe that the world of the future will be shaped as much by commercial and financial statesmen as by diplomats and politicians'.[18] IBM's Jacques Maisonrouge agreed, looking to businesspeople being in the 'vanguard ... helping to build a new world economic system'.[19]

Beyond the state

David Rockefeller is the epitome of this new breed of corporate statesmen. By drawing together members of the business and political elites into the Trilateral

Commission, in 1972 he created a powerful vehicle for the new globalists to influence the policy agenda.

A captain in the US intelligence service, in August 1944 Rockefeller was posted to Paris. He did his best work in Le Grand Véfour, one of that city's finest restaurants, wining and dining important European dignitaries – at some cost to his waistline – who were a useful source of information, which he fed to his controllers in the US Embassy. He was also an excellent host: affable, attentive, genuinely interested in what people had to say, and, coming from a fabulously wealthy family, he always picked up the tab.

The provenance of Rockefeller's internationalism dates back to this time. 'Like many in my generation, I returned from World War II believing a new international architecture had to be erected and ... I was determined to play a role in that process.'[20]

After the war, Rockefeller joined the family business, Chase National Bank, and by 1969, he was its chairman and chief executive. With many of the bank's operations overseas, Rockefeller used business trips to build an extensive network of contacts among influential political leaders, CEOs and a smattering of kings, queens and plenipotentiaries. Soon, his electrically powered Rolodex, and measuring four feet by five feet, contained in excess of 100,000 business cards.

From time to time, Rockefeller joined the chorus of new globalists speaking out in favour of greater international cooperation and against government regulations that fragmented global markets and frustrated the ability of transnational corporations to operate freely around the world. Loath to directly criticise the political elite, in private, he worried that government leaders had lost their passion for reforming, let alone expanding the international order.

By the start of the 1970s, Rockefeller saw more immediate reasons to worry. They included the Nixon Shock, which gutted the Bretton Woods system, the growing dysfunction of the UN and the propensity of the US to act unilaterally. He blamed 'isolationism and narrow nationalism', which he feared could reverse 'the growing internationalism and economic cooperation we have experienced for two decades and more'.[21] Resolved to counter this troublesome trend, he set about rallying other new globalists to the cause.

With few precedents to draw on, Rockefeller found inspiration in a book published in 1970 by his good friend Zbigniew Brzezinski, a professor of government at Columbia University. Titled *Between Two Ages*, it proposed the formation of a 'Community of the Developed Nations', consisting of three influential players in Western Europe, the United States and Japan. This community would develop 'long-range strategy for international development based on the emerging global consciousness'.[22] Importantly, Brzezinski argued that besides politicians, its policies should be driven by 'international businessmen, scholars, professional men, and public officials'.[23]

Using Brzezinski's proposition as his starting point, in July 1972, Rockefeller hosted a meeting at his Pocantico Hills estate during which participants decided to create a platform that these elites could use to contribute to global policymaking. In looking for an organisational model, Rockefeller consciously borrowed from Monnet's Action Committee for the United States of Europe, but with a much broader membership, drawn from the three major economic regions in the world (hence the name 'Trilateral Commission'). It aimed to encourage greater cooperation on political, economic and social problems and during the 1980s started to look at promoting sustainable development. With no global policy group filling this niche, the Trilateral Commission broke new ground.[24]

Making his case for the new body, Rockefeller argued: 'Governments don't have time to think about the broader long-range issues.' Having identified a void in international strategic policymaking, Rockefeller said that it made 'sense to persuade a group of private, qualified citizens to get together to identify the key issues affecting the world and possible solutions'. He went on to suggest that 'private citizens are often able to act with greater flexibility than governments in the search of new and better forms of international cooperation'.[25]

Next, Rockefeller consulted his Rolodex to identify whom he might approach from the crème de la crème of the political, business and intellectual elites. For example, he recruited Jimmy Carter and George H.W. Bush (future US presidents), Raymond Barre (former vice president of the European Commission and future prime minister of France), Kiichi Miyazawa (leading Liberal Democratic Party politician and future prime minister of Japan), as well as important politicians within government and opposition parties. Global mandarins from the UN agencies, IMF, GATT, Organization for Economic Co-operation and Development (OECD) and EU also accepted Rockefeller's invitations to join.

Everyone, even politicians, joined in their private capacity, which proved necessary if the Trilateral Commission was not to repeat the mistakes of the United Nations, which Rockefeller accused of having been reduced 'to a forum for the expression and promotion of narrow national or bloc interests'.[26]

Rockefeller was particularly keen that corporate statesmen should be part of his new project. George Ball joined, as did CEOs from major transnational corporations, making up 44 per cent of the Trilateral Commission's members (called 'commissioners').[27] With the private sector so strongly represented, Princeton law professor Richard Falk concluded that 'the vistas of the Trilateral Commission can be understood as the ideological perspective representing the transnational outlook of the multinational corporation'.[28] The Trilateral Commission, therefore, marked an important juncture in globalisation: it saw the corporate sector publicly accepted as a legitimate partner in shaping policies. This challenged an important assumption behind the international liberal order: that it should be built around governments working on concert to address global problems.

Justifying their contribution, Rockefeller argued that businesspeople owed a special duty – 'sagesse oblige' – to use their 'special capabilities and our access to knowledge ... [to] contribute to human development'.[29]

By bringing together members of the global elites, Rockefeller created a powerful organisation, although one not easily categorised. The Trilateral Commission operated neither as a traditional lobby group nor think tank, yet it shared features with both. Its well-researched reports provided fresh and sometimes controversial perspectives on how to make the world a safer and better place. They were influential because commissioners had direct access to decision-makers, and some went on to hold high office themselves. Best described as a transnational policy club, it established a model that others followed.

At its first plenary meeting, held in Kyoto in 1975, Brzezinski was appointed its director. Addressing his fellow commissioners, he told them that the Trilateral Commission had embarked on a historic mission: Just as '1945 marked the beginning of the existing international system', the creation of the Trilateral Commission would be 'the beginning of its renovation and readjustment'.[30] From this statement, we see that Brzezinski believed that they were the successors of the postwar generation of architects who constructed the foundations of internationalism at Bretton Woods and San Francisco. This time, however, the task would no longer be the preserve of the Anglo-American political establishment, but involve the business and political elites together with senior bureaucrats from international agencies.

As the Trilateral Commission was bedded down, international bureaucrats discovered that they had a strong affinity with CEOs, probably because they both had the most to gain from the expansion of the global project. They also absorbed ideas from one another and held remarkably similar views on how to strengthen the global superstructure. These factors would become important during the 1990s, when the two would work closely together to free trade and expand protection for foreign investment.

Greatest parade on earth

David Rockefeller's model of a transnational policy club inspired others. None have been more successful in size or reach than the World Economic Forum, the brainchild of a Swiss professor, Klaus Schwab. Such is its influence over the global policy agenda that *Time* magazine remarked that the Forum 'is probably the closest thing globalisation has to world headquarters'.[31]

Born on 30 March 1938, in Ravensburg, Germany, Klaus Schwab credited his enthusiasm for internationalism to his father. A member of Rotary, during summer vacations, his father arranged for Klaus to be billeted with Rotary members in other parts of Europe, not wanting his son to 'grow up in a narrow, national corset'.[32]

Despite doing well at school, Klaus was a loner. He recalls a painful incident during the Rutenfest, a street parade held during the last weekend of the summer holidays. The highlight of the festivities occurred when students marched through the streets beating drums (*Rutentrommler*). Much to his disappointment, Klaus was never asked to join the parade and watched on, envying the camaraderie of those marching. Reflecting on this many years later, he said that it was 'one of the biggest failures and setbacks in my life'.[33]

After obtaining doctorates in economics and technological sciences, as well as a Master in Public Administration from Harvard University, Schwab enjoyed a short, but stellar career in business before returning to academia in 1969 as a professor for business policy at the University of Geneva.

Having spent some time in the US studying American business methods, he was determined to help European companies lift their game in order to successfully compete on world markets. To help them, he decided to organise a symposium to introduce European CEOs to the latest management techniques from the US.

Schwab received seed funding from the European Economic Community, but still came up short. By a stroke of luck, during a golf game he interested Eugen Claussner in his project. Managing director of Hukla, a German furniture company, Claussner agreed to loan Schwab 50,000 Swiss francs – on one condition. Schwab had to either pay him back or join his company, which Schwab was not keen to do. His hands tied, Schwab accepted the deal.

Schwab chose Davos as his venue. It is a ski resort in the Swiss Alps, with excellent conference facilities and plenty of accommodation. He particularly liked the town's relative seclusion, which he hoped would cut busy CEOs off from their offices, encouraging participants to immerse themselves in the symposium's programme and to network after the day's lectures were finished.

Held in January 1971, 440 executives attended the conference. With the profits, Schwab quickly settled his debt with Claussner, thus avoiding an unwelcome career in the furniture business. Now confident that a sufficient demand existed for such events, Schwab decided to organise annual meetings of the newly named Forum européen de management (European management forum).

Unfortunately, after two years, the numbers started to drop, as the Forum faced competition. Looking for a way to reverse this trend, Schwab noticed that 'people were not so much interested in pure management methods but in the challenges of running companies in the broader global context'.[34] To freshen up the programme, Schwab included briefings on geopolitical issues delivered by prominent politicians and international affairs experts. He also added sessions led by social, consumer and environmental activists. '[I]f you live in a community of destiny, you have to respond to the expectations of different stakeholders', he explained.[35] By teaching CEOs to collaborate with key stakeholders, Schwab believed that European companies would not only meet the American challenge, but gain a competitive advantage over their rivals. While members of his business audience felt uncomfortable at what were often confronting sessions, many came to appreciate the value of these face-to-face encounters with their critics.

The new format revitalised the Forum, and in 1976, attendance rose to around 1,500. To accommodate its popularity, Schwab organised additional regional meetings outside Europe and encouraged non-European companies to join, with IBM chairman Tom Watson Jr. and Pepsi-Cola CEO Don Kendall among the first.

Next, Schwab courted political leaders and top international bureaucrats, believing that they would benefit from mixing with CEOs and that they too would appreciate the opportunity to discuss the state of the world. Leaders of international economic agencies were particularly grateful to Schwab, who set up closed-door, off-the-record side meetings where they could discuss common problems. As Schwab explained, this permitted 'participants to get to know each other, exchange ideas and work on ongoing issues and problems without having to produce a communiqué, treaty, press statement or any other document at its conclusion'.[36]

By 1987, the original name no longer suited, so Schwab changed it to the World Economic Forum. Run by a private foundation out of Geneva, its mission is no less than 'improving the state of the world'.[37] While the Forum has no formal authority, it is nevertheless influential, as Schwab explains:

> We are not a decision-making body – decisions in our world are made by those who have the necessary mandate to do so ... We offer, however, a decision-facilitating mechanism. In fact, there is no other organization that is so involved in the pre-decision-making and post-decision-making phases.[38]

The Forum possesses an unparalleled ability to generate creative solutions to global problems, which often find their way into those meetings where decisions are made. Similarly, after a programme is launched, Davos is often the place where partnerships between the private and public sectors are brokered, providing resources to implement that programme. It is only able to achieve its influence by maintaining a high profile, and its credibility is built on being able to attract the world's shakers and movers to Davos.

The popularity of the World Economic Forum rests on Schwab's ability to put together a programme that features top-shelf speakers, including a who's who of political leaders and heads of international agencies. After a day of formal sessions, those attending appreciate the opportunity to socialise with their peers and make connections that, one day, may prove to be useful.

The World Economic Forum maintains its currency through Schwab's unerring talent to capture the global zeitgeist. He also uses his opening speech to challenge his audience. For example, on a number of occasions, he has reproached politicians for their failure to tackle climate change. After the global financial crisis, he took aim at the excesses of unbalanced capitalism. And in 2014, speaking to the Forum's theme, 'The Reshaping of the World', he called on leaders to reform global governance so that it better addressed inequality and volatility.[39]

The success of the World Economic Forum also owes much to its exclusiveness, and Schwab unapologetically refers to it as the 'Davos Club'.[40] As Schwab explained, 'In order to reinforce the club character of its networks, the Foundation limits its activities to members and their special guests only.'[41] Selection is ruthless. An invite one year is no guarantee that this will be automatically repeated the next. Even the most high-flying individuals can find that they no longer make the cut once their star dims. 'Not always an easy thing to do, shooting old elephants, but how else did one stay current with the trend and temper of the times?' reflected Schwab.[42]

With the Davos Club now the domain of the global elites, one can easily overlook the fact that the World Economic Forum is run and bankrolled by major corporations, which are its only members. Everyone else is a guest, and they depend on Schwab and his organising committee for invites to join the parade. So while Davos may have become the unofficial headquarters of globalisation, the World Economic Forum is a privately-owned club, and its agenda obviously reflects many of the values held by CEOs, who lean towards neoliberal solutions like deregulation, limited government and free markets and trade.

Despite the rise of neoliberalism, Schwab has not always gone along with the predominant paradigm. In 1996, he penned an opinion piece for the *New York Times* in which he warned of a brewing backlash against globalisation and offered some ideas on how to prevent it:

> [T]he globalized economy must not become synonymous with 'free market on the rampage,' a brakeless train wreaking havoc. The social responsibilities of corporations

(and governments) remain as important as ever. What is on the agenda is the need to redefine and recalibrate them.⁴³

It was not until the end of 1999, after demonstrations closed down the WTO meeting in Seattle that members of the World Economic Forum started to heed Schwab's warnings and the tenor of sessions soon changed, as participants began to seriously consider how to moderate the downside of globalisation.

House of world order

Following the success of the Trilateral Commission and the World Economic Forum, policy networks have proliferated, swelling the ranks of the global elite. They include the annual Bo'ao Conference held in Hainan, China, the triennial Fathers and Sons meeting of plutocrats in Latin America, the Monaco Media Forum for media moguls and the World Business Council for Sustainable Development. For those desiring to soak up the latest technologies or business innovations, they can tap into events like the Aspen Festival of Ideas, Google's Zeitgeist and the Allen & Company Sun Valley Conference held annually in Idaho. The most popular of these is TED Talks, which attracts over 500 million hits for its online broadcasts, leading its owner and curator, Chris Anderson, to claim that 'combined, our contacts reach pretty much everyone who's interesting in the country, if not the planet'.⁴⁴ Other events discuss particular global issues and are organised by universities, think tanks and other non-governmental groups.

Not everyone welcomes the advent of the global elite. One of its sternest critics is political scientist Samuel Huntington, who talks dismissively of the 'Davos Man'. By his definition, the Davos Man does not have to be involved with the World Economic Forum or other transnational clubs, or even be male. What distinguishes him or her is that they 'have little need for national loyalty, view national boundaries as obstacles that, thankfully, are vanishing, and see national governments as residues from the past whose only useful function is to facilitate the elite's global operations'.⁴⁵ For all the reasons that Huntington came to disparage the Davos Man, members of the elite take pride in being harbingers of a new global civilisation.

The new generation of globalists, however, was not convinced that the model laid out in the 1940s had been a success, as Klaus Schwab pointed out.

> The lack of global leadership is glaring, not least because the existing global governance institutions are hampered by archaic conventions and procedures devised, in some instances, at the end of World War II. Sovereign power still rests with

national governments, but authentic and effective global leadership has yet to emerge. Meanwhile, public governance at the local, national, regional, and international levels has weakened. Even the best leaders cannot operate successfully in a failed system.[46]

In part, Schwab was echoing the criticisms of the new globalists of the 1970s: that international governance cannot be built around the preservation of sovereignty without stifling the growth of global markets. The other problem is that governments never fulfilled their promise of expanding the international rule of law. As a result, intergovernmental cooperation has fallen well short of adequately addressing global threats.

The appearance of private networks and elite clubs, like the World Economic Forum, was seen by political scientist Richard N. Gardner as a way out of this impasse. Writing in 1974, he predicted:

> [T]he 'house of world order' will have to be built from the bottom up rather than from the top down. It will look like a great 'booming, buzzing confusion,' ... but an end run around national sovereignty, eroding it piece by piece, will accomplish much more than the old-fashioned frontal assault.[47]

Gardner turned out to be astonishingly prescient. In the years that followed, governments surrendered their monopoly over governance of the global commons, and while not being side-lined, non-governmental actors now play an important role in shaping the global architecture.

The subsequent history of globalisation, particularly during the 1990s when its construction enjoyed a growth spurt, therefore can only be understood by looking at the informal as well as the formal pathways in which the global architecture operates. While globalisation progressed through traditional international treaties, the ideas that they contained have often been drawn from non-governmental policy networks and clubs, which reflect a consensus among the elites. Particularly important to seeing some of the major economic treaties of the 1990s through to a successful conclusion has been the close relationship between the business elites and executives in international agencies, often nurtured within the confines of one or other of the transnational clubs. What might have once been perceived as lobbying is now viewed as cooperation between allies to liberalise the global marketplace. An added feature of global governance is the emergence of norms, which provided non-legal means of defining responsible behaviour of countries, transnational corporations and even non-governmental organisations (NGOs). Finally, markets exerted their own influence, as transnational corporations have been able to use their mobility to press government to engage in competitive deregulation.

Notes

1. R.D. McFadden, 'George W. Ball Dies at 84: Vietnam's Devil's Advocate', *New York Times* (28 May 1994).
2. S. Karnow, *Vietnam: A History* (New York: Penguin Books, 1984), p. 266.
3. G.W. Ball, 'Introduction', in Jean Monnet's *Memoirs* (London: Collins, 1978), p 11.
4. G.W. Ball, 'Cosmocorp: The Importance of Being Stateless', *Columbia Journal of World Business*, 2:6 (1967), 23–36.
5. G.W. Ball, 'Cosmocorp', 23–36.
6. A modified version of the speech 'Cosmocorp: The Importance of Being Stateless' was published in the *Columbia Journal of World Business*, 2:6 (1967), 23–36.
7. George Ball quoted by Peter Nehemkis in 'Supranational Control of the International Corporation: A Dissenting View', *Californian Western Law Review*, 10:2 (1974), 286–324. Threadneedle Street is the London equivalent of Wall Street.
8. L. Silk, 'The New Globalists', *New York Times* (25 October 1972), pp. 63 and 75.
9. A. Peccei, *Before it is Too Late* (London: Macmillan Company, 1969), pp. 48–9 and 152, respectively.
10. W.B. Wriston, 'People, Politics and Productivity: The World Corporation in the 1980s', speech presented to the Multinational Customer Conference in London, England on 15 September 1976.
11. D. Rockefeller, 'Multinationals Under Siege', *Atlantic Community Quarterly* (Fall, 1975), 312–22.
12. G.W. Ball, 'Cosmocorp', 23–36.
13. J.H. Jacoby, *Corporate Power and Social Responsibility* (New York: Macmillan Publishing, 1973), pp. 118–19.
14. W.B. Wriston, 'People, Politics and Productivity'.
15. Center for the Study of Democratic Institutions (1970) 'The Reluctant Death of National Sovereignty', programme 518. Historian Arnold J. Toynbee interviews Aurelio Peccei of Olivetti and Fiat and Eldridge Haynes and Orville Freeman. Digital recording retrieved from: http://digital.library.ucsb.edu/items/show/5803 (accessed 25 March 2014).
16. Carl A. Gerstacker quoted by Richard J. Barnet and Ronald E. Müller in *Global Reach: The Power of the Multinational Corporations* (London: Jonathan Cape, 1974), p. 16.
17. A. Rubner, *In the Twilight of the Multis* (Brighton: Pen Press Publishers, 2008), p. 60.
18. A.W. Clausen, 'The Internationalized Corporation: An Executive's View', *Annals of the American Academy of Political and Social Science*, 403:1 (1972), 12–21, quote on p. 13.
19. J.G. Maisonrouge, 'How a Multinational Corporation Appears to Its Managers', in George W. Ball (ed.), *Global Companies* (Englewood Cliffs, NJ: Prentice-Hall, 1975), pp. 11–20, quote on p. 14.
20. D. Rockefeller, *Memoirs* (New York: Random House, 2002), p. 406.
21. D. Rockefeller, 'Multinationals Under Siege', 312–22.
22. Z.K. Brzezinski, *Between Two Ages* (New York: Viking Press, 1970), pp. 293, 295–7, 308.

23 Z.K. Brzezinski, *Between Two Ages*, p. 29.
24 It could be argued that the Bilderberg Group was the first transnational policy club, but its focus in its early years was improving relations between the US and Europe rather than global policymaking.
25 David Rockefeller quoted in *Trialogue*, 2 (November 1973), 5.
26 D. Rockefeller, 'Multinationals Under Siege', 312–22.
27 H. Sklar and R. Everdell, 'Who's Who on the Trilateral Commission', in Holly Sklar (ed.), *Trilateralism* (Boston: South End Press), p. 99. Data based on the years 1973–79.
28 R. Falk, 'A New Paradigm for International Legal Studies: Prospects and Proposals', *Yale Law Journal*, 84 (1975), 969–1021, quote on p. 1005.
29 D. Rockefeller, 'International Financial Challenges', *Vital Speeches of the Day*, 36:3 (1969), 83–6, quote on p. 83.
30 Zbigniew Brzezinski quoted in *Trialogue*, 4 (May, 1975), 2.
31 D. Morrison, 'The Brilliance of the Brilliant', *Time Asia* (27 January 2000).
32 K.M. Schwab, 'Klaus Schwab hat die globale Wirtschaft im Blick und die oberschwäbische Heimat im Herzen', interview of Klaus Schwab published on 16 December 2012 in *schwäbische.de*.
33 K.M. Schwab, 'Klaus Schwab hat die globale Wirtschaft im Blick und die oberschwäbische Heimat im Herzen'.
34 Klaus Schwab quoted by Haig Simonian in 'Klaus Schwab', *FT.com* (22 January 2008), p. 1.
35 This section relies heavily on a case study written by Kristen Lundberg 'Convener or Player? The World Economic Forum and Davos', C15-04-1741.0 (Cambridge, MA: Kennedy School of Government, 2004). All quotes are taken from this case study.
36 World Economic Forum, *A Partner in Shaping History* (Geneva: World Economic Forum, 2009), p. 43.
37 Mission statement was accessed on 18 April 2013 from the Forum's website at www.weforum.org/. In full, it states: 'The World Economic Forum is an independent international organization committed to improving the state of the world by engaging business, political, academic and other leaders of society to shape global, regional and industry agendas.'
38 K.M. Schwab, 'Sustainable Capitalism', in Marc Benioff and Carlye Adler, *The Business of Changing the World* (New York: McGraw-Hill Professional, 2007), pp. 233–41, quote on p. 234–5.
39 K.M. Schwab, 'The Reshaping of the World', 17 January 2014. Retrieved from: https://agenda.weforum.org/2014/01/reshaping-world/ (accessed on 21 March 2015).
40 K.M. Schwab, Opening Address, European Management Symposium, delivered in Davos on 27 January 1977.
41 World Economic Forum, *Our History*. Retrieved from: www.rtmark.com/more/articles/gatt.org-weforum-links-to-it!!!!!!.html (accessed 15 December 2014).
42 Klaus Schwab quoted by L.H. Hapham in *The Agony of Mammon* (London: Verso, 1998), p. 39.

43 K.M. Schwab and C. Smadja, 'Start Taking the Backlash Against Globalization Seriously', *New York Times* (1 February 1996).
44 Chris Anderson on TED's non-profit transition. Broadcast video retrieved from: www.ted.com/talks/chris_anderson_shares_his_vision_for_ted.html (accessed 20 April 2013).
45 S.P. Huntington, *Who Are We?* (New York: Simon and Schuster, 2004), p. 268.
46 K.M. Schwab, 'Global Corporate Citizenship', *Foreign Affairs*, 87:1 (2008), 107–18, quote on pp. 108–9.
47 R.N. Gardner, 'The Hard Road to World Order', *Foreign Affairs*, 52:3 (1974), 556–76, quote on p. 558.

7
The anatomy of an insurgency

> The world is nothing more than a market, an immense fairground. (Jules Verne, *Paris in the Twentieth Century*)

Making of an insurgent

Walter Wriston was nothing like a typical 1940s banker. In that decade, bankers were easy-going, faithfully following the '3–6–3 rule': paying 3 per cent interest on deposits, lending money at 6 per cent, and teeing off at the golf course by 3 p.m. By contrast, Wriston was never going to settle for a comfortable, albeit dull, career. His natural inclination was to overturn the existing order, and his restless ambition cast him into the role of an insurgent.

At CitiBank,[1] Wriston began by chipping away at the bank's entrenched procedures and opening its eyes to new business vistas. As he climbed the corporate ladder, he also found time to conduct a highly effective guerrilla war against New Deal banking regulations. Finally, he helped place a bomb under the Bretton Woods international regulatory system, destroying many of its important safeguards and opening the way for neoliberal policies to saturate the global financial order.

Walter Bigelow Wriston – 'Walt' to his friends – was born in Middletown, Connecticut on 3 August 1919 into an austere, Methodist household in which Walt was forbidden to listen to the radio or go to movies on Sundays. As a young boy, his mother called him 'Skippy' as he had a habit of alternately walking, running and skipping through the streets of Appleton, Wisconsin where the family had moved when he was six years old.

The main influence on his life was his father, Henry 'Hank' Wriston, who passed on a love for history, economics and politics to his son. President of Brown University, Hank Wriston joined the Council on Foreign Relations in 1924 and served as its president between 1951 and 1964. Widely respected, he was often called on to advise President Dwight Eisenhower, members of his cabinet and senators on international affairs. He was even mooted as a possible secretary of state, but he never received the nod.

Hank's politics were conservative, and his economic ideas followed classical liberalism, putting him at odds with Roosevelt's New Deal. In 1943, he published *Challenge to Freedom* in which he criticised 'reactionary and stifling bureaucratic management', calling on government to 'restrict itself and not enterprise'.[2] He was also an internationalist who believed that an interdependent world was being created by new communication technologies that 'have been shrinking the effective size of the world beyond the dreams of our fathers'.[3]

Like his father, Walt believed that governments should not meddle in the market, and later in life he would embrace neoliberalism. His heroes were Adam Smith – he kept a leather-bound edition of *Wealth of Nations* in pride of place on his bookshelf – and Friedrich Hayek.

An episode that occurred when he and his family were on their summer holidays in Europe turned Walt's romantic enthusiasm for the free market into a deep-seated commitment. Just weeks before Germany provoked the Second World War, Walt found himself in Frankfurt. Coming out of the railway station, he was horrified to see goose-stepping members of the Nazi Youth marching by, carrying swastika banners and singing 'Deutschland über alles'.[4] Later, reflecting on the experience, Wriston said, 'I saw what happens with total regulation of people's lives, which starts with economic regulation and leaps over into politics and the abolition of free speech'.[5]

After graduating from Wesleyan, where he studied history, in 1941, Walt completed his education at Tufts University's Fletcher School of International Law and Diplomacy where, the following year, he received a master's degree. Wriston then joined the State Department as a junior Foreign Service officer. Soon after, he married his college sweetheart, Barbara 'Bobby' Brengle, with whom he had one daughter. Following Pearl Harbor, Wriston enlisted, and in 1945 found himself on the Philippine island of Cebu as part of the Signals Intelligence Service. There, he operated the SIGABA coding machine which instilled in him a lifelong wonderment with technology and communications.

After returning to civilian life, Walt decided that he did not want to live in the shadow of his formidable father, which ruled out a career in academia 'because you'd have nothing but comparisons', he complained.[6] Reluctant even to seek out his father's advice, Walt consulted his mother's physician who suggested he think about banking. Walt was not excited by this suggestion but for a young man thinking about starting a family, it made sense. 'I came looking for a job so I could eat. If I were to sit up at night making a list of everything dull, banking would come out on top.'[7] Nevertheless, he joined First National City Bank (which later became CitiBank).

On 29 June 1946, Wriston turned up for his first day at work at 55 Wall Street. The architecture of the building is unimaginative but impressive. Its grey granite façade is fronted by two tiers of massive Corinthian columns. The message was clear: behind its solid oak doors, depositors could feel confident that they would find dependable, conservative bankers who would safeguard their money. Ever the subversive, on his first day Wriston wore a striped shirt rather than the white one worn by everyone else in the building, without exception.

As he settled into the job, Wriston discovered he had few attributes to get ahead in the banking milieu of the 1940s. He found it difficult to hide his impatience with the conservatism he encountered. At social events, he did not mix easily, a distinct disadvantage for a young man in banking. And his golf handicap was indifferent. 'Banking was a kind of a nice club', he remarked. There was little latitude for creativity or even skill because 'the government told you how much you could pay on deposits'.[8] Unlike other new employees, Wriston was neither looking for a tranquil life nor a secure career. By nature, he was a risk-taker who delighted in shaking the tree – or even, if given the chance, chopping it down and using it as firewood.

One of Wriston's clients was Aristotle Onassis, a shipping entrepreneur with big dreams. Short of capital, Onassis looked to Wriston to raise the funds he needed to expand his fleet of oil tankers. Wriston saw Onassis as a kindred spirit, one who was not afraid to break conventions (or the law, for that matter) to reach his goals. As Onassis plotted his insurgency campaign to overthrow the cosy monopoly enjoyed by the established shipping companies, he came to appreciate Wriston's ingenious schemes that allowed him to rapidly expand his fleet. Wriston so impressed Onassis that he offered the banker a job that came with a salary of 1 million dollars. Wriston knocked back the tycoon's offer, but the two men nevertheless became good friends.

In 1966, when Wriston's wife Bobby died suddenly from a heart attack, Onassis was there to comfort his friend. Later, Onassis even played matchmaker. Deciding that Walt needed to move on, he tried to set him up with an attractive young widow: Jacqueline Lee Bouvier Kennedy. Wriston was not even interested in a date, and a year later Onassis married her himself.

After watching the swashbuckling Onassis cut through his opposition, Wriston was inspired to undertake his own insurgencies.

He first made a name for himself in 1961. Government regulations prevented commercial banks from offering high interest rates, preventing them from competing with investment banks for capital. Wriston's way around this obstacle was imaginative: by offering negotiable certificates of deposit (CDs) that could be traded and therefore were technically different from normal deposits, he skirted around banking regulations. CDs were one of the first synthetic financial products introduced into the market, and it was soon copied by other commercial banks. In the years to follow, Wriston would often employ newly invented products to skirt around the Depression-era system of regulations designed to keep commercial banks dull and safe.

Wriston's big break came in 1967 when CitiBank's chief executive, George Moore, retired. Having identified Wriston as someone who could modernise the bank, Moore anointed Wriston as his successor.

Rules are made for breaking

During his time at the top, Wriston transformed CitiBank from a stuffy commercial bank into a one-stop financial supermarket that provided a full range of products and services to clients, wherever they were in the world – a strategy destined to make CitiBank the largest in the world.

His success, however, would depend on scything through the thicket of regulations that stood in his way. None galled him more than the Glass-Steagall Act passed by the US Congress in 1933. A reaction to the speculative fever that led to the Great Depression, it separated commercial banks, which the law's authors believed should offer a safe haven for mum-and-dad depositors, from investment banks where sophisticated investors could trade more risky shares and bonds.

To help him shake the bank out of its conservatism, Wriston recruited a group of executives, selected for their aggression and entrepreneurial flair rather than their golf handicap. According to a former executive, Wriston nurtured a 'ready, fire, aim' approach. 'The credo [at Citi] was always kick ass, take no prisoners', said another. 'We're the biggest, we're the best, let's do deals.'[9]

Wriston also created a strike force of lawyers who he looked to help him execute an insurgency he planned. Their brief was to dismantle the existing regulatory system, brick by brick. Wriston left his new legal team in little doubt of what he expected from them: 'Clerks follow the rules. You guys are hired to break the rules.'[10] Bob Dinerstein, one of CitiBank's legal hit men, gleefully explained that working with the team was like 'walking into a meeting of anarchists'.[11]

CitiBank employed a variety of tactics in its running battles with the government to free the financial sector from troublesome regulations. Most of its successes came from squeezing through legal loopholes. Other times, it used new products or technologies to skirt the rules. When all else failed, CitiBank simply ignored regulations and defied authorities to take it on in court.

In July 1968, in one of his more audacious assaults on the Glass-Steagall

Act, Wriston restructured CitiBank, creating a holding company, known as CitiCorp,[12] under which CitiBank operated as a subsidiary. Legally, the offspring of CitiBank became the parent, and as a holding company (which happened to own a commercial bank), it was not restricted by the Glass-Steagall Act. CitiCorp quickly took advantage of its legal status to go on a buying spree. Its new acquisitions opened up business activities that CitiBank was forbidden to enter. As soon as his competitors realised that Wriston had found a way around the Glass-Steagall Act, they followed, and, within six months, over fifty banks had established holding companies.

Like many of Wriston's surprise attacks on regulations, legislators were slow to respond. Eventually, in February 1969, Congressman Wright Patman introduced amendments to the Bank Holding Company Act to plug this loophole. To help fight these amendments, Wriston called on the services of Jack Yingling, a smooth-talking lobbyist who successfully watered down Patman's bill in the Senate. Passed in December 1970, it was left to the Federal Reserve Board (the Fed) to approve each new purchase by a bank holding company.

A contest of wills followed. CitiCorp pushed ahead with numerous purchases and some succeeded while the Fed blocked others. For example, CitiCorp was forced to withdraw its offer to purchase Chubb, which would have given it a toehold in the insurance industry. In August 1973, Wriston was also frustrated in his first venture into the credit card business, although he would later find another way to break into this market.

To become the world's largest financial supermarket, Wriston knew that he would have to go offshore. In 1972, Wriston created Citicorp International Bank Limited (CIBL, pronounced 'Sybil'), which operated as an investment bank out of London. Being outside the jurisdiction of the US, CIBL was not subject to the Glass-Steagall Act, and Wriston was able to take up business opportunities that were not available to CitiCorp at home.

As a result, CIBL aggressively expanded into loan syndication, private placements, foreign exchange trading, government bond underwriting, and merger and acquisitions. Soon, CIBL's team of high-pressure salespeople were putting together multimillion dollar deals and creaming 10 per cent off the top in fees. By 1974, CIBL had $4.5 billion worth of deals on its books and was making a tidy profit.

CIBL also opened up the Eurodollar market, which had existed since the 1950s but had not seen much trading activity until the 1970s. As the US dollar was the world's reserve currency, large volumes of dollars circulated outside the US, mainly in Europe, hence the name. Rather than depositing their Eurodollars in US banks where regulations set low interest rates, investors found that they could receive much better returns offshore. This market received a fillip from the oil shock of 1973, as billions of petrodollars swelled the Eurocurrency pool, making CIBL a very profitable part of the Citi banking group.

With few regulations, Wriston celebrated this 'stateless' market:

> [The Eurodollar] can move instantly, and it does. It's also annoying to governments because the market isn't in any one place, geographically. It resides in cyberspace. London today is the centre of Euromarket trading, but if the British put on reserve requirements or other controls, Bahrain is waiting. In just a couple of keystrokes, the whole market could be gone.[13]

The problem was that the lack of regulation in the Euromarket also opened it up to manipulation, tax evasion and a way to circumvent national laws. In February 1975, suspicious trading was uncovered by CitiBank foreign exchange trader David Edwards who warned his superiors that the Paris branch was engaged in a systematic campaign to defraud host countries through a series of sham transactions via its Bahamas branch. After his allegations were investigated by CitiBank's victims, Switzerland forced it to pay $5.2 million in back taxes, France clawed back $1.1 million, and West Germany recovered $3.7 million. These penalties were simply the cost of doing business and, in all likelihood, the amount recovered was a fraction of what CitiBank profited from its fancy footwork.

Not discouraged by such misadventures, Wriston was keen to expand into overseas loans, which he saw as another source of lucrative profits. As a result, CitiBank lent heavily to developing countries, committing 174.5 per cent of its total capital.[14] Overexposed, CitiBank was extremely vulnerable, as were other major banks that had followed it lead by making loans to Mexico, Argentina, Brazil, Venezuela and a number of African countries. Wriston dismissed suggestions that such investments were foolhardy, arguing that 'countries don't go bankrupt'.[15] While technically correct, countries can default on their debts, as he soon found out.

In 12 August 1982, Mexico's finance minister, Jesús Silva-Herzog, called the US treasury secretary, Donald Regan, Federal Reserve Board chairman Paul Volker and Jacques de Larosière, managing director of the IMF, to tell them that Mexico was no longer able to service its debt. It soon became clear that a number of African and Latin American countries were also in dire straits. Rumours of sovereign bankruptcies started to fly around financial circles. Had they gone ahead, CitiBank could easily have been ruined along with the other banks that had followed its lead in lending to developing countries.

In September 1982, the IMF hosted a conference in Toronto to sort out the mess. Wriston described the scene: 'We had 150-odd finance ministers, 50-odd central bankers, 1000 journalists, 1000 commercial bankers, a large supply of whiskey and a reasonably small city that produced an enormous head of steam driving the engine called "the end of the world is coming".'[16] The conference called on Mexico to restructure its debt and implement an austerity programme so that it did not amass even more debt. This prescription later extended to Brazil and then to thirty-seven other Third World countries that found themselves unable to service their debts – whether they liked it or not.

What followed was a disguised bailout, in which the IMF, and the American, major European and Japanese central banks committed money to a massive emergency loan package to insolvent countries so that they could continue to pay interest on restructured loans to private lenders.

This constituted a partial win for the banks, and while they did not fully recover their money, they significantly reduced the magnitude of their losses, compared to what would have happened in the event of a full-blown default. While CitiBank did take a haircut, the bailout saved its hide. Sadly, this was not the last time governments would bail out CitiBank.

Despite the ups and downs Wriston experienced at CitiBank, his hands-on approach to introducing neoliberal policies through insurgency was markedly more muscular than the approach taken by other new globalists, like David Rockefeller and Klaus Schwab, who looked to co-opt politicians and opinion leaders rather than confronting them. And there is no denying that his insurgency produced results, making him one of the principal architects of the neoliberal financial order that slowly emerged during the 1970s, and that went a long way to enthroning the market.

In September 1984, Wriston retired on his sixty-fifth birthday, but this did not signal the end of his contributions to the public debate on the future of the global financial order. In the years that followed, he became a vocal warrior for the free market.

Sovereignty of the market

Upon his retirement from CitiBank, Wriston went from a frontline general in the war of ideas to giving speeches and writing extensively on questions that obsessed his generation of new globalists. How could markets be freed? What did new technologies, particularly computers, mean for the future of the financial sector? How could the regulatory state be cut back? How could the global ambitions of transnational corporations be reconciled with the sovereignty of nation-states?

An engaging and erudite author, he often quoted neoliberal heavyweights –

Friedrich Hayek, Milton Friedman and George Stigler – while also drawing on sources as diverse as Thucydides, Plutarch and Alexis de Tocqueville, demonstrating his wide knowledge of history. His magnum opus, *Twilight of Sovereignty*, in particular, caused quite a stir when it appeared in 1992, delighting Wriston, who told the *New York Times*, 'For some reason, my shelf life has been longer than Wheaties.'[17]

Underpinning his arguments was a belief that information technology 'is rapidly creating a situation that might be described as the twilight of sovereignty, since the absolute power of the state to act alone both internally against its own citizens and externally against other nations' affairs is rapidly being attenuated'.[18] While he never seriously entertained the proposition that nation-states would disappear any time soon, he presented a compelling picture of how global markets were using new information technologies to radically circumscribe national sovereignty.

One way that this new financial order asserts its authority over governments is by imposing its hegemony over the value of currencies, which have been allowed to float since the Nixon Shock of 1971. Wriston described how information on the economic health of countries was being used by markets to set currency values:

> The convergence of computers with telecommunications has produced a global trading system, which in turn has allowed creation of a new international monetary system I call the Information Standard. ... The new Information Standard, unlike all prior arrangements, is not subject to effective political tinkering. ... This state of affairs does not sit too well with many sovereign governments because they correctly perceive the new Information Standard as an attack on the very nature of sovereign power.[19]

Going further, he remarked that 'not only are governments losing control over money, but this newly free money ... is asserting its control over them, disciplining irresponsible policies'.[20] In 1992, the same year as Wriston made this observation, Franz Müntefering, Germany's vice chancellor, confessed to the *Financial Times*, 'We have fading borders and this means the instruments of the national states are being constantly eroded. It is no longer possible for the individual states to dictate the rules of the economic game.'[21]

The position of developing countries was even more dire, because they were 'losing some of their sovereignty to an evolving system of international governance', complained Nelson Mandela. 'The very mobility of capital and the globalisation of the capital and other markets make it impossible for countries, for instance, to decide national economic policy without regard to the likely response of these markets.'[22]

Less attention, however, is paid to Wriston's ideas on how the Information Standard is creating a new form of global governance, which he called 'economic democracy'.[23] In his construction, the 'electronic global market has produced what amounts to a giant vote-counting machine that conducts a running tally on what the world thinks of the government's diplomatic, fiscal, and monetary policies. That opinion is immediately reflected in the value the market places on a country's currency.'[24] Behind the computer screens of Wriston's voting machine are currency traders, bond holders and speculators, who governments must satisfy if they do not want the market to punish their policies, or as he explained, 'capital goes where it's wanted, and it stays where it's well treated'.[25]

Economic democracy is a radical redefinition of democracy. The 'votes' of market actors, transnational banks and financial institutions in the main, are the only ones that count in the global electorate. Legitimising the exercise of such private authority, Wriston argues that corporations are 'far more democratic, collegial, and tolerant than distant state bureaucracies inhabited by men and women who never seem to have enough knowledge to temper or justify their power', and he predicts that they will rise up and challenge the 'prerogatives of the sovereign state'.[26]

President Bill Clinton, for example, discovered the limits to his power when, in 1992, he was told that he would have to break his election promise to invest in the country's deteriorating infrastructure because the bond market would not approve such a massive expenditure. In response, Clinton fumed, 'You mean to tell me that the success of the program and my reelection hinges on the Federal Reserve and a bunch of fucking bond traders?'[27]

Economic democracy has not only been used to protect bondholders, but the voting power of transnational banks and financial institutions has also been used to pressure governments to deregulate their economies; reduce the size of their bureaucracies; wind back social security programmes; privatise their utilities and enterprises; reduce corporate taxes; and introduce pro-business policies. With each victory, the war of ideas changed the face of globalisation, replacing many of its liberal features with the neoliberal agenda, and promoting the sovereignty of global markets above national interests.

What hath Wriston wrought?

When Wriston retired in September 1984, the *Wall Street Journal*'s Charles Stabler wrote: 'For good or ill, banks today are free to be the financial-services conglomerates that Mr. Wriston envisioned and largely brought about.'[28] Also ambivalent, *Bloomberg Businessweek* magazine described Wriston as 'the pivotal figure in the transformation of the banking industry from a somnolent business straitjacketed by regulation into the global free-for-all it is today – a decidedly mixed blessing'.[29] The *Institutional Investor* was less uncertain, claiming that 'Wriston – more than any other individual – aggressively sought to redefine what a bank is and isn't, and, in so doing, lit the flame of the financial services revolution.'[30]

However, only when the financial crisis shook the world in 2007, and the years that followed, could his legacies be fully appreciated.

Wriston's insurgency helped sweep away Depression era regulations, which were introduced in the 1930s in the hope of preventing a repeat run on banks. They aimed to reduce market volatility, discourage speculation and contain systemic risk.

Wriston never bought the widely held explanation for the Depression. It was not triggered by irresponsible banks, speculation or excessive risk-taking but, he argued, 'by the Fed refusing to supply liquidity'.[31] Embracing a neoliberal worldview that was hostile to government interference in capital markets, Wriston believed that computer technologies which had started to become available during the 1970s were a game changer. With the rapid circulation of information, he believed that markets were more efficient and bankers could better identify and manage risks. For Wriston, the tangle of Depression-era regulations were not necessary, as 'risk taking was ... not synonymous with recklessness',[32] and with better information, markets were now inherently more efficient and stable.

Through Wriston's own efforts and those of others in the financial sector who followed in his footsteps, many banking regulations were removed. This allowed a new generation of global banks to become financial supermarkets, able to hunt down ever higher profits by taking on ever greater risks. Like Wriston, they believed they now possessed superior tools and skills required to manage ever-larger risks.

This newfound confidence was tested and found wanting when the financial crisis hit. Rather than exhibiting superior risk-management skills, the major banks had let their animal spirits carry them away, as Wriston's successor at CitiBank, Chuck Prince, explained to the *Financial Times* on the eve of the crisis, 'When the music stops, in terms of liquidity, things will be complicated. But as long as the music is playing, you've got to get up and dance. We're still dancing.'[33]

In the summer of 2007, with CitiBank twirling to the merriest of gigs, the subprime bubble burst and CitiBank lost $17.4 billion in its securities and banking divisions and admitted that it had an additional $49 billion in distressed assets on its books. In 2008, it lost a further $27.7 billion. Sadly, they were not alone, and around the world many megabanks were also in deep trouble.

Governments quickly reached the conclusion that they could not afford to let these megabanks go under as they were likely to take the rest of the economy with them. And so they started to bailout strategically important banks that were too-big-to-fail.

CitiBank was near the head of the queue, receiving $49 billion in two instalments in late 2008 followed by government guarantees for its toxic assets of up to $306 billion (later adjusted to $301 billion). It survived, but only by the skin of its teeth, leading *Washington Post* columnist, Steven Pearlstein, to write: 'Of all the rescues mounted by the government this year, none carries with it more symbolism, or more irony, than that of Citigroup.'[34]

The irony was that Wriston's insurgency had helped emasculate rules that stopped banks from growing too large. The most important was the Glass-Steagall Act. When it was finally repealed in 1999, after being fatally wounded by Wriston and his team of legal anarchists, US banks engaged in a rash of mergers and takeovers. To stay competitive, non-US banks followed suit. As a result, the ten leading global banks' share of total banking assets climbed from 14 per cent in 1999 to 19 per cent in 2007.[35]

Saving such large banks was an expensive exercise, and according to a World Bank report, based on a sample of forty countries, by 2000 bailouts had cost 'on average 12.8 per cent of national GDP to clean up their financial systems'.[36]

The worry is that megabanks now know that they will be bailed out should they get into trouble. While such interventions may stop the rot in the short term, it is not without long-term consequences, according to Kevin Dowd, a professor of economics at the University of Sheffield. He says, 'Too big to fail encourages irresponsible risk taking by financial firms, which makes them weaker and financial markets more fragile.'[37]

There are other problems with the proliferation of too-big-to-fail banks, according to US Attorney General Eric Holder:

> I am concerned that the size of some of these institutions becomes so large that it does become difficult for us to prosecute them when we are hit with indications that if we do prosecute – if we do bring a criminal charge – it will have a negative impact on the national economy, perhaps even the world economy. I think that is a function of the fact that some of these institutions have become too large.[38]

Such worries explain why so few bankers went to jail, despite ample evidence of malfeasance, and why cases that were brought against banks were often settled out of court, accompanied by large fines but no admissions of guilt.

So the open sore of banks that are too-big-to-fail is now joined by the problem of bankers who are too-important-to-jail.

Not surprisingly, bank executives do not think their institutions are too big. Making the case for the status quo, Prince's successor as CEO at Citi, Vikram Pandit, wrote an article that appeared in the *Financial Times* on 20 August 2012 in which he claimed that 'Citigroup is just the right size.'[39] To ensure that legislators did nothing to break up Citi, it bankrolled fifty-five lobbyists, more than any other big bank or financial industry trade association, and, together with other megabanks, they have spent $599 million lobbying since March 2008 to discourage the re-regulation of the financial sector.[40]

Emboldened by their success, in 2014 bankers began a new chapter in their campaign. Not content to resist new regulations, they started to lobby to wind back regulations that were introduced in the wake of the global financial crisis. On 11 December 2014, the US House of Representative passed a bill that repealed a key part of the Dodd-Frank Act, which aimed to stop banks from gambling in derivatives markets using insured deposits and other taxpayer subsidies and guarantees. Not only did CitiBank lobby to have the measure passed, but it drafted the new law, which was then adopted by legislators, with only a few voicing their objections.[41]

Any chance of reform, therefore, is remote because banking lobbyists have enjoyed remarkable success undermining legislation that might prevent another crisis, particularly in the US. As a result, we now have a new phenomenon: banks that are too-big-to-regulate, suggesting that Wriston's legacies are safe.

Notes

1. When Walter Wriston joined, the bank was called First National City Bank of New York, then First National City Bank of the City of New York in 1955, and finally CitiBank in 1976. In 1968, the bank created a holding company, First National City Corporation, which changed its name to CitiCorp in 1974. In 1998, CitiCorp merged with Travelers to become CitiGroup. So as not to confuse the narrative, I have generally used the Citi nomenclature other than when the correct name is important to the context.
2. H.M. Wriston, *Challenge to Freedom* (New York: Harper & Brothers Publishers, 1943), p. 75.
3. H.M. Wriston quoted by Phillip L. Zweig in *Walter Wriston, CitiBank, and the Rise and Fall of American Financial Supremacy* (New York: Crown Publishers, 1995), p. 8.
4. 'Deutschland über alles' is a song associated with Nazis as it literally means 'Germany above all'.

5   P.L. Zweig, *Walter Wriston, CitiBank, and the Rise and Fall of American Financial Supremacy*, p. 19.
6   Walter Wriston quoted by Jeff Madrick in *Age of Greed* (New York: Alfred A Knopf, 2011), p. 11.
7   Walter Wriston quoted by John Brooks in 'The Money Machine', *New Yorker* (5 January 1981), pp. 41–61.
8   P.L. Zweig, *Walter Wriston, CitiBank, and the Rise and Fall of American Financial Supremacy*, p. 46.
9   I. Picker and J.W. Milligan, 'The Collapse of CitiBank's Credit Culture', *Institutional Investor*, 25:14 (1991), 53–65.
10 P.L. Zweig, *Walter Wriston, CitiBank, and the Rise and Fall of American Financial Supremacy*, p. 305.
11 P.L. Zweig, *Walter Wriston, CitiBank, and the Rise and Fall of American Financial Supremacy*, p. 807.
12 At this point it was called the First National City Corporation and later changed its name to Citicorp. For simplicity, I refer to it by its latter name.
13 T.A. Bass, 'The Future of Money', *Wired*, 4:10 (October 1996).
14 W.R. Cline, *International Debt: Systemic Risk and Policy Response* (Washington, DC: Institute for International Economics, 1984), p. 24.
15 Walter Wriston quoted by Jeffrey Sachs in *Developing Country Debt and Economic Performance* (Chicago: University of Chicago Press, 1989), p. 8.
16 Walter Wriston quoted by Moira Johnston in *The Tumultuous History of the Bank of America* (Washington, DC: BeardBooks, 2000), p. 180.
17 B. Lyne, 'Two Ways to Cross Retirement's Bridge', *New York Times* (25 April 1993).
18 W.B. Wriston, *The Twilight of Sovereignty* (Bridgewater, NJ: Replica Books, 1992), p. xii.
19 W.B. Wriston, 'In Search of a Money Standard', *Wall Street Journal* (12 November 1985), p. 28.
20 W.B. Wriston, *The Twilight of Sovereignty*, p. 66.
21 B. Benoit, 'SPD Chief Stands By Call to Tackle "Locusts"', *Financial Times* (14 February 2007), p. 8.
22 'Report by the President of the ANC to the 50th National Conference of the African National Congress', delivered by Nelson Mandela on 16 December 1997 in Mafikeng (South Africa).
23 T. Bass, '"Want to Know About the Future of Money?" Talk to Walter Wriston', *Wired*, 4:10 (October 1996).
24 W.B. Wriston, *The Twilight of Sovereignty*, p. 9.
25 Walter Wriston interviewed by William F. Buckley Jr. on *Firing Line* on 30 May 1986 and broadcasted on PBS.
26 W.B. Wriston, *The Twilight of Sovereignty*, p. 121.
27 R. Woodward, *The Agenda: Inside the Clinton White House* (New York: Simon & Schuster, 1994), p. 73.

28 C.N. Stabler, 'Wriston Set Off and Avalanche in a Glacier-Like Industry', *Wall Street Journal* (30 August 1984), p. 18.
29 A. Bianco, 'What Wriston Wrought', *Bloomberg Businessweek Magazine* (6 February 2005), p. 36.
30 Anonymous introduction to article by Walter Wriston, 'Was I Exacting? Sure. Was I Occasionally Sarcastic? Of Course', *Institutional Investor*, 21:6 (June 1987), 16–20, quote on p. 16.
31 Walter Wriston interviewed by William F. Buckley Jr. on *Firing Line* on 30 May 1986 and broadcasted on PBS.
32 W.B. Wriston, *Risk & Other Four-letter Words* (New York: Harper & Row, 1986), p. ix.
33 M. Nakamoto and D. Wighton, 'Bullish Citigroup Is "Still Dancing" to the Beat of the Buy-Out Boom', *Financial Times* (10 July 2007), p. 1.
34 S. Pearlstein, 'A Bailout Steeped in Irony', *Washington Post* (5 November 2008), p. D01.
35 International Financial Services London Research, *Banking 2010* (London: International Financial Services London Research, February 2010).
36 P. Honohan and D. Klingebiel, 'Controlling the Fiscal Costs of Banking Crises', Policy Research Working Paper 2441 (Washington, DC: World Bank, September 2000), p. 3.
37 K. Dowd, 'Too Big to Fail? Long-Term Capital Management and the Federal Reserve', *Cato Institute Briefing Papers*, No. 52 (Washington, DC: Cato Institute, 23 September 1999), p. 2.
38 D. Douglas, 'Attorney General Says Big Banks' Size May Inhibit Prosecution', *Washington Post* (6 March 2013), p. A12.
39 P.J. Davies, 'Citi Chief Rejects Calls for Bank Splits', *FT.com* (20 August 2012).
40 K. Connor, *Big Bank Takeover* (Washington, DC: Institute for America's Future, 2010), pp. 1–2.
41 R. Blackwell, 'Why Citi May Soon Regret Its Big Victory on Capitol Hill', *American Banker* (11 December 2014).

8

Accelerated development

'Well, in our country,' said Alice, still panting a little, 'you'd generally get to somewhere else – if you run very fast for a long time, as we've been doing.'

'A slow sort of country!' said the Queen. 'Now, here, you see, it takes all the running you can do, to keep in the same place. If you want to get somewhere else, you must run at least twice as fast as that!' (Lewis Carroll, *Alice through the Looking Glass*)

Whiz kid

On 30 September 1980, after announcing his retirement from the World Bank, Robert McNamara borrowed a quote from George Bernard Shaw to capture his time as president: 'You see things and say why? But I dream things that never were and I say, "Why not?"'[1]

In just thirteen years, McNamara transformed the World Bank from a backwater with a loan portfolio of less than 1 billion dollars to the largest development agency in the world, lending over $13 billion to the poor. The official history was fulsome in its praise of McNamara's contributions: 'McNamara shaped the evolution of the Bank as no one before or after him.'[2] It was more coy about his other legacy: to assert the independence of the World Bank from the US, whose influence had eroded the credibility of the bank during the early years of the Cold War.

McNamara's importance to the history of globalisation, however, goes well beyond such contributions. He linked development with market liberalisation, pressing neoliberal reforms onto developing countries.

Robert McNamara's journey started over six decades earlier. Born on 9 June 1916, Bob was reared in modest circumstances in the San Francisco Bay Area. His father, the son of Irish immigrants, managed a wholesale shoe shop, but the main influence on the young boy was his mother, Clara Nell, who instilled in Bob a fierce drive to succeed.

Extremely bright, Bob shone in school, where he displayed restless intellectual curiosity. While short-sighted and uncoordinated as a child, he took to tennis with a vengeance as an outlet for his seemingly unquenchable energy. Anyone watching him play would have seen a character trait both admirable and foolhardy. Refusing to give up, he chased down every ball, no matter how hopeless his chances of returning it. Later in life, he would turn this into a management mantra: 'Better to have tried and failed than never to have tried.'[3]

Well read, McNamara developed a liberal social outlook at the University of California at Berkeley, where he graduated with top marks in economics. In 1937, McNamara attended Harvard Business School, studying towards a Master of Business Administration. At Harvard, McNamara discovered what would become a lifelong fascination, if not obsession: the power of numbers. He fervently believed that quantitative data and statistical analysis could be used to solve management problems and make organisations more efficient.

During the war, McNamara served stateside, in the Far East and Pacific theatres of war between 1943 and 1946, where he demonstrated that by crunching numbers, he could improve military logistics.

Discharged a colonel, he returned briefly to Harvard, before joining the Ford Motor Company as part of a team of consultants employed to revitalise the ailing company. Knowing little about the car industry, he and the other consultants showered executives, engineers and other staff members with an endless stream of questions, leading employees to call them the 'quiz kids' after the child prodigies in a popular radio programme. Annoyed at this unflatteringly moniker, McNamara suggested the name 'whiz kids', and it followed him for the rest of his life, although not always used in a kindly way.

Over the next few years, the whiz kids revolutionised logistics and production systems, as well as introducing cost accounting. Largely due to their efforts, by 1948, Ford made a profit of $94.3 million, after years of losses.

His appearance mirrored his self-image as a rational man. The first thing one noticed about Robert McNamara in his prime was a tall, taut man, with a full head of black hair, immaculately coiffed with a precise parting just a little left of centre and he wore big wire-rimmed glasses. During meetings, he would overwhelm his opponents with data and statistics, fashioning them into a scalpel that he used to vivisect opposing arguments.

Early in his career he knew exactly where he was going. According to historian David Halbertam, who studied McNamara's time at Ford, 'He sought truth, but in search for truth he sought power as well.'[4] His undoubted ability, as well as a talent for Machiavellian machinations, found McNamara moving up the corporate ladder quickly. In November 1960, he was named president of the Ford Motor Company, the first outside the Ford family.

Just as McNamara reached the summit at Ford, president-elect John F. Kennedy was looking to recruit the brightest and the best for his incoming administration. McNamara's name cropped up, not for his aptitude for producing cars but for his reputation as a whiz kid adept at turning large organisations around. Having inherited a bloated military establishment, Kennedy wanted someone who would tame America's industrial-military complex.

JFK was not disappointed. His new secretary for defence tore through the Pentagon like a tornado, dismantling fiefdoms, weeding out waste and redundancy, and, for the first time, holding the military to account. Using statistics and charts, McNamara was determined to extract value out of every dollar spent.

While his reforms of the US military succeeded, McNamara's reputation suffered when America became mired in the disastrous Vietnam War, which his critics cruelly called 'McNamara's War'. By 1967, after vigorously prosecuting the war, McNamara started to have doubts that the war could be won. Seeing that his secretary for defence had 'gone dovish on me',[5] President Lyndon Johnson put McNamara's name forward for the vacant position as president of the World Bank.

For supporters of the World Bank, however, the prospect of McNamara becoming its president was not well received; after all, wasn't LBJ getting rid of his troublesome secretary for defence? The appointment was not, however, as odd as it first appeared. What his critics had failed to notice was that McNamara had been thinking for some time about how poverty had contributed to global insecurity. Before the American Society of Newspaper Editors in Montreal on 18 May 1966, McNamara argued:

> Without internal development of at least a minimal degree, order and stability are simply not possible. They are not possible because human nature cannot be frustrated beyond intrinsic limits. It reacts because it must.[6]

Speaking from the heart, he went on to say that peace and stability in the world depended far less on armament levels than on raising the standards of living of the poorer two-thirds of the world. Reporting on this speech for the *New York Times*, James Reston, who had previously attacked the secretary for defence for his prosecution of the war, revised his opinion of McNamara. 'McNamara is reaching beyond the draft, beyond the Pentagon, beyond the administration policy, beyond the present, even beyond the concept of sovereign nation states ... He is searching for a unifying principle.'[7]

McNamara once again challenged those who saw him as a warmonger when, on 24 February 1967, he told a convocation audience at Millsaps College in Mississippi:

If the wealthy nations of the world ... [d]o not do more to close this sundering economic split, which cleaves the abundant north half of the planet from the hungering southern hemisphere, none of us will ultimately be secure no matter how large our stocks of arms.[8]

These speeches revealed that McNamara was a liberal at heart with a strong international perspective and a nuanced view on the value of war in sorting out geopolitical conflicts and unrest, more than his critics gave him credit for. So rather than treat his new job as a comfortable sinecure, McNamara saw the World Bank as an opportunity to make a positive contribution to humanity.

McNamara's other wars

On 1 April 1968, McNamara took up his new position, determined to fight poverty. To win this new war, he needed to win a few important battles first.

McNamara waged the opening skirmish against the bank itself. Proud of its AAA rating, its bankers jealously guarded their reputation as prudent lenders. William Clark, McNamara's director of information and later the bank's vice president for external relations, described the 'Old Guard' as giving the bank an 'air of a boarding school such as Eton'. With few projects on their books, they administered their loans with 'leisurely perfectionism'. Moreover, the mainly Anglo-American staff often patronised the governments of newly decolonised nations that came knocking on the bank's door.[9]

On 18 June 1968, McNamara presented his first five-year plan to his Board of Governors. When they read that it proposed doubling lending, all hell broke loose as governors did not share McNamara's ambition to turn what was a conservative bank into a fully-fledged development agency, with an ambitious programme of loans. This was the first test to his authority, and McNamara successfully stared down his opponents to get his way.

During the next three months, his staff scoured the bottom drawers of dusty filing cabinets for projects, discovering applications that had been rejected for lack of funds. They also encouraged countries that had already been well looked after by the World Bank to ask for more. They even worked up new proposals for countries that had previously been considered too backward to cope with bank-style development.

To assist him in this battle, in May 1970, McNamara recruited Hollis Chenery from Harvard to lead the new research section. Soon, Chenery's whiz kids were feeding McNamara with quantitative data, tables and graphs, which he used to apply his results-oriented management techniques to the World Bank's business. Justifying his obsession with statistics, McNamara explained: 'We are in the business of dealing with numbers – numbers of people, numbers of dollars, numbers of food produced. How on earth can you run this place without thinking about numbers?'[10]

During his three terms at the head of the World Bank, McNamara would use numbers not only to manage his growing empire, but to harass staff members to meet targets. As a result, the World Bank approved more loans and processed them faster than ever before.

To carry out his ambitious plans, McNamara needed new sources of funding. To help him, he head-hunted Eugene Rotberg from the US Securities and Exchange Commission, who proved to be an enterprising whiz kid. Not coming from Wall Street, and with little background in finance, Rotberg had no idea he had been given a near hopeless job: 'I knew so little I did not know enough to say it could not be done.'[11] This suited McNamara, who did not want someone who would start off with the premise that it was going to be impossible to raise substantial new funds. His faith in Rotberg was justified when his new treasurer brought an aggressive approach to raising funds, finding imaginative ways to access new sources. Rotberg successfully arranged bond offerings in Canada, Switzerland, the UK, West Germany, the Netherlands, Belgium, Italy and Sweden. Such was his success that Rotberg increased borrowings from $735 million to $1,368 million between 1968 and 1971, and this figure soared to $5,068 million in 1981.

Finding new sources of funds served a second purpose. McNamara was aware that in the past the US had used it financial muscle within the World Bank to help its Cold War allies, and punish its enemies.

McNamara was seeing at first hand the outcome of the first meeting of the World Bank in Savannah, where John Maynard Keynes had unsuccessfully warned of the dangers of 'becoming American concerns, run by gigantic American staff, with the rest of us very much on the sideline'.[12]

Although it was not its primary purpose, Rotberg's fundraising reduced the relative proportion of the US's direct contributions from 32 per cent in 1968 to 23 per cent in 1981, while borrowing from Wall Street dropped from 42 per cent in 1969 to just 17 per cent in 1981. As its contributions decreased, so too did America influence. Although the US persisted in trying to throw its weight around, McNamara was ready for them.

> I had a hell of a time with the U.S., and I developed a strategy. My strategy was going without them. A lot of people thought that was wrong. It wasn't wrong. I knew damn well if I went ahead without them they'd be pulled along eventually. And they were, every time.[13]

McNamara's next major test of the bank's independence came in 1971, when India and Pakistan faced off over Bangladesh's fight for self-determination. In his oral history, McNamara records what happened when William P. Rogers, the then-secretary of state, tried to pressure the bank to ignore a loan application from India, which was no friend of the US. Unwilling to be intimidated, McNamara told Rogers: 'Hell, you're so biased toward Pakistan, you don't know which way is up. Those are good loans; they're good credits, and I'm not going to take them off the agenda.' Although Rogers tried to bully McNamara, 'We won't allow it', McNamara shot back, 'Look, you get your votes, and I'll get mine.'[14] After this confrontation, McNamara lobbied his board and was able to secure sufficient support to override the US.

This incident became a turning point, and while the US still foiled a few loans – most notably to the Marxist government of Salvador Allende in Chile in the early 1970s and to Vietnam in 1979 – McNamara's bank moved steadily closer to Keynes's original vision of an institution free of political interference.

McNamara's battle to assert his independence also owed a debt to his Machiavellian machinations. During his time at the World Bank he manipulated his board of forty-two directors, who represented member countries. Describing his modus operandi, McNamara observed that his directors could act as 'a negative constraint on achieving a sound program'. When one of his programmes was threatened, McNamara would circulate among the directors and 'divide and conquer'.[15] During his time as president, only about twenty-five matters came to the vote, and in most, McNamara won. The significance of these victories is that the US found itself in the unfamiliar position of being on the losing side.

In 1991, reflecting on the position of the head of an international agency, particularly faced with a board that was willing to put national interests ahead of the agency's charter, he offered advice based on his experience:

> [When an] agency director, whatever you call him, the executive, CEO in one of these international organizations must, in his own mind, be sufficiently free so that he can put his job on the line if he feels it necessary to do so.[16]

Determined to run his own agenda, McNamara first made sure that his board would support his campaign to ramp up the World Bank's attack on poverty.

Attack on poverty

Reappointed in 1973 to a second term, McNamara wanted a more sophisticated strategy that would allow the bank to aggressively attack underdevelopment.

In September 1973, McNamara unveiled his new agenda. In Nairobi, he told his Board of Governors that during his next term he would focus on attacking 'absolute poverty', which he defined as a condition of deprivation that 'falls below any rational definition of human decency'.[17] The key to his strategy was to shift development away from GDP growth, which often did not benefit the poor but just created greater inequality. Instead, he wanted the bank to directly help individuals improve their environment and well-being. In particular, the bank would lend to projects that would directly help the rural poor, so that they could take advantage of the Green Revolution, in which miracle crops increased yields. He also boosted funding to education, population control, and improved access to clean water and good nutrition.

More than just a new strategy, for McNamara it was a crusade, as he explained to his board:

> The whole of human history has recognized the principle – at least in the abstract – that the rich and the powerful have a moral obligation to assist the poor and the weak. That is what the sense of community is all about – any community: the community of the family, the community of the village, the community of the nation, the community of nations itself.[18]

Still in a rush to help the world's poor, McNamara set the bank an audacious target: 'We should strive to eradicate absolute poverty by the end of this century.'[19]

What followed was a remarkable escalation of the bank's anti-poverty programmes, with some triumphs; but there were also some heart-wrenching failures. Loans were diverted into the pockets of corrupt officials, environments were damaged by poorly designed infrastructure projects, and ideologically driven adjustment programmes increased inequality, lowered growth and brought misery in their wake. Many of his mistakes could be put down to McNamara's enthusiasm, wanting to push the bank to expand its lending portfolio quickly. Had he not been in such a rush, it is possible that he might have enjoyed more success.

Through no fault of its own, McNamara's plan ran into trouble before it had a chance to make a difference. Less than two weeks after his Nairobi speech, the Yom Kippur War broke out between Israel and a coalition of Arab states led by Egypt and Syria. After the ceasefire, the Arab members of OPEC quadrupled the price of oil to punish the west for its support of Israel. Caught in the crossfire, developing nations were also hit hard. To make matters worse, wealthy countries, weakened by stagflation, reduced their aid contributions. The 1970s also witnessed a reduction in global trade as protectionism increased. As if that was not enough, agricultural exports from developing countries were devastated when the European Economic Community and the US started to dump surplus grain into international markets. As a result, Third World debt soared, increasing 25 per cent per annum from 1976 to 1980, reaching an unsustainable $500 billion by 1981.

With its own borrowing drying up, the World Bank assumed the role of matchmaker, bringing together commercial banks with needy developing countries. As the oil-rich countries searched for outlets to invest their newfound wealth, McNamara encouraged developing countries to tap into petrodollar loans, defying US objections.

While the World Bank had staunched the immediate impact of the oil price shock, McNamara knew this was a temporary expedient, and that developing countries also needed to turn their attention to boosting exports and stimulating the private sector. Without radical reform, McNamara anticipated that their debts would just continue to grow, as new loans funded interest rates on existing ones.

Aware that escalating debt could turn into a death spiral, McNamara decided to attack the problem by fixing structural weaknesses. As he explained to his Board of Governors at its annual get-together in Washington, DC, in September 1975:

> All too often their policies of subsidized capital, overvalued exchange rates, and excessive regulation discourage entrepreneurial incentive to sell abroad.[20]

Returning to this theme, the bank's 1977 annual report called for developing countries to embark on 'policy adjustments' to deal with their long-term debt problems. In private, McNamara was less diplomatic and laid the blame on 'internal mismanagement' by governments.[21]

McNamara's numerous calls for macroeconomic reform, however, fell on deaf ears, as governments simply were not interested in reforming the structure of their economies. McNamara felt he could not push the issue, as a strict reading of the bank's Articles of Agreement prohibited it from interfering in the political affairs of its members.

McNamara decided that the only way out of this impasse was to offer incentives to countries willing to undertake macroeconomic reform. In May 1979, McNamara announced a new programme in which the bank would offer clients structural adjustment loans. These were designed to help developing countries adopt reforms that would cultivate free markets and create a friendly environment for private investment, foreign capital and trade.[22]

Slow to take up structural adjustment loans at first, developing countries soon found that they had little choice when they were hit by a second oil price hike in 1979. Desperate for funds to stay afloat, a number of developing countries applied for structural adjustment loans. The first recipient, Turkey, received $200 million in March 1980 to finance reforms to enhance the effectiveness of its agricultural and industrial productive capacity by placing 'greater reliance on market forces and less on direct state intervention and control'.[23] Kenya and the Philippines soon followed, as did Bolivia, which was pressured to privatise its state-owned enterprises.

Turning his attention to another matter, McNamara was keen to draw China into the World Bank. In April 1980, he led the World Bank's first official mission to China to discuss its membership. Welcoming him, general secretary of the Communist Party of China, Deng Xiaoping explained:

> We are very poor. We have lost touch with the world. We need the World Bank to catch up. We can do it without you, but we can do it quicker and better with you.[24]

Despite US opposition, McNamara once again demonstrated his independence by personally pushing through China's membership in record time. On 15 May 1980, he proudly announced that the People's Republic of China had joined the World Bank Group. This initiative not only brought a major developing country into the bank, but also provided a counterbalance to US influence.

With his wife ill, in June 1980, McNamara gave notice that he would leave the World Bank two years before his third term expired, thus giving him twelve months to tie up loose ends and allow sufficient time for the Board of Governors to find a successor.

Unlike his quiet exit from his position as secretary of defence in the wake of the Vietnam debacle, McNamara left the World Bank with his head held high, satisfied that he had done what he could to help the poor.

On 6 June 1981, McNamara walked out of the World Bank for the last time, handing the reins over to Tom Clausen, a former chief executive officer of Bank of America. Clausen was a dependable Reaganite, and during his term he went much further than McNamara, aggressively imposing free market solutions on developing countries looking for loans.

Faustian bargain

Clausen's first few months were uncomfortable. The incoming US Republican administration was hostile towards the World Bank, viewing its 'poverty alleviation' programmes as 'welfare giveaway' and it wanted to cut America's contributions.[25] On 29 September 1981, President Reagan lectured the Boards of Governors of the World Bank and IMF at their annual meeting: 'The societies which have achieved the most spectacular broad-based economic progress in the shortest period of time are ... [those willing] to believe in the magic of the marketplace.'[26]

To get the Reagan administration on side, Clausen decided he needed to take a more muscular approach to structural adjustments by pushing the limits of the legacy programme he had inherited from McNamara. Unlike McNamara, Clausen did not worry about the bank's articles that prevented interference with the 'political affairs of any member'.[27] In fact, he made development loans *conditional* on macroeconomic reforms, along neoliberal lines.

The thinking behind this policy shift was that the bank's mission of tackling global poverty could be reframed as an economic issue. Rather than just providing aid, it would tackle the causes of poverty: failure to promote exports, encourage private enterprise and attract foreign investment.

One of Clausen's first acts was to replace McNamara's chief economist, Hollis Chenery, with neoliberal ideologue Anne Krueger. She, in turn, replaced most of the bank's research and policy staff with like-minded economists. Under Krueger, the prevailing orthodoxy at the World Bank was that government was the problem and free markets were the solution to the troubles besetting developing countries.

The policy, later known as the 'Washington Consensus',[28] forced governments to reduce their spending, such as expenditure on education and healthcare, while phasing out food and fuel subsidies and privatising public enterprises, including power utilities, telecommunication companies and water suppliers. Finally, it pressured governments to substantially reduce barriers in areas like foreign investment and trade, eliminate restrictions on capital inflows and deregulate the labour market. Deep in debt, developing countries had little choice but to accept these loans and the conditions that came with them.

After the Third World debt crisis, which started in 1982 with Mexico and continued throughout the 1980s, these conditional loans became a major component of North–South capital flows, and, over the next two decades, extended to nearly ninety developing countries as different as Argentina, Romania, Ghana and South Korea.

In 1985, Reagan's secretary of the treasury, James Baker, gave the Washington Consensus a fillip when he offered fifteen major debtor nations access to $29 billion, provided they embraced market-orientated macroeconomic reforms.

Soon, loans from regional development banks and aid from bilateral donors took their lead from the Washington Consensus and attached conditions to loans. The World Bank and IMF[29] coordinated loans from all sources so that recipient countries could not avoid taking their medicine.

As the number of loans proliferated, it became clear that they were often poorly designed, leading to unintended consequences.

Jamaica is typical of how the bank's adjustment programme could go wrong. Jamaica received its first conditional loan in the late 1970s and then three more between 1982 and 1984. President Michael Manley criticised these loans, explaining that they had forced his government into a 'Faustian bargain'.[30] While the bank's loans rescued the country from its immediate financial woes, cheap imports from the US killed off Jamaica's domestic agriculture, dairy and poultry industries. After savage cuts to its bureaucracy, debt levels declined, but so, too, did total output. In addition, growth plunged from around 3 per cent in the early 1970s to a dismal 1.3 per cent by 1991. Sharp increases in utility rates and the cost of fuel hit the poor particularly hard, and, in January 1985, riots erupted in the streets of Kingston, resulting in seven people being shot dead.

Unfortunately, this was not an isolated example. Other developing countries suffered through painful adjustment programmes and emerged in no better position. Some even found that their debt levels had actually risen.

By the time Clausen left in 1986, the World Bank had committed a total of almost $12.5 billion on adjustment projects. Despite all this criticism, Clausen boasted, 'I loved structural adjustment loans, and I made a lot of them.'[31]

With the passage of time, its main architect, Anne Krueger had second thoughts about the wisdom of the programme. In a lecture she delivered at New York University titled: 'Meant Well, Tried Little, Failed Much', she reflected on the reasons why the Washington Consensus failed to meet the expectations of its neoliberal sponsors.

> In some cases, tough commitments were made without a full understanding of what was involved. In other cases, the commitment was only skin-deep: rhetoric seen as alternative to real reform, or at least as a way of buying time. Public opposition to policies that have painful implications for some sections of the population can also weaken political resolve.[32]

This mea culpa came as no surprise to Joseph Stiglitz, the chief economist of the World Bank. After leaving the bank, he provided a measured analysis of its flaws.

> Not all the downsides of the Washington Consensus policies for the poor could have been foreseen, but by now they are clear. We have seen how trade liberalization *accompanied by high interest rates* is an almost certain recipe for job destruction and

unemployment creation – at the expense of the poor. Financial market liberalization *unaccompanied by appropriate regulatory structure* is an almost certain recipe for economic instability – and may well lead to higher, not lower interest rates, making it harder for poor farmers to buy the seeds and fertilizer that can raise them above subsistence. Privatization, *unaccompanied by competition policies and oversight to ensure that monopoly powers are not abused*, can lead to higher, not lower, prices for consumers. Fiscal austerity, *pursued blindly*, in the wrong circumstances, can lead to high unemployment and a shedding of the social contract.[33]

While the value of the Washington Consensus is much debated, there is no doubt that it proved to be a boon for the private sector. Reforms compelled countries to liberalise trade, reduce barriers to foreign direct investment and remove regulations that discouraged the entry of foreign firms. All of these reforms helped transnational corporations expand into developing countries. In addition, forced privatisations of utilities and other government-owned businesses ensured that the private sector controlled much larger parts of the economies of developing countries than they did before this policy started.

While McNamara's policies opened the way for the neoliberal Washington Consensus, at heart he was a liberal internationalist who believed that governments were the primary agencies that would reduce poverty and provide for the welfare of their citizens. He urged governments in developing countries to pursue growth targets 'in terms of nutrition, housing, literacy, and employment'. Aware of the problem of inequality, he went on to argue that growth should not favour 'highly privileged sectors whose benefits accrue to the few'.[34] To be fair, his successor took structural loans much further than he ever envisaged.

McNamara's thirteen years as president left other legacies much more deserving of praise. By increasing funds available to the world's poor, he revived the fortunes of the World Bank at a time when it stood in real danger of sinking into irrelevance.

McNamara should also be given credit for breaking the stranglehold the US had over the bank, allowing it to better serve the needs of the world's poor rather than kowtowing to US policymakers.

Notes

1 Address by Robert S. McNamara to the Board of Governors, delivered on 30 September 1980 in Washington, DC.
2 J. Kraske, *Bankers with a Mission* (New York: Oxford University Press, 1996), p. 161.

3   B. Brower, 'McNamara Seen Now, Full Length', *Life* magazine (10 May 1968), pp. 76–100, quote on p. 100.
4   D. Halberstam, *The Reckoning* (London: Bloomsbury, 1987), p. 208.
5   D. Halberstam, *The Best and the Brightest* (New York: Random House, 1973), p. 645.
6   R.S. McNamara, 'Security in the Contemporary World', speech delivered to the American Society of Newspaper Editors on 18 May 1966 in Montreal, Canada.
7   James Reston is quoted by Deborah Shapley in *Promise and Power* (Boston: Little, Brown and Company, 1993), p. 383.
8   Address by Robert S. McNamara to the Millsaps College Convocation on 24 February 1967 in Jackson, Mississippi.
9   Excerpts from William Clark's diary are quoted by Deborah Shapley in *Promise and Power: The Life and Times of Robert McNamara* (Boston: Little, Brown and Company, 1993) p. 477.
10 Quoted in J. Kraske, *Bankers with a Mission*, p. 173.
11 Interview with Eugene H. Rotberg, 22 April 1994 (Washington, DC: World Bank History Project, Brookings Institute), p. 10.
12 D.E. Moggridge (ed.), *The Collected Writings of John Maynard Keynes* (Cambridge: Macmillan/Cambridge University Press, 1980), Vol. XXVI, p. 217.
13 Interview with Robert S. McNamara, 1 April, 10 May, and 3 October 1991 (Washington, DC: World Bank History Project, Brookings Institute), p. 56.
14 Interview with Robert S. McNamara, 1 April, 10 May, and 3 October 1991, p. 50.
15 Interview with Robert S. McNamara, 1 April, 10 May, and 3 October 1991, p. 10.
16 Interview with Robert S. McNamara, 1 April, 10 May, and 3 October 1991, p. 12.
17 Address by Robert S. McNamara to the Board of Governors, delivered on 24 September 1973 in Nairobi, Kenya.
18 Address by Robert S. McNamara to the Board of Governors, delivered on 24 September 1973 in Nairobi, Kenya.
19 Address by Robert S. McNamara to the Board of Governors, delivered on 24 September 1973 in Nairobi, Kenya.
20 Address by Robert S. McNamara to the Board of Governors, delivered on 1 September 1975 in Washington, DC.
21 P.A. Sharma, *Globalizing Development: Robert McNamara at the World Bank*, Doctor of Philosophy dissertation (Los Angeles: University of California, 2010), p. 253.
22 Address by Robert S. McNamara to the Board of Governors, delivered on 2 October 1979 in Belgrade.
23 P.A. Sharma, *Globalizing Development*, p. 441.
24 Deng Xiaoping quoted by Pieter Bottelier in 'China and the World Bank: How a Partnership Was Built', Working Paper No. 277 (Stanford, CA: Stanford Center for International Development, 2006), p. 4.
25 World Bank, 'Alden Winship ("Tom") Clausen', profile posted on the World Bank website. Retrieved from: http://web.worldbank.org/WBSITE/EXTERNAL/EXTABOUTUS/EXTARCHIVES/0,,contentMDK:20487071~pagePK:36726~piPK:437378~theSitePK:29506,00.html (accessed 16 December 2014).

26 Remarks made by President Ronald Reagan at the Annual Meeting of the Boards of Governors of the World Bank Group and International Monetary Fund delivered on 29 September 1981 in Washington, DC.
27 International Bank for Reconstruction and Development, Articles of Agreement Art. IV, § 10 (1989).
28 Retrospectively, in 1989, John Williamson coined the term 'Washington Consensus' to describe the neoliberal prescription associated with these programmes.
29 The IMF had pioneered its Extended Fund Facility in 1974, which was similar to the structural adjustment loans given by the World Bank.
30 Quoted in S. Black, *Life and Debt*, video recording by Tuff Gong Pictures Production, 2001.
31 Quoted in A. Fitzgerald and H. Murphy, 'World Bank's "Wrong Advice" Left Silos Empty in Poor Countries', *Bloomberg.com* (9 December 2008).
32 A.O. Krueger, 'Meant Well, Tried Little, Failed Much: Policy Reforms in Emerging Market Economies', remarks at the Roundtable Lecture at the Economic Honors Society, delivered on 23 March 2004 in New York University.
33 J.E. Stiglitz, *Globalization and its Discontents* (London: Penguin Books, 2002), p. 84. Italics in the original.
34 Address by Robert S. McNamara, to the Board of Governors of the World Bank, delivered on 25 September 1972 in Washington, DC.

9
Free trade follies

I have seen many a bear led by a man; but I never before saw a man led by a bear.
(James Boswell, *The Life of Samuel Johnson*)

Suds on the rise

On 15 December 1993, Irishman Peter Sutherland brought down his gavel, ending seven and a half years of hard negotiations that created the World Trade Organization. While only involved for the last six months, Sutherland played the endgame like a chess grandmaster.

Once it opened for business, the WTO liberalised trade to an unprecedented level, leading Mickey Kantor, the US Trade Representative to hail Sutherland as the 'father of globalization'.[1]

Born on 25 April 1946, into an upper middle-class family, Peter Denis 'Suds' Sutherland was raised in the affluent suburb of Foxrock in south Dublin with his brother and two sisters. Brought up Catholic, Suds attended Dublin's Gonzaga College, a Jesuit day school with a liberal curriculum and a reputation for intellectual rigor. 'We were expected to lead in society if we could and to do so in the right direction', recalls Sutherland.[2] Academically, he hit his straps at University College Dublin, where he excelled in his law studies. He always made time, however, for rugby, earning a reputation as a ferocious competitor.

Suds went on to captain the Lansdowne Football Club in 1970 and 1971 as his father 'Billy' Sutherland had thirty years earlier. Well suited to the physical game, Sutherland was beefy with strong, broad shoulders. His position as prop required brute strength. Lining up in the front row of the scrum, the prop acts as a battering ram, muscling the opposition backwards. It also involves putting one's head where it can be hurt and Suds boasted that his nose was broken nine times, 'probably with justification', he joked.[3] On the field, however Sutherland was deadly serious about his rugby, and team mates recall that he did not like to lose.

At a rugby match, he met an attractive Spanish senorita, who was studying

English while working in Dublin as an au pair. Although he was just twenty years old and spoke little Spanish, Suds fell head over heels for María ('Maruja') Cabria de Valcarcel. After she returned home, Suds worked as a bricklayer to earn his fare to Madrid. When he arrived on the Plymouth ferry at Santander, he had enough time before the train for Madrid left, so he bided his time at a local bar. While enjoying ale, he chatted with the barman, Paco. When he explained why he was in Spain, Paco told Suds that he was wasting his time because 'no Spanish father would allow his daughter to marry someone like me', recalls Sutherland.[4] However, he was not one to be told that something he wanted was impossible, and on 18 September 1971 they married at the home of her parents in Northern Spain.

After university, Sutherland started his law career at the Dublin bar. His first break came in 1981 when Prime Minister Garret FitzGerald asked the brilliant young barrister to be his Attorney General. After the government's re-election, Sutherland served another term as Ireland's top legal officer.

He then went on to become the youngest-ever European Commissioner in 1985, which Sutherland claimed 'was a defining moment, if there was one, in my life'. Describing himself as 'notoriously European', he took to his new job with relish.[5]

In Brussels, Sutherland made his name as a formidable negotiator. Depending on the situation, he could execute the most delicate of manoeuvres or he could tear through the opposition, much as he had done on the rugby field. Massively built and well over six feet tall, he could be an intimidating presence during a negotiating session. In private, puffing away at a large cigar, he was a garrulous, entertaining raconteur and erudite conversationalist, equally comfortable mixing with the political and business elites as he was with the rugby crowd at the Lansdowne pub where he enjoyed the occasional pint.

In the second half of the 1980s, European Community president Jacques Delors depended on Sutherland to help create a single European market. This meant removing government assistance from local industries, breaking open national cartels and eliminating barriers to trade between member countries. He fully understood that the European experiment depended on his success.

As Commissioner in charge of competition, Sutherland enjoyed the legislative backing of the Single European Act. Fully willing to exercise its legislative powers to the fullest, Sutherland went toe-to-toe with vested interests by fearlessly attacking illegal price-fixing, breaking up national cartels and monopolies and rolling back state subsidies, earning him the nickname: 'that turbulent priest'.[6]

We can get the flavour of his negotiating style from a Brussels insider, who described an occasion when Sutherland confronted European transport ministers.

To use the Irish vernacular – 'went through them for a short cut' over air passenger transport restrictions. He said, 'I'm going to take each and every one of you to court'. It was a question of being able to stand up to them. He was using language which was different to that of the usual Commissioner – he tore strips off them. 'Who is this guy?' they were saying afterwards.[7]

He applied the same approach to other major industry sectors, conducting dawn raids and hauling corporate executives before the European Court of Justice, leading Delors to fondly call Sutherland his 'sheriff'.[8] Such was his success that in 1988 Sutherland received the Robert Schuman Medal for his contributions to creating a single European market.

A prominent member of cosmopolitan elite clubs like the Bilderberg Group, the Trilateral Commission, the European Round Table of Industrialists and the World Economic Forum, Sutherland worked these networks to garner support for European integration. 'To me, knowing people, networking with people has been a key to whatever limited success I have had', he explains.[9] These clubs would also prove invaluable later, when he negotiated the creation of the WTO, which superseded the GATT (General Agreement on Tariffs and Trade).

In 1989, as Sutherland was coming to the end of his term as commissioner, he was already thinking ahead. While having a final coffee with members of his cabinet, Sutherland was asked: 'What's next?' to which he replied: 'There was only one game in town – GATT.'[10] But Sutherland would have to wait four years to realise that ambition, and in the interim he was kept busy by various executive and board positions in Irish firms.

Endgame

Sutherland was eyeing GATT because it was in the midst of the Uruguay Round of negotiations, which promised to dramatically reduce trade barriers around the world. Unsurprisingly, as an ardent free trader and enthusiastic supporter of globalisation, he wanted to be part of the biggest game in town.

In September 1986, in Punta del Este, Uruguay, GATT ministers settled on an ambitious agenda of reforms, which they believed would benefit rich and poor nations alike. Developing countries wanted rules that would open up markets in Japan, Europe and the US for their agriculture and other products like textiles, where they held a competitive advantage. Developed countries wanted access to new markets for their manufactured goods and, as negotiations progressed, they added services and intellectual property to the agenda.

By the 1990s, GATT negotiations had stalled under the leadership of Arthur

Dunkel, as the US, Japan and Europe were at odds over a number of major issues. Dunkel eschewed conflict and relied on gentle diplomacy to encourage the parties to resolve their differences. By 1993, he was burnt out and negotiations appeared to be dead in the water.

Unwilling to accept failure, the American head of the GATT delegation, Mickey Kantor, and his and European counterpart, Sir Leon Brittan, decided that a more vigorous negotiating style was needed, and they parachuted Sutherland into the director-general's job, which he took up on 1 July 1993. When asked by a Scottish journalist why he thought he would succeed when others had failed, Sutherland said that he had the 'skill to run to the line once he gets possession of the ball'.[11] And as director-general of GATT, he was determined to get the ball over the try line.[12]

To generate momentum, Sutherland used the media to link free trade with economic success and job growth. He went on to accuse politicians of pandering to vested interests of producers with subsidies and tariffs, forcing consumers to bear unnecessary costs.[13] He also embarrassed obstructionist governments, publicly accusing them of not negotiating in good faith. This strategy softened up negotiators for what Sutherland was determined to make the endgame.

To end the interminable round of fruitless talks that had marred the previous six years, Sutherland insisted that an agreement be finalised by 15 December 1993, a date he insisted was 'engraved in stone'.[14]

During negotiations, Sutherland seemed to be everywhere. A master of minutiae, he helped broker deals. And when a major disagreement arose, he would muscle his way through opposition, as if it were a rugby scrum. Reflecting back, Sutherland admits at times he was a 'bully', but insists that he always acted with the best of intentions.[15]

If necessary, he would phone ministers, even the US president, when he needed support to remove an obstacle. Understandably, many delegates resented Sutherland because he often went over their heads. Nevertheless, this tactic worked well, as political leaders often overcame difficulties that their negotiating teams could not. After a few such calls, delegates became more pliable when they realised that Sutherland could cut the ground from under them.

One anecdote illustrates Sutherland's propensity to browbeat recalcitrant negotiators. At the eleventh hour, the Japanese ambassador got cold feet, uncertain whether his government would be comfortable with the final agreement. Sutherland shocked the ambassador by demanding his prime minister's phone number. The ambassador told Sutherland that he did not have it, and in any case, it was early morning in Tokyo. Sutherland immediately returned to the podium and announced that, as there was no instruction to the contrary, Japan presumably had no objection to the final treaty. Amazingly, they did not call his bluff.

In less than six months, Peter Sutherland achieved the equivalent of herding wasps, as he convinced 118 countries to unanimously agree to establish the WTO.[16] Before it could become law, it still needed to be ratified by legislatures. Once this was completed, government ministers gathered in Marrakech, Morocco, on 15 April 1994 to sign the final treaty. In the ensuing euphoria, Mickey Kantor wrapped Sutherland in a bear hug. No less jubilant, Sutherland threatened to dance an Irish jig on one of the flower-decked tables. Now much heavier than in his playing days, everyone was much relieved when he decided to celebrate with a cigar instead.

Many viewed the WTO as the completion of the task started in Havana in 1948, when a treaty to form the International Trade Organization was finalised. While the ITO was a child of the international liberal order, the WTO marked a seismic shift towards neoliberal globalisation, as Harvard economist Dani Rodrik explained: 'Domestic economic management was to become subservient to international trade and finance rather than the other way around.'[17]

On closer examination, the WTO was not an unqualified victory for the neoliberal global order. Instead, it contained compromises and special deals that had little to do with free trade. In particular, side agreements were written into the WTO 'to cater to special interests', according to Diana Tussie, director of the Latin American Trade Network. As a result, she claims, 'trade rules have been dominated by behind-the-curtain global corporate interests'.[18] The largest of these are Trade-Related Aspects of Intellectual Property Rights (TRIPS) and the General Agreement of Trade in Services (GATS).

The secret history of the WTO

The successful passage of TRIPS was largely due to the time and efforts expended by companies with heavy investments in intellectual property (IP).

One of the lobbyists who spent some time working on this side agreement was James Enyart and we are fortunate to have his account of the campaign, which he published in the little-known magazine of the Licensing Executives Society International, *Les Nouvelles*. He started by providing an overview of the lobbying strategy: 'The industry and traders of world commerce have played simultaneously the role of patient, the diagnosticians and the prescribing physicians.'[19]

Enyart worked for Monsanto, which, during the late 1970s, was hurting because its patented chemicals and pesticides were being 'pirated'.[20] Monsanto was also worried that the genetically modified crops it was developing would face the same fate. The fault, Monsanto believed, lay in international law, which provided insufficient protection to IP owners in many parts of the world.

Monsanto was not the only 'patient' that was worried. Other companies were also losing millions of dollars. Bootlegged video tapes of the latest films could be picked up for a dollar in the alleyways of Bangkok and Singapore; fake Levi jeans, Louis Vuitton handbags and Rolex watches were sold for a pittance in flea markets; students photocopied chapters of school textbooks; and just about any software could be obtained for about the cost of a floppy disk. Even copies of prescription drugs and agricultural chemicals were being peddled for a fraction of the price of branded equivalents.

Describing the first phase of this campaign, Enyart writes, 'Changing foreign IP laws was viewed by many as impossible. It took a few fanatics in some big companies to take on the impossible.'[21]

One of those 'fanatics' was Ed Pratt, CEO of Pfizer. In 1981, when he took over the chair of the powerful Advisory Committee for Trade Negotiations, he urged President Reagan to fight international IP piracy. Joining Pratt's crusade were John Opel, CEO of IBM; John Young, CEO of Hewlett-Packard; and Jack Valenti from the Motion Picture Association of America. They enjoyed the support of the International Intellectual Property Alliance (IIPA), which represented copyright and trademark interests, and the newly formed Intellectual Property Committee (IPC), which included CEOs from companies like DuPont, Monsanto, Merck, CBS and General Motors.

To diagnose the patient's disorders, the IPC commissioned economist and IP expert Jacques Gorlin to identify remedies to the industry's malady. Gorlin's report concluded that the international legal regime to protect IP was patchy and inconsistent, and that enforcement in many parts of the world was non-existent. The medicine he prescribed was a side agreement on IP in the upcoming Uruguay Round, which would standardise protection periods – preferably for as long as possible – require countries to legislate new international standards, catch and prosecute pirates, and create a dispute resolution process that would discipline countries that failed to protect the rights of IP owners.[22]

In September 1985, the US Trade Representative, Clayton Yeutter, used Gorlin's report to lobby other GATT members, hoping they would support US efforts to include IP on the agenda of the upcoming Uruguay Round. Much to his frustration, Yeutter found little interest among the Quad, whom he believed had the most to gain from protecting IP. The Quad was a loose alliance of the US, Europe, Canada and Japan, which was a major bloc within GATT. At this point, Yeutter approached Pratt for help: 'I'm convinced on intellectual property but when I go to Quad meetings, they are under no pressure from their industry. Can you get it?'[23]

In response, as Enyart recounts, US businesses marshalled 'coalitions, across companies, across industries, across oceans in order to build the critical mass necessary to move governments'.[24] Most of the coalition-building occurred during June and August 1986, when members of IPC and IIPA used their connections to arrange a series of international meetings with corporate heavyweights. They succeeded in enlisting the support of the Confederation of British Industries; Bundesverband der Duetschen Industries in Germany; Patronat in France; the Union of Industrial and Employers' Confederations (UNICE), an umbrella organisation that represents European business associations; Keidanren, a federation of Japanese business organisations; and the International Chamber of Commerce. They, in turn, lobbied their governments over the next month. One by one, Quad countries came on-board, and by 1986, they succeeded in placing IP on the agenda for the Uruguay Round. Reflecting on the creation of this grand coalition, Enyart observed, 'It is amazing what momentum can be created when a few committed CEOs personally contact their counterparts.'[25]

Once the Uruguay Round commenced, the IPC, Keidanren and UNICE used Gorlin's original prescription to prepare the 'Basic Framework of GATT Provisions on Intellectual Property',[26] which was used by negotiators from Quad countries to prepare their position.

Opposition mainly came from ten developing countries, led by India and Brazil.[27] They argued that GATT's jurisdiction was limited to tangible goods and it lacked the legal competence to address IP. This opposition was muscled aside by the US, which 'used its unilateral trade sanctions to force many countries to yield ahead of the TRIPS negotiations. ... When some refused to yield, the US took action in the form of denial of duty free access under its GSP [Generalized System of Preferences] schemes',[28] reported Chakravarthi Raghavan in the *South-North Development Monitor*.[29]

By April 1989, those opposing TRIPS had all but given up, and four years later, when Sutherland lowered his gavel for the last time, TRIPS was part of the final WTO package. Such was the success of industry's lobbying that Gorlin remarked, with some satisfaction, 'We got 95% of what we wanted.'[30]

Concluding his account of the operation, Enyart drew a more general lesson from this campaign. '[T]he rules of international commerce are far too important to leave up to government bureaucrats and their academic advisors.' Instead, '[i]t's time for the people who actually make development happen to have an appropriate voice'.[31][31]

Trading invisibles

Like TRIPS, lobbying to include GATS in the Uruguay Round started many years earlier. An OECD report published in 1973 first floated the idea that 'trade in services', like goods, could be subject to international competition and that it constituted a large untapped market.[32] Prior to this, services were regarded as intangibles or, in the words of *The Economist* magazine, 'something you can buy and sell but not drop on your foot'.[33] This is why they are sometimes called 'invisibles'.

While this report did not have an immediate impact, some executives understood its importance. One of those was Harry Freeman, vice president of American Express. Facing barriers to his plans to expand his company's business overseas, Freeman believed he had the solution:

> We were having problems, which we now call market access problems (we did not have this kind of terminology at that time), in thirty or forty countries. We had no remedy under the trade laws or under the General Agreement on Tariffs and Trade (GATT), which only covered goods. To make a long story short, we decided that we would have to change that, which meant starting a new round of trade negotiations including services.[34]

In 1979 he took his idea to his CEO, Jim Robinson, who asked Freeman 'to start a new trade round as soon as possible'. Freeman recounts the conversation that followed:

> He asked, 'How long will it take?' I said, 'I don't know, ten years maybe. I don't know. I have never done it' ... He said, 'Well, do it as soon as you can.' I said, 'I need some money.' He said, 'Don't worry about money. This is so important, you will have an unlimited budget.' If there was one phrase that really pushed trade and services, that was it. We put a person in Brussels, a person in Tokyo, two or three people in Washington, three people in New York, and so forth.[35]

A few months later, Freeman organised a meeting for fellow true believers. Held at Ditchley Park, an eighteenth-century manor house in southern England, they explored ways to create a free market for services.

Key to this campaign was Geza Feketekuty, a counsellor to the US Trade Representative. He had undertaken pioneering work at OECD in the early 1970s and would become a leading advocate for free trade of services within government. As an insider, Feketekuty also provided a critical link between government and the private sector. According to Jane Kelsey's history of GATS, 'Geza Feketekuty ... played an important leadership role throughout the process of taking an idea and a glimmer in the eyes of a few farsighted business leaders to a negotiation on the world stage.'[36]

In the ensuing years, at conferences and meetings held at places like Ditchley Park, Bellagio in northern Italy and Winston House near Steyning in West

Sussex, industry lobbyists and government trade officials coalesced into what they indiscreetly referred to as the 'trade services Mafia'.[37]

In the US, John Reed from CitiCorp and Hank Greenberg from AIG joined Freeman to create the US Coalition of Service Industries in 1982, which led the lobbying. Freeman became its foundation chairperson, tasked with including a side agreement on the trade in services on the agenda of the Uruguay Round.

This 'mafia' also was strong in the UK, led by the Liberalisation of Trade in Services (LOTIS) Committee, which drew together senior bureaucrats, senior officials from the Bank of England and executives from prominent companies, including Goldman Sachs International, Barclay, Lloyds and HSBC. One of the key figures in LOTIS was Sir Leon Brittan, who explains how the committee operated:

> There was a time when international trade negotiations in the GATT rounds were very much left to government officials. The Uruguay Round began to change that, in particular because trade in services posed more complex problems when it came to liberalisation. Private sector views on issues and priorities became important inputs for government negotiators.[38]

Over the next few years, lobby groups formed in Canada, Hong Kong, Sweden, New Zealand, Argentina, Australia and the European Union. The International Chamber of Commerce also offered its support, issuing a statement urging 'all governments to enter into reciprocal and mutually advantageous undertakings to reduce impediments to international trade in services'.[39]

Opposition came from developing countries. Led by India and Brazil, a bloc of developing countries contested the inclusion of trade in services in the negotiating work programme for the Uruguay Round. As one Brazilian delegate observed:

> From a developing country's perception, [the Americans] are now trying to have a new outlet with services so that they can expand their trade to areas where they think they still have comparative advantage. On other areas they are defensive.[40]

They also worried that GATS would provide transnational corporations with new ways to dominate their local economies, undermine subsidies for the poor, and force them to privatise state-owned utilities, including banks and insurance companies. Finally, from a purely practical viewpoint, with limited resources and expertise, they knew that they would be stretched negotiating new and complex issues thrown up by trade in services.

Despite this opposition, GATS made it onto the agenda, which was the cue for the services 'mafia' to help the agreement over the line. Harry Freeman recounted their lobbying effort.

> The US private sector on trade in services is probably the most powerful trade lobby, not only in the United States but also in the world. ... At the close of the Uruguay Round, we lobbied and lobbied. We had about 400 people from the US private sector. There were perhaps four Canadians and nobody from any other private sector. The private sector advocacy operations in the US government are radically different from those in every other government in the world.[41]

Once the Uruguay Round was completed, but still needed to be ratified, John Reed and Hank Greenberg flew to Washington, where they told both Republicans and Democrats that GATS was a very good deal for American businesses. According to WTO Trade in Services Division director, David Hartridge, these efforts proved critical to the outcome:

> [W]ithout the enormous pressure generated by the US financial services sector, particularly companies like American Express and Citicorp, there would have been no services agreement.[42]

The high cost of free trade

Once negotiations ended, Peter Sutherland proudly announced that the WTO represented the 'belated completion of the Bretton Woods structure of IMF, World Bank and the WTO', which he hoped would turn 'words about a new world economic order into reality'.[43] And like the Bretton Woods agreement, which its architects designed to prevent a repeat of the economic battles that had raged during the 1930s and contributed to the Second World War, Sutherland claimed that the WTO had 'largely eliminated commercial ambition as a cause of war. ... Now businesspeople conquer markets, not navies.'[44]

In an important speech delivered to the Institute of Economic Affairs in London on 16 June 1994, Sutherland acknowledged the ideological legacy the WTO owed Friedrich Hayek. The WTO's 'rules and disciplines reflect the view that a decentralised system of market-determined prices is the best way of ensuring an efficient allocation of resources, ... [by] laying down the conditions of competition for a free enterprise system', he told his audience.[45]

Sutherland was particularly proud of the WTO's dispute settlement mechanism, which represented for him the crowning achievement of the new trade regime by imposing the rule of law. For the first time, less developed countries had a legal avenue to address unfair trade, where before they had been victims of bullying by the major powers. The WTO also had the ability to approve sanctions on any country that breached its rules.[46] Sutherland welcomed these rules 'as defender of the rights of the weak and the vulnerable among its members'.[47]

The WTO's unique enforcement mechanism involved trade tribunals, which adjudicated disputes. While they lacked the power to punish violators, injured parties could impose retaliatory trade restrictions on the offending country. Such sanctions only work if they hurt the offending country.

Not everyone agreed with Sutherland that poor and rich countries were equal within the WTO. Magna Shahin, who represented Egypt during the Uruguay Round, explained the problem faced by developing countries. 'China could [use it], but what about a country like Egypt or even a smaller one against the US, the EU or even Japan?'[48]

Antigua and Barbuda provides a test case on whether, in practice, a small country can take on a superpower. In 2007, the WTO ruled against US prohibitions against offshore internet gambling, and the judgment allowed the twin-island nation to recover $21 million per year from the US. With little trade with the US, Antigua and Barbuda was not in a position to levy retaliatory duties on American goods. Instead, the WTO allowed it the right to suspend US intellectual property rights, which meant that they could sell to the world US patented and copyright products free of royalties. Not only did the US refuse to pay the damages, it then took to bullying the Caribbean micro-nation. 'Government-authorised piracy would undermine chances for a settlement', warned Nkenge Harmon, a spokeswoman for the US Trade Representative's office. This was a hollow threat as the US had refused to negotiate in good faith since the judgment went against it. Harmon went on to make a veiled threat. 'It also would serve as a major impediment to foreign investment in the Antiguan economy, particularly in high-tech industries.'[49] Frustrated, on 25 April 2014, Antigua and Barbuda issued a statement to a meeting of the Dispute Settlement Body.

> It seems, perhaps the harsh light of this prolonged action by one of the weakest against the strongest is on the verge of condemning the multilateral trading system established here some two decades ago as what its critics then feared – a vehicle by which the strong economies could extract concessions from the weak while at the same time effectively stone-walling – no, in fairness, denying – the ability of small economies to obtain any meaningful recourse when wronged by others.[50]

After the June 2014 election, the new government of Gaston Browne further reduced his country's claim, stating that 'the reality of the situation' was to get 'the best result for the people of Antigua and Barbuda', which involved little by way of a cash settlement but in-kind contributions, such as the establishment of a US satellite visa office and additional scholarships for the American University of Antigua.[51]

The other major claim made by Sutherland was that the WTO created a new era of free trade. The new trading regime did impose a rules-based system and significantly reduced tariffs, but it did not introduced trade that was free or fair.

Evidence that the WTO did not deliver free trade is not hard to find. Within the final package of sixty agreements, there are 560 pages of complex legalese and another 23,000 pages of codicils, many of which are special deals and exceptions that serve vested and national interests. If genuine free trade was the objective, a much simpler (and much briefer) set of rules would have emerged from the Uruguay Round.

With so many concessions, compromises and deals part of the final agreement, at best, the WTO is about *freer* trade not *free* trade, with the major powers the big winners. For the rest, 'opening up markets in the developing countries to goods from the advanced industrial countries without full reciprocation', claims former World Bank economist and Nobel Prize winner, Joseph Stiglitz, 'left them worse off than they would be with a truly free and fair trade regime'.[52]

TRIPS, in particular, has been criticised as unfair to developing countries. Evelyne Hong, from the Malaysia based NGO, Third World Network, argued that 'TRIPs will affect the Third World by increasing the knowledge gap; and by shifting bargaining power towards the producers of knowledge most of whom are in the industrialised North.'[53] It is also possible that rather than diffusing technologies to developing countries, transnational corporations will optimise their profits by exporting only finished products, all at a premium price. The World Bank estimates it will cost developing countries $20 billion more for pharmaceuticals and other products that are protected by patents and copyright, with profits banked by transnational corporations based in developed countries.[54]

There has also been criticism of TRIPS from free trade advocates. Jagdish Bhagwati, Sutherland's economics policy advisor, attacked the agreement, which he argued has nothing to do with market liberalisation but represented a victory for corporate interests:

> For virtually the first time, the corporate lobbies in pharmaceuticals and software had distorted and deformed an important multilateral institution, turning it away from its trade mission and rationale and transforming it into a royalty collection agency.[55]

By royalties, Bhagwati means that corporations use legislative monopolies provided by patents, trademarks and copyrights to sell or license products at premium prices not set by the marketplace.

Developing countries also had a number of serious problems with GATS. One of the more vocal opponents was India. Its ambassador to GATT, Shrirang Shukla, said, 'The issue of services ... had the potential of rendering [GATS] into an effective instrument to support and promote the activities of transnational corporations.'[56] In particular, developing countries believed that GATS would allow international banks to dominate their economies and that foreign utilities would force them to open up government services, like water and electricity, to private competition.

Nevertheless, developing countries achieved one minor victory during the Uruguay Round by limiting the scope of the Trade-Related Investment Measures Agreement (TRIMS). This side agreement contained rules that required governments to apply the same regulations to foreign investors as they do to local businesses. It also protected foreign investments from confiscation without compensation. Opposing TRIMS, developing countries argued that it had nothing to do with trade, but was solely designed to protect corporate property and investments. While TRIMS was part of the final WTO package, the amendments stripped it of its effectiveness. Rather than accepting this defeat, over the last twenty years or so, the US in particular has aggressively pursued regional and bilateral investment agreements that include strong protections for foreign investment.

Notes

1. Professor Kenneth J. Costa in his introduction to Peter Sutherland, who delivered the Gresham Lecture, 'Leadership at a Time of Transition and Turbulence', at Barnard's Inn Hall on 8 March 2011.
2. P.D. Sutherland, 'Peter Sutherland's Reflections on his Education at Gonzaga College', in *Gonzaga at Sixty* (Dublin: Messenger Publications, 2010), pp. 26–30, quote on p. 27.
3. J. Ashworth, 'Influential Irishman Who Has a "Fairy Godmother" on His Side', *The Times* (14 February 2005), p. 44.
4. Quoted in B. Bergareche, 'El riesgo ahora está en Italia, pero a medio plazo el problema es Francia', *ABC.es* (18 March 2013).
5. P.D. Sutherland, 'Sud's Law', *UCD Connections* (2010–11), pp. 22–7.
6. P.D. Sutherland, 'Leadership at a Time of Transition and Turbulence', Gresham Lecture, delivered in London on 8 March 2011.
7. A. Murdoch, 'Profile: Champion of Free Trade', *Independent* (11 July 1993).
8. J. Gillingham, *European Integration, 1950–2003* (Cambridge: Cambridge University Press, 2003), p. 251.
9. M. Hannigan, 'Sutherland, a Man with All the Luck, Some Fame and Finally a Fortune', *Irish Times* (15 August 1998), p. 6.

10 S. Carswell, 'The Ultimate Social Networker', *Irish Times* (30 January 2010), p. 7.
11 J. Cooney, '"Super Suds" Returns to the Political Corridors of Power', *Herald Scotland* (10 June 1993).
12 Equivalent to the end-zone in gridiron football.
13 *GATT, The Sting: How Governments Buy Votes on Trade with the Consumer's Money* (Geneva: GATT, August 1993).
14 T. Redburn, 'Paris Pressed to Ease Stance on Trade Deal', *New York Times* (9 September 1993).
15 P.T. Larsen, 'Peter Sutherland: The Charming Enforcer', *FT.com* (28 July 2008).
16 The Marrakech Agreement was signed by 116 GATT members plus Algeria and Honduras.
17 D. Rodrik, *The Globalization Paradox* (New York: W.W. Norton & Company, 2011), p. 76.
18 Opening remarks by Diana Tussie, on 'The WTO and Development: The Challenges of Trust and Empowerment in Governing Global Trade', the Geneva Lectures on Global Economic Governance, Global Economic Governance Programme, University College, delivered in Oxford on 3 October 2007.
19 J. Enyart, 'A GATT Intellectual Property Code', *Les Nouvelles*, 25:2 (1990), 54–6, quote on p. 56.
20 'Pirated' is a pejorative word and inaccurate, as is explained by Harry Blutstein in 'Shalt Thou Pirate Thy Neighbours' Movies?', *Arena* magazine (February 2015), pp. 38–40.
21 J. Enyart, 'A GATT Intellectual Property Code', p. 54.
22 J.J. Gorlin, 'A Trade-Based Approach for the International Copyright Protection for Computer Software', unpublished report (1 September 1985).
23 Clayton K. Yeutter quoted by Peter Drahos and John Braithwaite in *Information Feudalism* (London: Earthscan, 2002), p. 117.
24 J. Enyart, 'A GATT Intellectual Property Code', p. 54.
25 J. Enyart, 'A GATT Intellectual Property Code', p. 54.
26 The Intellectual Property Committee, Keidanren, UNICE, 'Basic Framework of GATT Provisions on Intellectual Property: Statement of Views of the European, Japanese and United States Business Communities', June 1988.
27 The others were Argentina, Cuba, Egypt, Nicaragua, Nigeria, Peru, Tanzania and Yugoslavia.
28 The Generalized System of Preferences, or GSP, is a formal system of exemption from the more general rules of the GATT, allowing developed countries to lower tariffs for the least developed countries, without also lowering tariffs for rich countries. It is left to the discretion of each developed country whether or not they apply GSP. The US has used this system widely, and also abused it, using the threat of withdrawing GSP to pressure clients to support it in international negotiations.
29 C. Raghavan, 'Did Uruguay Round Resolve Anything?', *South-North Development Monitor* (14 February 1994).

30 Jacques Gorlin quoted by Susan Sell in *Private Power, Public Law: The Globalization of Intellectual Property Rights* (Cambridge: Cambridge University Press, 2003), p. 55.
31 J. Enyart, 'A GATT Intellectual Property Code', pp. 53 and 55.
32 OECD, *Policy Perspectives for International Trade and Economic Relations*, report by the High Level Group on trade and related problems to the Secretary General of OECD (Paris: OECD, 1973).
33 Quoted by William J. Drake and Kalypso Nicolaïdis, 'Ideas, Interests and Institutionalization: "Trade in Services" and the Uruguay Round', *International Organization*, 46:1 (1992), 37–100, quote on p. 43.
34 H.L. Freeman, 'Comments on "Financial Services and the GATS 2000 Round" by Pierre Sauvé and James Gillespie' (Brookings-Wharton Papers on Financial Services 2000), p. 456.
35 H.L. Freeman, 'Comments on "Financial Services and the GATS 2000 Round"', p. 456.
36 J. Kelsey, *Serving Whose Interests?* (Oxon: Routledge Cavendish, 2008), p. xix.
37 W.J. Drake and K. Nicolaïdis, 'Ideas, Interests and Institutionalization', 61.
38 L. Brittan, 'Europe's Prescriptions for the Global Trade Agenda', speech delivered to the Annual Meeting of the US Coalition of Service Industries, in Washington, DC, on 24 September 1998.
39 Statement by the International Chamber of Commerce is quoted by Patrick F.J. Macrory, Arthur Edmond Appleton and Michael G. Plummer in *The World Trade Organization: Legal, Economic and Political Analysis*, Vol. 3 (New York: Springer-Verlag, 2005), p. 306.
40 The unnamed Brazilian delegate is quoted by William J. Drake and Kalypso Nicolaïdis, 'Ideas, Interests and Institutionalization', 52.
41 H.L. Freeman, 'Comments on "Financial Services and the GATS 2000 Round"', p. 458.
42 D. Timms, 'Are You Being Served?', *The Guardian* (23 January 2001).
43 P.D. Sutherland, 'The New Multilateral Trading System: What Is at stake', speech given to the Swedish-American Chamber of Commerce in New York on 3 March 1994.
44 P.D. Sutherland, 'Avoiding Stalemate in the Doha Round', Tacitus Lecture delivered in London on 15 April 2003.
45 P.D. Sutherland, 'A New Framework for International Economic Relations', the Third Hayek Memorial Lecture delivered at the Institute of Economic Affairs in London on 14 June 1994.
46 This mechanism allows an aggrieved WTO member to bring a case against any other country that it believes breached WTO rules. Such disputes are heard by semi-judicial trade panels that adjudicate on the merits of each case. If a panel's findings are not implemented, then the Dispute Settlement Body will automatically authorise retaliation. In the next step, the wronged party can set tariffs or get even in other ways to recover damages suffered. This was a considerable improvement on the previous GATT agreement, which had no way of disciplining members that broke its rules.

47 Peter Sutherland quoted by Kendall W. Stiles in 'New WTO Regime: The Victory of Pragmatism', *International Law & Practice*, 4 (1995), 36–7.
48 M. Shahin, 'From Marrakech to Singapore: The WTO and Developing Countries', *Third World Network* (1996), 22–7.
49 D. Palmer, 'U.S. Warns Antigua Against "Government-authorized Piracy"', *Reuters* (28 January 2013).
50 W. New and C. Saez, 'Antigua Questions Efficacy of WTO Dispute System over IP-Related Case', *Intellectual Property Watch* (26 April 2014).
51 S. Stradbrooke, 'Antigua Fires Attorney Mark Mendel, Makes New $100m offer to End US WTO Dispute', *CalvinAyre.com* (9 September 2014).
52 J.E. Stiglitz, *Making Globalization Work* (New York: W.W. Norton, 2007), p. 62.
53 E. Hong, 'Globalisation and the Impact on Health – A Third World View', paper prepared for the Peoples' Health Assembly, held between 4–8 December 2000 in Savar, Bangladesh.
54 World Bank, *Global Economic Prospects and the Developing Countries 2002* (Washington, DC: World Bank, 2001), Chapter 5.
55 J.N. Bhagwati, *In Defense of Globalization* (Oxford: Oxford University Press, 2004), p. 183
56 S.P. Shukla, *From GATT to WTO and Beyond*, Working Paper 195 (Helsinki: United Nations University and World Institute for Development Economics Research, 2000), p. 14.

10
Global Fifth Amendment

> You are my creator, but I am your master – obey.
> ... Beware; for I am fearless, and therefore powerful. (Mary Shelley, *Frankenstein*)

The accidental libertarian

Having spent his professional life as an academic, public intellectual and media commentator, Richard Epstein built his reputation on his uncompromising libertarian interpretations of the US constitution. His views are almost always controversial, attracting attacks from academics, politicians and even conservatives.

His expertise and passion are for the US legal system, out of which Epstein developed a revolutionary legal doctrine, built around the takings clause of the Fifth Amendment of the US constitution. Remarkably, it has taken on a life of its own, gaining currency as a global norm. Applied to regional and bilateral investment treaties, Epstein's interpretation of takings allowed transnational corporations to sue governments for losses when national regulations reduced the value of their foreign investments or property. This doctrine of regulatory takings has been incorporated into an emerging global legal order, challenging traditional privileges associated with national sovereignty.

Richard Epstein was born on 17 April 1943, spending his early years in Brooklyn before the family moved to Great Neck, Long Island. His father, Bernard, was a radiologist, and his mother, Catherine, ran her husband's office. Despite his mother's strong political view as a New Deal liberal, with a deep distrust of the Republican Party, Richard's political ideas while he was growing up were largely unformed.

At school, Richard displayed no early brilliance, but made up for any academic deficiency with his enthusiasm, bouncing out of his seat to blurt out answers before his teacher had a chance to ask who in the class knew the answer. 'I had a bunch of teachers who prophesied an ugly end to my academic career', he recalls.[1]

Despite his teachers' dire prediction, Richard did well enough to get into

Columbia University. It was the 1960s and the campus was a hotbed of left-wing radicalism. 'I've always been a contrarian intellectual, and when I see lots of people out there chanting and screaming, my first reaction is that they've got to be wrong', he says.[2]

The very unpopularity of libertarianism may well have appealed to Richard's iconoclasm. With tongue firmly planted in cheek, Epstein speculated that he might have fallen under the influence of a friend of his Uncle Sammy, 'who was a strong social Darwinist who inveighed how charity weakened the spine of the system, but he died, tragically, from a bee sting, which always seemed to me to warn against the perils of excessive individualism'.[3]

In truth, he became what he calls an 'accidental libertarian' at Oxford University,[4] where he went in 1964 on a Kellett Fellowship. Shaping his philosophy was the great liberal thinker, John Locke, who wrote about the natural rights of property. He also immersed himself in Blackstone's *Commentaries*, an eighteenth-century compendium of legal judgments that underpin British common law. As his libertarianism took root, Epstein came to believe in 'individual autonomy, as self-rule, but not unconstrained by the rights of others; private property, with an eye to the commons; freedom of contract, with an eye to externalities; limited government, with a fear of excessive concentration of power'.[5]

When Epstein did not have his head buried in a legal book, he would dip into the English newspapers each morning, turning first to the sports pages. This would allow him to converse intelligently with other students about cricket, a sport unfamiliar to many Americans. In 1966, Epstein left Oxford for Yale Law School, where he graduated cum laude two years later. In 1968, he joined the law faculty at the University of Southern California when he was just twenty-five years old.

In 1972, Epstein married Eileen Wolfe, and that same year they settled in Illinois, where he became a member of the University of Chicago's law faculty.

Epstein quickly built his reputation as a brilliant and original thinker, unwilling to confine himself to a narrow specialisation. '[I]ntellectual glaucoma, or the constant narrowing of vision that creeps in if you do not constantly expose yourself to new challenges', he warns. 'Unless you are willing to make new investments in intellectual capital, you will lose your intellectual appetite and your intellectual edge.'[6]

His knowledge of a wide range of subjects has also made Epstein a formidable debater and a stimulating lecturer whose ideas come cascading out in such a way that 'taking notes in his class is like trying to fill a Dixie cup with water from Niagara Falls', one student recollected.[7] He is also a formidable public intellectual, whose ideas challenge conventional wisdom.

Game changer

It was Epstein's 1985 book *Takings*[8] that first brought him notoriety, and the controversy it generated still rages to this day. It presents original arguments that radically reinterpret the Fifth Amendment of the US Constitution. Long-established case law holds that governments only have to pay 'just compensation' when they appropriate private property, such as when land is confiscated in order to build a new highway or airport. Epstein extends this principle to what he calls 'regulatory takings', explaining: 'All regulations, all taxes, and all modifications of liability rules are takings of private property, and prima facie compensable by the state.'[9] The only exceptions are when the state uses its police power to protect society from common threats.[10]

Professor of law and professor of history at Vanderbilt University, James Ely, applauds *Takings* for challenging settled law. 'Professor Epstein was the primary intellectual force in changing the terms of debate over property in the constitutional order.'[11] That debate raged inside and outside academe because Epstein, unlike most scholars, was willing to reach a popular audience through lectures, public debates and newspaper articles.

By promoting regulatory takings, Epstein hoped to provide libertarians with the intellectual ammunition they needed to blow out of the water 'many of the heralded reforms and institutions of the twentieth century: zoning, rent control, workers, compensation laws, transfer payments, [and] progressive taxation'.[12] In these instances, the government could only regulate if 'it's willing to buy off its dissenters at a fair valuation'.[13] For advocates of limited government, regulatory takings is a highly attractive legal doctrine.

> [T]he requirement of just compensation for government takings should constitute a powerful and useful check on the growth of the state, which if consistently applied would effectively clip the wings of the modern welfare state.[14]

Epstein's doctrine on property rights soon drew strong reactions from both the left and right, as both sides realised that it represented a new battleground in the war of ideas. The stakes were high. If adopted, regulatory takings 'invalidates much of the twentieth century legislation', Epstein announced with some satisfaction.[15]

Accused of dangerous revisionism, *Takings* was attacked when it was first published, often viciously. Epstein's ideas evidently got under the skin of otherwise sober academics. A sample of comments includes accusations that it is 'a disturbing book', a 'patent and howling failure', and an 'intellectual wasteland'.[16] Liberal-leaning Professor Thomas Grey from Stanford Law School fumed, '*Takings* belongs with the output of the constitutional lunatic fringe, the effusions of gold bugs, tax protestors, and gun-toting survivalists',[17] while Mark Kelman, also from Stanford, condemned its ideology: 'The book's only useful contribution may be to expose more fully the moral venality and intellectual vacuity of formal, legalized libertarianism.'[18]

These attacks only spurred Epstein on. In a 2009 article commenting on Epstein's resilience, Professor Robert C. Ellickson, a former colleague and friend, wrote:

> For decades, he has challenged conventional opinion on a host of topics, knowing that he would draw fierce criticism from many commentators. Although most law professors nominally support the existence of a vigorous marketplace of ideas, most feel some discomfort when they venture a nonconformist opinion. Richard, by contrast, revels in the heat of academic battle. ... Richard sometimes may appear to have an excessive self-confidence. This is an affect that helps him in settings where he is outnumbered by his critics.[19]

On his side, Epstein had a good number of supporters. For example, the *Wall Street Journal* named Epstein's book one of the ten best of 1985,[20] while conservative Paul Gottfried, Raffensperger Professor of Humanities at Elizabethtown College, lauded Epstein's ability to combine 'legal scholarship and libertarian conviction to produce a brief against the destruction of property rights in modern America'.[21] It is outside academia, however, that the doctrine of regulatory takings has created a political firestorm.

Takings Project

Activist lawyers Doug Kendall and Charles Lord have uncovered what the authors called the 'Takings Project',[22] a campaign to enshrine regulatory takings in legislation. While not a conspiracy or even a coordinated campaign, the Takings Project has attracted a wide range of supporters among American conservatives.

> With supportive judges sitting in crucial places in the federal judiciary, a large and still growing collection of corporations, non-profit law firms, and think tanks has assembled to assist developers in bringing takings cases through the court system and to these judges. ... At the center of the Takings Project is a nationwide network of prodevelopment, non-profit legal foundations that bring takings cases free-of-charge to their clients.[23]

An early fan of regulatory takings was Edwin Meese III, whom President Ronald Reagan appointed as attorney general in 1985. By applying Epstein's legal doctrine, Meese hoped to roll back regulations on an industrial scale. In his memoir, Charles Fried, solicitor general in the Reagan Administration, provides an insider's account of Meese's role in the Takings Project:

> Attorney General Meese and his young advisors – many drawn from the ranks of the then fledgling Federalist Societies and often devotees of the extreme libertarian views of Chicago law professor Richard Epstein – had a specific, aggressive, and, it seemed to me, quite radical project in mind: to use the Takings Clause of the Fifth Amendment as a severe brake upon federal and state regulation of business and property. The grand plan was to make government pay compensation as for a taking of property every time its regulations impinged too severely on a property right – limiting the possible uses for a parcel of land or restricting or tying up a business in regulatory red tape. If the government labored under so severe an obligation, there would be, to say the least, much less regulation.[24]

Disturbed by what he witnessed, Fried challenged Meese, who responded: 'Maybe it is a radical departure from the regulatory mess we are in right now, but it's not a radical departure from the Constitution.'[25] Meese hoped that the Takings Project would reshape the regulatory landscape, just as Epstein had dreamed it would.

Meese's first move was to prepare for President Reagan's signature on Executive Order 12,630, which stated that '[e]xecutive departments and agencies should review their actions carefully to prevent unnecessary takings that are necessitated by statutory mandate'.[26] While not imposing compensation when regulatory takings occur, it signalled the first step towards legitimising Epstein's legal doctrine. First introduced in 1988, it fell victim to politics when the Clinton Administration rescinded this measure in 1994.[27]

After leaving the Administration, Meese occasionally worked with Richard Epstein and others on the Takings Project, often linking up with public interest law groups. The most prominent of these were the Institute of Justice, the Pacific Legal Foundation, the Federalist Society, the Mountain States Legal Foundation, Cato Institute, Heritage Foundation and the Wise Use movement. These groups enjoyed modest success, as they pursued the Takings Project by supporting test cases in state and federal courts and providing model laws to state legislatures.

The breakthrough in the federal sphere occurred in 1994, when the Republicans won the Congressional majority. The 104th Session of the House passed the Private Property Protection Act that forced the government to provide compensation when the value of anyone's private property was reduced by more than 20 per cent.[28] Predictably, it died in the Democrat-controlled Senate.

In 2006, Epstein reflected on what he had achieved, displaying mixed emotions:

> [I]t is strictly a case of two steps forward and one step backwards, if that. But writing a book like *Takings* can never be called a failure because it is unable to reverse the direction of judicial thinking that has lasted for over fifty years. It is quite enough to break the intellectual monopoly that once backed up the New Deal order. The overall political and intellectual debate will be conducted, in my view, at a far higher level precisely because political competition has replaced monolithic liberal orthodoxy. And the impacts will be felt at all levels, because political officials and private parties now have to think twice about whether they want to engage in the kinds of activities that *Takings* condemns.[29]

In the US, Epstein effectively challenged conventional wisdom on takings, but on the ground, little changed because the Supreme Court failed to accept this doctrine. Outside the US, however, the Takings Project gained traction, as regional and bilateral investment treaties were built on the principle of regulatory takings.

Going regional

Frustrated in the US, proponents of the Takings Project managed to enshrine its legal doctrine in the investment section of the North American Free Trade Agreement (NAFTA). This agreement joined the US, Canada and Mexico into a regional free trade zone and came into force on 1 January 1994. By creating a model that others followed, the Takings Project won a major victory, leading law academics Vicki Been and Joel Beauvais to suggest that NAFTA gave birth to the 'Global Fifth Amendment'.[30]

NAFTA included a regulatory takings clause (Chapter 11) at the insistence of American and Canadian negotiators, with good reason. In 1938, the Mexican government expropriated all reserves, facilities and assets of foreign oil companies. Then, in 1982, the government nationalised foreign banks. While no one expected Mexico to go down the same track again, negotiators worried that a future Mexican government might use oppressive regulations or impose punitive taxes as a way to confiscate foreign assets by stealth.

In line with the Takings Project, Chapter 11 compelled governments to make restitutions to foreign companies for 'measure[s] tantamount to nationalization or expropriation'.[31] It also included a revolutionary 'investor-to-state' mechanism to deal with disputes.³² This allowed corporations to take a government to an independent tribunal, whose judgments were binding. While the tribunal could not force a government to withdraw the offending regulation, it could compel a recalcitrant government to pay compensation to the injured corporation, not just for loss of property but for future profits and other damages as well.

Edwin Williamson, one of the authors of Chapter 11, had previously promoted the Takings Project through his activities with the Federalist Society. Accounts of behind-the-scene drafting of Chapter 11 suggested that he was instrumental in broadening its coverage. 'What we're really trying to protect here are property rights ... [which have] always gotten short shrift from an international standpoint because the international legal community is very left-wing and doesn't care about property rights', Williamson claimed.³³

Within a few years of NAFTA coming into force, the provisions of Chapter 11 were tested. And no one was surprised when the Mexican government wound up in the line of fire.

In 1997, California-based Metalclad Corporation had planned to establish a waste-disposal plant in San Luis Potosí, Mexico. With approvals from the national and state government in hand, Metalclad simply needed a building permit from the municipal council, which the company believed was a formality. Rather than narrowly considering whether the plant was properly constructed, the municipality refused the permit because it feared that the plant could harm the environment and poison the local water supply.

As public protests in Mexico grew, the government realised its mistake. In a policy shift, it supported the municipality by declaring the site part of a specially protected ecological zone, which effectively prevented Metalclad from operating its facility. As a result, the company sued the Mexican government and won. In 1999, a NAFTA tribunal awarded Metalclad $16.7 million in damages.

To everyone's surprise, Mexico was not the only target of Chapter 11 actions. In 1997, the Canadian government passed a bill banning the import and trade of petrol-additive MMT³⁴ because it posed an environmental risk. MMT is produced only in the US by the Ethyl Corporation of Virginia. Because the company exported MMT to Canada, it was able to invoke NAFTA's Chapter 11 to fight the ban.

Ethyl submitted a claim for $251 million, which the company alleged represented lost profits and damage it had suffered from the ban. Anticipating a defeat before the NAFTA tribunal, the Canadian government decided to cut its losses. In July 1998, the government reversed its ban on MMT and paid Ethyl $13 million in legal fees and damages. A humiliating letter from the minister of the environment, Christine Stewart, to Ethyl capped off this sorry episode:

> Current scientific information fails to demonstrate that MMT impairs the proper functioning of automotive on-board diagnostic systems. Furthermore, there is no new scientific evidence to modify conclusions drawn by Health Canada in 1994 that MMT poses no health risk.[35]

This letter shocked health and environmental experts, who believed that the scientific case against MMT was sound. One study, for example, showed that exposure could lead to symptoms similar to Parkinson's disease.[36] Automakers also harboured concerns that MMT damaged catalytic converters in their cars.[37]

After this shameful cave-in, the public and politicians in North America asked how this dangerous clause had become part of NAFTA without anyone sounding the alarm. The answer is most disturbing. Joseph Stiglitz, who was on the Council of Economic Advisers during the NAFTA negotiations, claimed:

> Had President Clinton known about this, I feel confident that he would, at a minimum, have demanded a side-letter providing an interpretation of Chapter 11 that precluded such an interpretation. But we never had a discussion on the topic in the White House, and I am convinced that President Clinton was not apprised of the risk of such an interpretation.[38]

The same went for Capitol Hill. Abner Mikva, White House Counsel between 1994 and 1995, told the *New York Times*, 'If Congress had known that there was anything like this in NAFTA, they would never have voted for it.'[39]

Dan Price, the other principal author of Chapter 11, has a different story, claiming, 'The parties did not stumble into this.' The truth is probably that the negotiators knew what they were doing, but their political masters did not. This did not particularly bother Price, who went on to say, 'My only advice is, get over it.'[40]

Conscious that other Chapter 11 cases were in the pipeline after the Ethyl debacle, critics feared that Chapter 11 posed a real and immediate danger to the democratic system. David Haigh, who represented Canada on NAFTA's Advisory Committee on Private Commercial Disputes, described the nature of the threat:

> Chapter 11 potentially creates an opportunity for foreign corporations ... to influence the legislative process and potentially even to impede the passage of legislation or the exercise of regulatory power.[41]

Rather than perceiving this as a problem, Price praised Chapter 11 as an effective way of 'depoliticizing ... disputes'. He further explains:

The idea was to take them [disputes] out of the political realm and put them more into the realm of commercial arbitration. The idea was that the investor, by having the avenue of bringing the dispute itself, could resolve the dispute in a way that did not engage the political organs of ... governments.[42]

Just the threat of a Chapter 11 action, Price suggested, will be sufficient to temper the enthusiasm of legislators for new regulations:

[W]hen the Congress is considering legislation that is inconsistent with our international obligations, the first thing we, in this case we is the United States Trade Representative (USTR), or the legal advisor's office, do is trot up to the Hill and tell them, if you do this, a claim will be asserted against us either in the WTO or by a private party under agreement and there will be a claim for damages. It is one of the most powerful arguments against passing a measure inconsistent with international obligations.[43]

The wider implications of Chapter 11 were not lost on the corporate sector, as Lydia Lazar, a commercial attorney, told the *Global Financial Markets* magazine: 'When just the threat of a chapter 11 action may suffice to wrest a financial settlement from a government, investors have unprecedented leverage against states.'[44]

Barry Appleton, who served as counsel for the Ethyl Corporation, chortled that Chapter 11 is 'a dream come true for business ... This is the part of NAFTA that nobody read ... Governments that want to protect their own citizens have to pay for it under NAFTA.'[45]

On the other hand, NGOs were left in a state of shock. 'As a legal concept, NAFTA really is mind-boggling in its potential scope', lamented Daniel Seligman, director of the Sierra Club's Responsible Trade Program. 'What we can envision here is a wholesale overturning of the regulatory state, which took 100 years to build.'[46] Seligman's comments uncannily echo those of Epstein's, who predicted that regulatory takings could invalidate 'much of the twentieth century legislation'.[47]

Soon, law firms that specialised in trade law alerted their corporate clients to the possibilities. As a result, a number of cases started to percolate their way through the legal system. By November 2014, pending claims under Chapter 11 added up to over $38 billion.[48]

Not directly involved in these legal actions, Epstein is somewhat peeved at being forgotten by the movement that was launched off the back of his 1985 book *Takings*.

I am aware that what I have said has been very influential in the NAFTA debate and that, strangely enough, much of what I say seems to have more resonance in the international context than it did in the domestic context. Nobody from any of those [business] organizations even thought to ask me to give an opinion, let alone hire me as a consultant. I think they should have asked me.[49]

Going global

At the same time as the Takings Project could claim a success with NAFTA's Chapter 11, it also suffered a major defeat when developing countries gutted the TRIMS during the Uruguay Round.

Still determined to create a strong legal regime to protect foreign investment, in June 1995 the OECD started work on a Multilateral Agreement on Investment (MAI). This treaty notionally only applied to OECD countries, but as its members controlled around 90 per cent of foreign investment, it had every chance of becoming a de facto international agreement.

Businesses liked the idea that such a treaty would remain in the safe hands of the OECD. Stephen Canner, spokesperson for the US Council for International Business, explained why. 'OECD member countries were keenly aware of the successful efforts by LDCs [less developed countries] to water down the TRIMS negotiations and it did not want to ignite a "race to the bottom["].'[50]

A drafting committee of government trade and investment negotiators, assisted by experts from the International Chamber of Commerce and Industry Advisory Committee to the OECD, started work in September 1995. Treating the negotiations as a technical exercise, the OECD did not bother making any announcements about the MAI, keeping the public in the dark. Even more disturbing, ministers who had been charged with overseeing the process seemed to be unaware of the radical nature of the MAI.

This changed in March 1997 when Tony Clarke from the Polaris Institute obtained a leaked draft of the MAI. Accusing the OECD and the business sector of engineering 'a silent coup',[51] Clarke posted the document on the internet,[52] triggering protests around the world. This campaign spread quickly, helped along by the internet, which was used to recruit and mobilise activists. The resultant movement, which built up momentum quickly, exploited already widespread anti-globalisation sentiments that, up until the MAI, had lacked a cause it could latch onto.

Like NAFTA's Chapter 11, the draft MAI provided strong protections for investors against regulatory takings, leading Lori Wallach, director of the Public Citizen's *Global Trade Watch*, to describe the agreement as 'NAFTA on steroids'.[53]

Then next two years witnessed anti-MAI protests in the US, Canada,

Australia and several European countries. In the face of this concerted campaign, in early December 1998, the OECD abandoned its MAI. The ease with which politicians walked away from the MAI suggest that, like NAFTA's Chapter 11, they were not fully aware what negotiators were agreeing to on their behalf. And when they took the trouble to enquire, they were unwilling to publicly defend the principle of regulatory takings.

The failure of TRIMs and MAI, however, did not spell the end of the Global Fifth Amendment. Instead, new bilateral investment treaties (BITs) saw it spread around the world. Negotiated behind closed doors, BITs seldom attracted attention, and therefore avoided controversy, even though they contained many of the features of NAFTA's Chapter 11 and the MAI. This small-target strategy, while hardly elegant, nevertheless allowed the Global Fifth Amendment to flourish, and by December 2014 there were 2,816 BITs, signed or pending.[54]

Developing countries are invariably at a disadvantage when they negotiate BITs with industrial countries. Negotiating with the US, for example, 'is not a discussion between sovereign equals', explains José Alvarez, an international law professor from the New York University School of Law. 'It is more like an intensive training seminar conducted by the United States, on U.S. terms, on what it would take to comply with the U.S. draft.'[55] European countries are no better. For example, before a developing country receives development aid from Germany, it must first sign a BIT.

The result is the proliferation of unequal agreements, leaving governments in developing countries in a poor position to meet the needs of their populations, as Oxfam explained:

> [T]he current international investment regime can do a lot of harm to the public welfare because it hampers the ability of governments to act in response to broader concerns of human development or environmental sustainability. The investment arbitration system takes some important public policy decisions out of the hands of domestic courts and institutions, which in the case of developing countries leads to a further weakening of democratic institutions.[56]

Like NAFTA, it was only when policies and legislation of developed countries were challenged that the wisdom of BITs was questioned. For example, in 2011 tobacco giant Philip Morris sued Australia over their anti-smoking laws using its bilateral trade agreement with Hong Kong.[57] In 2012, Swedish energy multinational Vattenfall sued the German government, seeking €3.7 billion for lost profits from its nuclear power plants, which would be forced to close following the government's decision to phase-out nuclear energy.[58] And in 2013, Lone Pine Resources Inc. launched a $250 million claim against the Quebec government when it imposed a moratorium on hydraulic fracturing (fracking), which led to revocation of the company's gas exploration permits.[59]

Corporate sovereignty

International investment agreements represent a major advance in the application of the rule of law by including direct sanctions for regulatory takings. For the first time, transnational corporations have legal standing to sue governments, putting them on an equal footing with sovereign states. Should a government be found guilty of regulatory takings, it is placed in the invidious position of either repealing its laws or compensating corporations for injuries to their business. According to Wenhua Shan, Yangtze River Chair Professor of International Economic Law at Xi'an Jiaotong University, 'under BITs and other investment instruments, it is not too much of an exaggeration to say that they [corporations] enjoy certain elements of "sovereignty"'.[60]

Gus van Harten, law professor at York University, sees the emergence of corporate sovereignty as a victory for neoliberalism, as 'it imposes exceptionally powerful legal and economic constraints on governments and, by extension, on democratic choice, in order to protect from regulation the assets of multinational firms'.[61] David Schneiderman, a professor of law and political science at the University of Toronto, also sees a threat to democracy from new transnational legal rules and institutions that impose 'constitution-like limits on the exercise of local political authority far into the future'.[62] Unsurprisingly, neoliberals have become strong defenders of regulatory takings, such as Sir Ferdinand Mount, a stalwart of the Thatcher government. He argued that by constitutionally entrenching free markets, 'the less they are subjected to the day-to-day barter of the political process, [and] the better their chances of being put into practice'.[63]

The problem with this argument is that, unlike constitutions, which usually require overwhelming approval from a universal plebiscite, economic treaties lack legitimacy because they are negotiated in secret and in places far removed from public scrutiny, and, on occasions, are not even fully understood by the politicians signing them into law.

Despite these concerns, neoliberal constitutionalism is well on its way to constraining governments from interfering with the Hayekian 'spontaneous order', built on the neoliberal sacred trinity of preservation of property rights, free trade and deregulation of capital movements.

Notes

1. J.S. Frey, 'Introducing Richard Epstein', *The Law School Magazine* (2009). Retrieved from: http://blogs.law.nyu.edu/magazine/2009/profile-richard-epstein/ (accessed 26 March 2015).
2. J.S. Frey, 'Introducing Richard Epstein'.
3. R.A. Epstein, 'The Accidental Libertarian', in *I Choose Liberty*, compiled by Walter Block (Auburn, AL: Mises Institute, 2010), pp. 106–16, quote on p. 108.
4. R.A. Epstein, 'The Accidental Libertarian', pp. 107–16.
5. R.A. Epstein, 'The Accidental Libertarian', p. 107.
6. R.A. Epstein, 'The Reflections and Responses of a Legal Contrarian', *Tulsa Law Review*, 44 (2008–9), 647–75, quote on p. 649.
7. J.S. Frey, 'Introducing Richard Epstein'.
8. R.A. Epstein, *Takings: Private Property and the Power of Eminent Domain* (Cambridge MA: Harvard University Press, 1985)
9. R.A. Epstein, *Takings*, p. 95.
10. R.A. Epstein, *Takings*, p. 109.
11. J.W. Ely, 'Impact of Richard A. Epstein', *William & Mary Bill of Rights Journal*, 15:2 (2006), 421–8, quote on p. 426.
12. R.A. Epstein, *Takings*, p. x.
13. Richard Epstein quoted in William Greider, 'The Right and US Trade Law: Invalidating the 20th Century', *The Nation* (15 October 2001). Retrieved from: www.thenation.com/article/right-and-us-trade-law-invalidating-20th-century (accessed 26 March 2015).
14. R.A. Epstein, 'Takings', in *The New Palgrave Dictionary of Economics and the Law*, ed. P. Newman, Vol. 3 (New York: Stockton Press, 1998), p. 561.
15. R.A. Epstein, *Takings*, p. 281.
16. Reviews quoted by Eric R. Claeys in 'Takings: An Appreciative Retrospective', *William & Mary Bill of Rights Journal*, 15:2 (2006), 439–56.
17. T.C. Grey, 'The Malthusian Constitution', *University of Miami Law Review*, 41 (1986), 21–48, quote on p. 23.
18. M.G. Kelman, 'Taking *Takings* Seriously: An Essay for Centrists', *California Law Review*, 74 (1986), 1829–63, quote on p. 1829.
19. R.C. Ellickson, 'Federalism and Kelo: A Question for Richard Epstein', *Tulsa Law Review*, 44 (2008–9), 751–63, quote on p. 752.
20. C. Rosett, 'The Year's Best Books', *Wall Street Journal* (24 December 1985), p. 7.
21. P. Gottfried, 'Takings: Private Property and the Power of Eminent Domain', *National Review*, 23 (May 1986), 40–2, quote on p. 40.
22. D.T. Kendall and C.P. Lord, 'The Takings Project: A Critical Analysis and Assessment of the Progress So Far', *Boston College Affairs Environmental Affairs Law Review*, 25 (Spring 1998), 509–87.
23. D.T. Kendall and C.P. Lord, 'The Takings Project', 539.

24   C. Fried, *Order and Law: Arguing the Reagan Revolution. A Firsthand Account* (New York: Simon & Schuster, 1991), p. 183.
25   T. Castleton, 'Claims Court Crusader: Chief Judge Puts Property Rights Up Front', *Legal Times* (17 August 1992), p. 1.
26   Executive Order No. 12,630, 3 C.F.R. section 554 (1988), reprinted in 5 U.S.C. section 601 app. at 319–21 (18 March 1989).
27   Office of Management and Budget Circular No. A–11 (revised July 1994).
28   Private Property Protection Act of 1995, H.R. 925, 104th Congress, § 2.
29   R.A. Epstein, 'Taking Stock of Takings: An Author's Retrospective', *William & Mary Bill of Rights Journal*, 15:20 (2006), 407–20, quote on p. 412.
30   V. Been and J.C. Beauvais, 'The Global Fifth Amendment: NAFTA's Investment Protections and the Misguided Quest for an International 'Regulatory Takings' Doctrine', New York University Centre for Law and Business, Working Paper CLB-02-06, 2009.
31   North American Free Trade Agreement, Article 1110.
32   Technically, this mechanism first appears in Argentina-US BIT signed in 1991, but it only became effective in July 1998. NAFTA, however, was the first multilateral free trade agreement with this type of dispute settlement mechanism involving three states with major national economies.
33   Edwin Williamson quoted in William Greider, 'The Right and US Trade Law'.
34   MMT is the popular name for methylcyclopentadienyl manganese tricarbonyl.
35   Christine Stewart quoted by Shawn McCarthy in 'Failed Ban Becomes Selling Point for MMT', *The Globe and Mail* (21 July 1998), p. A3.
36   P.J. Landrigan, 'MMT, Déjà Vu and National Security', *American Journal of Industrial Medicine*, 39:4 (2001), 434–5.
37   J.M. Davis, 'Methylcyclopentadienyl Manganese-Tricarbonyl: Health Risk Uncertainties and Research Directions', *Environmental Health Perspectives*, 106, Supplement 1 (February 1998), 191.
38   J.E. Stiglitz, 'Multinational Corporations: Balancing Rights and Responsibilities', *Proceedings of the Annual Meeting – American Society of International Law*, Vol. 101 (2007), 3–60.
39   A. Liptak, 'Nafta Tribunals Stir U.S. Worries', *New York Times* (18 April 2004), p. A1.
40   Dan Price quoted in William Greider, 'The Right and US Trade Law'.
41   D.R. Haigh, 'Chapter 11 – Private Party vs. Governments, Investor-State Dispute Settlement: Frankenstein or Safety Valve?', *Canada-United States Law Journal*, 26 (2000), 115–34, quote on p. 125.
42   D.M. Price, 'Chapter 11 – Private Party vs. Government, Investor-State Dispute Settlement: Frankenstein or Safety Valve?', *Canada–United States Law Journal*, 26 (2000), 107–14, quote on p. 112.
43   D.M. Price, 'Discussion Following the Remarks of Mr. Price and Mr. Haigh', *Canada–United States Law Journal*, 26 (2000), 135–40.
44   Lydia Lazar quoted by William Greider in 'Sovereign Corporations', *The Nation* (30 April 2001).

45 Anon., 'NAFTA's Investor-Protection Clause Faces Test', *San Diego Union-Tribune* (13 July 1997), I–1.
46 Daniel Seligman quoted by Dennis Pfaff, in 'Trade Winds', *California Lawyer* (September 2000), p. 25.
47 R.A. Epstein, *Takings*, p. 281.
48 'Table of Foreign Investor-State Cases and Claims under NAFTA and other U.S. "Trade" Deals' (Washington, DC: Public Citizen, November 2014).
49 Richard Epstein quoted by William Greider in 'The Right and US Trade Law'.
50 S.J. Canner, 'Multilateral Agreement on Investment', *Cornell International Law Journal*, 31 (1998), 657–81, quote on p. 666.
51 A. Clarke, *Silent Coup: Confronting the Big Business Takeover of Canada* (Ottawa and Toronto: James Lorimer & Company, 1997).
52 Clarke posted the document on an international email distribution list called *Le Forum International sur la Globalisation*.
53 Testimony given by Lori Wallach, Director, Public Citizen's Global Trade Watch before the House Committee on International Relations Subcommittee of International Economic Policy and Trade on 5 March 1998.
54 International Investment Agreements Navigator, UNCTAD database. Retrieved from: http://investmentpolicyhub.unctad.org/IIA (accessed 22 December 2014).
55 J.E. Alvarez 'The Development and Expansion of Bilateral Investment Treaties: Remarks', *Proceedings of the Annual Meeting – American Society of International Law Annual*, 86 (1992), 532–57, quote on p. 553.
56 J. Perez, M. Gistelinck and D. Karbala, *Sleeping Lions: International Investment Treaties, State-Investor Disputes and Access to Food, Land and Water* (Oxford, UK: Oxfam International, 2011), p. 31.
57 T. Voon, and A. Mitchell, 'Face Off: Assessing WTO Challenges to Australia's Scheme for Plain Tobacco Packaging', *Public Law Review*, 22 (2011), 218–36.
58 *Vattenfall AB and Others v Federal Republic of Germany*, Notice of Arbitration, ICSID Case No. ARB/12/12 (31 May 2013).
59 Lone Pine Resources Inc. v Government of Canada, Notice of Arbitration, UNCITRAL (6 September 2013).
60 W. Shan, 'From North-South Divide to Private-Public Debate: Revival of the Calvo Doctrine and the Changing Landscape in International Investment Law', *Northwester Journal International Law & Business*, 27 (2006–7), 631–64, quote on p. 664.
61 G. Van Harten, 'Five Justifications for Investment Treaties: A Critical Discussion, *Trade Law and Development*, 2:1 (2010), 19–58, quote on p. 24.
62 D. Schneiderman, 'Transnational Legality and the Immobilization of Local Agency', *Annual Reviews of Law and Social Science*, 2 (2006), 387–408, quote on pp. 387–8.
63 F. Mount, *British Constitution Now* (London: Heinemann, 1992), p. 242.

Part III

The human face of globalisation

On a sunny Thursday afternoon in the summer of 1999, José Bové arrived in the French village of Millau atop his blue Ford tractor, puffing on his favourite pipe and wearing a straw hat. Accompanying him were about 300 friends and supporters from the village and surrounding countryside, intent on protesting against globalisation.

'The objective was to have a non-violent but symbolically forceful action, in broad daylight and with the largest participation possible', explained Bové.[1] His strategy was to carefully dismantle a partially completed McDonald's fast-food outlet, so it could be re-assembled at a later date, to avoid accusations of wanton destruction of property. To show their peaceful intent, Bové even gave notice to the local gendarme, who sent ten officers to keep watch and take photos.

Everyone was in a festive mood, and over the next few hours they dismantled the building, removing doors, roofing and electrical plates. They then loaded the parts onto trucks. Some kids then hopped on top and banged sticks on the sides as the procession made its way through the streets of Millau. Their destination was the regional prefecture, where they deposited the materials of their afternoon's travails. Afterwards, many found refuge in a local cafe, where they enjoyed a glass or two of white wine from the nearby vineyards of Languedoc.

The injustice that drove Bové and his compadres was a recent decision of the World Trade Organization to support the US, which had argued that Europe's ban on hormone-injected meat was illegal under free trade rules. With the blessing of the WTO, the US was authorised to impose retaliatory tariffs. To inflict maximum political pain, the Americans levied 100 per cent tariffs on Roquefort cheese, foie gras and Dijon mustard. If the US chose to attack iconic food items of France, then Bové decided he would target the iconic cuisine of America: McDonald's hamburgers and the incongruously named French fries.

Soon after, Bové and ten other activists were charged with causing criminal damage. On the day of his trial, Bové arrived on an oxcart holding aloft a large wheel of cheese from his own farm, and shouted to the crowd, 'We shall overcome – save our Roquefort and down with junk food!'[2] Later, as he emerged from the courthouse, he raised his handcuffed hands to the cheers of

45,000 supporters. This moment was captured by the international media, and as this image was circulated around the world, it transformed Bové into a folk hero and the most recognisable face of the counter-globalisation movement.

It did not take long before the media referred to Bové as a modern Astérix,[3] drawing parallels with the much-loved cartoon character who led the ancient Gauls against the overwhelming might of the Roman imperium. There is even a slight physical resemblance: Bové is a short man with a long drooping moustache and receding sandy hair.

Bové's protest against globalisation, however, was not the first. Since the 1980s, other discontents have taken to the streets. Often, their anger was narrowly focused on transnational corporations, which were perceived as the embodiment of everything wrong with the global order.

Enjoying international celebrity, in November 1999 Bové flew into Seattle to protest the Third Ministerial meeting of the WTO. Showing characteristic flair for self-promotion, Bové smuggled 500 kilos of Roquefort into the US, handing out samples of the cheese to members of the media and whomever he met on the streets.

Bové, like most of the other demonstrators, hoped for a peaceful protest, but that was not to be. At what has become known as the 'Battle of Seattle', windows at Starbucks and McDonalds were smashed, Niketown was looted and elegant shops downtown trashed. In response, the mayor unleashed the National Guard onto the protesters, using armoured vehicles, with black-clad riot police riding shot gun on the sides. What followed were pitched battles, with police dispersing protesters with tear gas, pepper spray, stun grenades and rubber bullets.

The Battle of Seattle was just one of many demonstrations that occurred around the same time. Targets included the joint meetings of the IMF and the World Bank in Washington (April 2000) and Prague (September 2000), the World Economic Forum in Melbourne (September 2000) and Davos (January 2003), the Quebec Summit on the Free Trade Agreement of the Americas (April 2001), the European Union gatherings in Gothenburg (June 2001) and Barcelona (March 2002), and the G-8 summit in Genoa (July 2001). By selecting these events, protesters were making a clear statement that they were unhappy with the existing global institutional architecture and its rules.

There was no single position that the protesters shared, but contrary to popular belief, few totally rejected globalisation. Instead, most wanted radical reform. Under the slogan, 'Another world is possible',[4] the *alter-mondialisation* (alternative globalisation) movement took aim at transnational corporations, which had profited at the expense of environmental and labour standards; inequitable trade rules that disadvantaged developing countries; and an economic system that widened the gap between the rich and poor. For Bové, globalisation needed to be placed under democratic control to produce an 'economy in the service of men, and not men in the service of the economy'.[5]

Members of the political elite started to take notice when they realised that these demonstrations were attracting public support. One 1999 French poll showed that 45 per cent of respondents supported Bové's views on globalisation, with just 4 per cent hostile.[6] A Sofres poll, commissioned by *Le Monde* two years later, asked 'Who benefits most from globalisation?,' to which 55 per cent said 'transnational corporations', 47 per cent said 'financial markets' and 7 per cent said 'consumers'.[7]

On the other side of the Atlantic, many ordinary Americans surprisingly supported the Seattle protest despite the violence, with a 1999 Harris Poll finding 52 per cent sympathetic to the protesters and the same percentage agreed that businesses held too much power and influence. Surprisingly, 22 per cent said that they viewed globalisation less favourably as a result of the demonstrations.[8] Unable to ignore this shift in public opinion, politicians responded.

In France, the left called for 'mondialisation maîtrisée' (managed globalisation), while the right favoured 'mondialisation humaine' (globalisation with a human face).[9] One of the most unexpected converts was President Jacques Chirac, who had introduced neoliberal reforms into France during the late 1990s. After protesters attacked the G-8 meeting in Genoa, which he had just attended, Chirac acknowledged that the popular opposition was being fed by 'the uncertainties created by the development of globalization and the ability of States to control, humanize it'.[10] In an effort to come up with practical alternatives to neoliberal globalisation, in October 2001, the prime minister of Belgium, Guy Verhofstadt, convened a special conference that explored how 'ethical globalization' might be promoted.[11]

In the US, Sandy Berge, national security advisor in the Clinton Administration, remarked that it was necessary to 'shape globalization so that it spurs growth and lifts the poor as well as the rich, improves the dignity of labor and strengthens the protection of the environment'.[12] James Wolfensohn, president of the World Bank, added that globalisation needed to be reformed so that it 'offset its less positive aspects for those adversely affected' and 'promotes social equity and works for the poor'.[13]

The momentum for civilising globalisation waned after 9/11, as politicians and the public became preoccupied with questions on how globalisation was sustaining terrorism. How did the free flow of capital and complex bank transactions allow terrorist networks to access laundered money? How were immigrants from Islamic countries being radicalised and recruited by fundamentalists?

How could shipments of atomic, biological and chemical weapons be spotted in a world in which sea transport was poorly monitored and customs were overwhelmed by the volume of goods passing through ports? How could security agencies detect terrorist plots before that were carried out?

While the preoccupation with terrorism raised the public's anxiety about globalisation, it also presented solutions. After 9/11 there was increased international cooperation, with no-fly lists, new anti-laundering protocols and renewed efforts to detect and intercept shipments of illegal armaments.

Rather than directly leading to protests against globalisation, the anxieties raised by terrorism have been sublimated into Islamophobia and anti-immigrant campaigns on the right, and fears of the growth of the security state on the left.

The tide of opinion changed again in 2008, when the global economy nearly collapsed, causing a new crisis of confidence in globalisation.

As a new wave of protests broke out – the most prominent being the Occupy movement – politicians once again turned their attention to the problems of economic globalisation. For example, on the eve of the G-20 summit, held in London in April 2009, British Prime Minister Gordon Brown stated, 'Instead of a globalization that threatens to become values-free and rules-free, we need a world of shared global rules founded on shared global values'.[14] Robert Zoellick, World Bank president, suggested that 'the goal must be to build a more inclusive and sustainable globalization'.[15] India's prime minister, Dr Manmohan Singh, observed that the benefits of globalisation were not equitably distributed: 'Ensuring inclusive growth within nations, and inclusive globalization across nations, is a central challenge that faces us.'[16]

The movement to civilise globalisation represents a separate, but complementary approach to the liberal and neoliberal global orders. It has relied mainly on norms – standards of expected behaviour – to discipline transnational corporations and promote more ethical behaviour. A number of programmes launched since the Second World War have endeavoured to harness international cooperation to address non-economic issues like protection of human rights, labour conditions and the environment, and the improvement of human health. Only during the late 1990s did the idea that globalisation needed to be civilised take root as a conscious strategy.

Notes

1. J. Bové and F. Dufour, *The World Is Not for Sale: Farmers Against Junk Food* (London: Verso, 2001), p. 5.
2. W. Northcutt, 'José Bové vs. McDonald's: The Making of a National Hero in the

French Anti-Globalization Movement', *Proceedings of the Western Society for French History*, 31 (2003), 326–45, quote on p. 331.
3   Anon., 'Jose Bove: A Latter-Day Astérix Taking on New Global Empire', *Agence France–Presse* (28 June 2000).
4   The unofficial home of the *alter-mondialistes* movement is the World Social Forum, which adopted this slogan.
5   José Bové is quoted by Vicki Birchfield in 'José Bové and the Globalisation Countermovement in France and Beyond', *Review of International Studies*, 31:3 (2005), 581–98, quote on p. 592.
6   P. Gordon and S. Meinier, *The French Challenge: Adapting to Globalization* (Washington, DC: Brookings Institution Press, 2001), p. 143.
7   Anon., 'Une menace ou une chance?', *Le Monde* (19 July 2001), p. 3.
8   Anon., 'Business Week/Harris Poll: A Survey of Discontent', *Business Week Online* (27 December 1999).
9   N. Jabko and S. Menuier, 'Global Clevages? How Globalization and Europeanization Redefine Domestic Politics in Europe', paper delivered at the Biennial Conference of the European Union Studies Association on 27–29 March 2003.
10 Press briefing given by M. Jacques Chirac, President of the Republic, in Genoa on 20 July 2001 at the meeting of the G-8.
11 G. Verhofstadt, 'Towards Ethical Globalization', *OECD Observer*, No. 231/232 (May 2002).
12 S.R. Berger, 'American Leadership in the 21st Century', remarks at the National Press Club, delivered in Washington, DC on 6 January 2000.
13 Remarks made by James Wolfensohn at the Tenth Ministerial Meeting of UNCTAD in Bangkok on 16 February 2000.
14 G.G. Brown, *The Change We Choose: Speeches 2007–2009* (Edinburgh: Mainstream Publisher). Speech delivered to the St Paul's Institute in London on 31 March 2009.
15 R.B. Zoellick, 'A New Kind of Globalization', *Newsweek* (31 December 2008), p. 8.
16 M. Singh, Statement by Prime Minister of India at the General Debate of the 63rd UN General Assembly, delivered in New York on 27 September 2008.

11

When the saints come marching in

EVER ONWARD – EVER ONWARD!
That's the spirit that has brought us fame!
We're big, but bigger we will be
We can't fail for all can see
That to serve humanity has been our aim! (IBM corporate song, 1935)

Stand on your feet, black boy

Certain that God was at his side, in 1977 Reverend Leon Sullivan launched a crusade to end apartheid in South Africa. He applied economic pressure on the regime by convincing a large number of firms to first eliminate racial inequality in their workplaces and then challenge apartheid directly. Central to his crusade was a voluntary code of conduct, which has since evolved into a model followed by transnational corporations. Under the rubric of 'corporate social responsibility' (CSR), this new body of ethical norms has become a prominent feature on the global business landscape, used to soften the sharper edges of globalisation.

Sullivan's later preoccupation with helping his black brethren in South Africa can be traced to his own upbringing, during which he saw how racism could erode the souls of its victims, and how it could be defied and overcome.

Leon Sullivan was born on 16 October 1922, in Charleston, West Virginia, in the heart of Dixie. His parents, Charles and Helen Sullivan, were divorced when he was just three, after which he was raised by his adored grandmother, whom he called 'Mama'. She worked as a domestic maid and also took in others' washings to make ends meet. A devout Christian, Mama taught him that 'nothing is impossible if you believe in your mind and heart it can be done', he recalled.[1]

Leon and Mama lived in a clapboard house with no plumbing, fronting a dirt alley. Desperately poor, he recounted: 'We had no welfare so everybody sort of looked out for each other.'[2] Central to the sense of community was religion, and on warm Sunday evenings, women would sit on their porches singing hymns and spirituals, which made Leon feel that God was always by his side.

An event that made a deep impression on Leon occurred when he was just eight. It was a warm day and so the young boy sauntered into a drugstore on Capitol Street and, sitting down, put a dime on the counter, saying, 'I wanna Coke.' The proprietor yelled, 'Stand on your feet, black boy! You can't sit down here!' This experience stayed with him, and shaped his character and career. 'That was my first real confrontation with bigotry, prejudice and discrimination', he bristled. '[A]t that moment, as I stood there, glaring back at the big man's burning eyes, I decided that I would stand on my feet against this kind of thing as long as I lived.'[3]

And so he did. Over the next few years, the young boy defied the unwritten rule of West Virginia that segregated whites from blacks by entering restaurants, movie houses and other whites-only establishments to demand service. Often he did not have a penny to his name, but that hardly mattered as he expected to be thrown out, and he was almost never disappointed.

On one occasion, inspired by what he had just learned in Civics class, Leon decided to try a new tactic. At a greasy spoon on Quarrier Street, he sat down at the counter to place his order. When the white owner, predictably, insisted he leave, Leon stood his ground. At age twelve, he was already six feet tall; needless to say, everyone noticed. In a loud voice, the young boy then recited the preamble to the United States Constitution, word perfect. After he had finished, to his surprise, everyone stood up and applauded. One man then came over to shake Leon's hand and, sitting the boy down at the counter, told him, 'Anybody who can recite that stuff doesn't have to pay.'[4] Leon was rewarded with a serving of West Virginia donuts, the specialty of the house, washed down with a coke.

Leon also faced institutional discrimination. In high school, he entered the Boys State programme that honoured civic leadership. The competition was divided into white and black categories. The white boy who won became a page in the Capital building and got to meet the mayor, so that he might aspire to that position one day. Sullivan, who won the prize for blacks, was rewarded with a job cleaning the sewers of Charleston and got to meet the black labourers, who never aspired to hold a job any better than the one they had. 'I was only 16 but it was a burning memory', he recalled.[5]

At the all-black West Virginia State College, Leon met Moses Newsome, a pastor at the First Baptist Church of Charleston, who encouraged the young man to seek a career in the church. Leon quickly proved he was a natural. Blessed with a sonorous baritone voice and confidence that belied his tender years, he soon found himself preaching at two churches on alternate Sundays: one in the foothills of the Appalachians and the other in a coal mining town. One paid him in fuel, eggs, occasional suppers with parishioners and some loose change, while the other paid him twelve dollars a fortnight, which helped Leon cover his tuition fees.

Although he was destined to become a pastor, it was his Mama who profoundly influenced the direction of his vocation. While in his sophomore year, he was urgently called home. His grandmother was suffering from tuberculosis, also known as the 'child of poverty'. By the faint light of the oil lamp, Leon kept vigil by her bed, with the smell of death in the air. 'Leonie, help your people', she rasped with her remaining strength. 'And don't let this kind of thing happen to anybody else.'[6] Taking her last words to heart, Sullivan built his ministry around applying Christianity to the pressing social problems of the day. 'I felt that God didn't just want people to have milk and honey in heaven, he wanted them to have some ham and eggs on earth', he explained.[7]

In 1943, Leon Sullivan moved to Harlem, where he enrolled in New York's Union Theological Seminary. He also became assistant minister at the Abyssinian Baptist Church, and then pastor at the small Fandell Presbyterian Church. While in New York, he rubbed shoulders with giants of the civil rights movement: A. Philip Randolph, Adam Clayton Powell Jr. and Martin Luther King Jr.. Identifying with their struggle, Sullivan resolved to use his ministry to fight segregation, racism and other obstacles that stopped African-Americans from getting ahead.

Armed with that conviction, in 1950, Sullivan moved to Philadelphia, and took up the position of pastor of the historic Zion Baptist Church. What he discovered shocked him. 'Wherever my eyes fell, I saw little black boys and girls ... trying to find childish joy and fun in the midst of dirt, roaches and garbage', he said.[8] Sullivan channelled his rage into what would become his life's work: creating economic opportunities that would lead his community out of poverty.

Looking where to begin, Sullivan noticed that most white business owners refused to give African-Americans good jobs. Determined to confront such racism, in early 1958, Sullivan brought together 400 local pastors to support his campaign of 'selective patronage'. Employing the slogan 'Don't buy where you don't work', their first target was Tastykake cupcakes. After three months of lost sales over the summer high-season, it surrendered, as did other companies that depended on black customers. Over the next four years, Sullivan was able to convince Coca-Cola, Esso and Sun Oil, among others, to employ more African-Americans.

Although an outstanding success, it created a new problem. Most African-Americans lacked the skills to take up the new jobs on offer. To address this shortcoming, in January 1964, Sullivan founded the first of what would become a worldwide network of Opportunities Industrialization Centers.[9] Launched in an abandoned jailhouse in a North Philadelphia ghetto, it provided training for those who lacked the necessary work skills.

In the years that followed, this and other campaigns that Sullivan launched were aimed at economic empowerment of minority groups, an area that he carved out for himself among his generation of civil rights leaders. For Sullivan, capitalism needed to be harnessed to lead the black community out of poverty.

Sullivan's support of the private sector made him an attractive candidate in the eyes of General Motors (GM), when it was looking to appoint an African-American to its board. Sullivan gladly accepted the position in early 1971, but GM's choice surprised those that knew him, including his long-time friend, writer and satirist Dick Gregory: 'Jesus Christ! How did they make that mistake! Of all the Negroes they could get, why him? They don't know what they're in for.'[10] President Lyndon Johnson, who had worked with Sullivan on the War on Poverty in the 1960s, gave out a whoop of delight when he heard the news, and immediately put through a call to Sullivan, telling him, 'Now what's good for General Motors really is good for America.'[11]

Challenging apartheid

At GM, Sullivan found a new cause to pursue. The company was a major employer of blacks in South Africa, and like all other businesses in South Africa, its factories were segregated. This was just one of the ugly features of apartheid, which embedded racism in the laws of the land. This system was much crueller than anything Sullivan had seen growing up with Jim Crow laws, and so he decided 'that working to end apartheid was God's plan for my life'.[12]

His first opportunity came at GM's annual general meeting, held on 21 May 1971. Controversy broke out when Bishop John Hines, the head of the Episcopal Church, filed a shareholder resolution that called on the company to withdraw completely from South Africa. Unable to contain himself, Sullivan stood up to speak. 'American industry cannot morally continue to do business in a country that so blatantly and ruthlessly and clearly maintains such dehumanizing practices against such large numbers of its people', he thundered.[13] Unfortunately, his intervention had little effect, and stockholder activists could only marshal a shade over 1 per cent of the votes.

During the next four years, Sullivan kept at GM, but without any success, as GM was never going to divest its holdings in South Africa. Sensing this, he revised his strategy during the summer of 1975, after customs officials in Johannesburg humiliated him on his way out of the country. The incident that triggered his detention was a meeting he had just held with union, civic and business leaders. There, he met Adam Klein from the National Union of Clothing Workers, who told Sullivan that divestment 'would not have 100% success and is therefore a meaningless gesture'. Instead, he urged Sullivan to launch a campaign to compel US companies to eliminate discrimination in the workplace. After this meeting, a security officer pulled Sullivan aside and, in an interview room, ordered him to disrobe down to his underwear. They were looking for his notes of his meetings with South African activists, which they had hoped would include names. 'I was standing there, stripped, and I thought to myself, when I leave I will do what I have to do.'[14]

On his return, Sullivan jotted down: 'Principles of Equal Rights for United States Firms in the Republic of South Africa', a draft of a code of conduct that he hoped companies would adopt. The code urged US subsidiaries to desegregate their South African workplaces, improve conditions for their black employees, and train, then promote them into well-paid jobs that had been traditionally reserved for whites. Less radical than divestment Sullivan anticipated that his code would be more palatable to businesses, yet still achieve the objectives of the anti-apartheid movement.

He first approached GM, threatening to resign if they did not subscribe to his principles. That threat was met with consternation, as GM knew that it would be a PR disaster if its only black director quit over the company's racist operations in South Africa. On the other hand, they were pleased that Sullivan was no longer insisting on divestment. The proposition that they sell up their highly profitable operations, probably at fire sale prices, was not on the cards. And so, on 9 July 1975 the board adopted a code, though not the exact one drafted by Sullivan. GM insisted he drop a requirement that the company recognise black unions and another that called on firms to publicly voice their opposition to apartheid

Buoyed by this success, Sullivan then approached other US companies, which were no more comfortable with the code than GM, but accepted it nonetheless, out of the belief that by signing his code they could alleviate pressure from activists to divest. Like GM, they would only sign a watered-down version of Sullivan's code.

Reasoning that this was the best deal he was going to get, Sullivan reluctantly accepted the changes, but having lost this skirmish he had a plan that would eventually give him what he wanted.

> I designed the Principles in a way that I could modify them. I called it 'amplification' and I amplified them step-by-step every six months. The executives of the companies did not like it because they said I kept raising the bar, changing the goal-posts. They said they didn't have the authority to do that. I said, it says here in the Principles, I am the authority with the help of God, and who could oppose it![15]

On 1 March 1977, twelve companies signed the 'Principles of Equal Rights', which soon became known as the 'Sullivan Principles'. They included GM, Ford, 3M, IBM, Mobil and CitiBank, but many others refused, worried that the code would curtail their freedom to manage their businesses.

Behind the scenes, Sullivan had a stormy relationship with many of the signatories, who believed that all they had to do was remove the 'whites only' signs on bathrooms.[16] In truth, the very practices that the code aimed to end were what had attracted transnational corporations to invest in South Africa in the first place: low wages, a compliant workforce, outlawed black unions and strikers fearful that they could be jailed. For these reasons, companies were in no hurry to fully implement the Sullivan Principles.

Keen to stamp out tokenism, Sullivan pressed ahead with two amplifications, which he issued on 6 July 1978 and 1 May 1979. They introduced independent monitoring and public reporting in the hope of shaming companies that failed to live up to the letter of the code. He also wanted to include measureable targets to hold companies accountable, but dropped this condition after facing stiff resistance.

By 1983, 146 firms had signed up. Although progress was patchy, some companies pushed ahead by training and placing blacks in management positions, and raising the wages of black workers so they started to catch up with those of whites, although the gap remained large.

Even as the Sullivan Principles were making some headway in workplaces, the political situation in South Africa was deteriorating. During the early 1980s, students boycotted classes, protesters filled the streets of black townships and workers went on strike, while the police responded with violence and mass arrests.

These circumstances led Sullivan to harden his position, and on 7 May 1985 he gave the South African government an ultimatum: it had just two years to end statutory apartheid, release Nelson Mandela and afford black Africans full suffrage. Otherwise, he would call on companies, without exception, to disinvest and for foreign governments to impose a total trade embargo on South Africa.

Rather than improving, violence and repression escalated to the extent that, on 20 July 1985, President P.W. Botha declared a state of emergency in thirty-six magisterial districts to contain the violence. Botha further showed that he was not in any mood to compromise when, on 15 August, he announced to the Natal Provincial Congress of his National Party, 'I am not prepared to lead white South Africans and other minority groups on a road of abdication and suicide!'[17] This speech seemed to shut the door on meaningful reform.

When the deadline expired with his demands unmet, Sullivan abandoned his code and exhorted companies to divest.[18] Through his efforts, and those of other anti-apartheid leaders, a major exodus out of South Africa began on the part of foreign companies. Coca-Cola, GM and IBM were among the first. It would be heartening to think these firms were driven by ethical considerations. But the cost of staying in South Africa was becoming too high. First, as a result of Sullivan's lobbying, pension funds were punishing companies that refused to leave South Africa by selling up their shares. By the early 1990s, with the South African economy in dire straits and violence escalating, the decision to sell up was easy.

To everyone's surprise, the end came peacefully when Botha's successor, F.W. de Klerk, came to the conclusion that white minority rule was untenable. Facing the inevitable, on 11 February 1990, the government freed Nelson Mandela and entered into negotiations with black leaders on majority rule. Following elections in 1994, Mandela became president of a democratic and free South Africa on 8 May. Sullivan was invited to the inauguration, but decided to stay home and watch it on TV. 'I'll go over when everybody else is gone and after all the pictures have been taken', he said. 'It'll be more meaningful for me to go when I can do something to help.'[19]

When Sullivan did visit, it was to found branches of the Opportunities Industrialization Center in each of South Africa's nine provinces. 'Without education, economic apartheid will replace political apartheid', Sullivan warned.[20]

Looking back, it is difficult to say whether the Sullivan Principles accelerated or delayed the downfall of apartheid. On one hand, the Sullivan Principles did contribute to the endgame by shaking the South African government's confidence, once it saw that foreign companies were willing to challenge apartheid laws and eventually decamp, wrecking its economy. On the other hand, it may well have postponed disinvestment in the country, allowing companies to continue business as usual, making only cosmetic changes to their operations and allowing the apartheid regime to hang on.

Aspiring to sainthood

Sullivan's legacy, however, goes beyond his fight against apartheid, according to S. Prakash Sethi and Father Oliver Williams, business ethicists who had worked with Sullivan on his code.

> [T]he Sullivan Principles represented the crucial turning point in the then-ongoing debate about societal expectations for corporate conduct; the Sullivan Principles marked the beginning of a new era, one in which corporate social responsibility was no longer controversial, but an accepted norm. ... [I]t was no longer a question of

whether corporations, as important social institutions, should be responsible for the community's well-being or for negative externalities that corporations create as a consequence of their normal business operations. Instead, the locus of debate permanently shifted to how and what extent corporations should be held accountable for their societal impact of their business operations.[21]

The Sullivan Principles took CSR into the international domain and his strategy was adapted by a generation of newly formed international NGOs to expose and tackle corporate misbehaviour through deft manipulation of international media, in the hope of righting environmental and social wrongs. They had mixed successes, as the following three early campaigns demonstrate.

One of the first was launched by the Infant Formula Action Coalition, which organised a boycott of Nestlé products in July 1977, prompted by the publication of *The Baby Killer*.[22] Written by Mike Muller from the London-based NGO, War on Want, the pamphlet accused powdered milk companies, Nestlé in particular, of unethical marketing of formula milk into developing countries, leading to malnutrition and even death of babies. In May 1981, following discussions with the industry and NGOs, the World Health Organization (WHO) issued its *International Code of Marketing of Breast-milk Substitutes*. In this instance, the code targeted a whole industry sector rather than the activities of transnational corporations active in a particular country, as Sullivan had. Implementation, however, proved to be problematic. In 2004, a worldwide study was conducted to analyse compliance with the WHO code. Its report, *Breaking the Rules, Stretching the Rules*, detailed over 3,000 breaches of the code.[23]

Another early adopter of industry norms was the International Federation of Pharmaceutical Manufacturers Associations, which, in March 1981, produced its *Code of Pharmaceutical Marketing Practices*. This code served two purposes. It was used to counter criticism from Third World countries that drug companies engaged in unethical promotion of drugs. It was also used to forestall action by the WHO, which threatened to issue its own code, which in all likelihood would have been much tougher than the industry would have liked. Dr Wilbert Bannenberg, trustee of the Amsterdam-based Health Action International, attacked the industry's code for being far too weak. 'Just waiting for complaints to come in is not enough: there must be an active monitoring system and a way of enforcing respect for the code', he complained. 'National authorities in developing countries often don't have the facilities to do this.'[24]

One of the most ambitious CSR programmes in the world was launched following an explosion in Bhopal (India) at the Union Carbide plant in December 1984. With over 2,500 fatalities and many more injured, the industry (not just Union Carbide) faced high levels of distrust and hostility wherever they operated large hazardous chemical plants. To repair its reputation, the chemical industry launched Responsible Care® in January 1985. Unfortunately, this code has been shown to have feet of clay. In a survey of 2,735 US chemical plants, Shanti Gamper-Rabindran from the University of Pittsburgh and Stephen Finger from the University of South Carolina found no statistical reduction in pollution among those that followed the industry's code compared to those that did not.[25]

Other transnational corporations and industry sectors have followed a similar course, reasoning that they needed to control the agenda by issuing their own voluntary codes, rather than have one imposed on them. But implementing a CSR programme, in itself, does not demonstrate that former sinners have reformed their ways. Instead, as the above examples illustrate, we should take heed of George Orwell's warning: 'Saints should always be judged guilty until they are proved innocent.'[26]

Ex-World Bank chief economist, Joseph Stiglitz's criticism goes deeper. He argues that 'in a world of ruthless competition, incentives often work against even those with the best intentions'. Corporations have evolved to become extremely proficient profit-making organisations, and CSR diverts them from this core function. This does not stop companies adopting the aura of sainthood. '[E]ven the worst polluter and those with the worst labor record', Stiglitz suggested, cover their tracks by cynically hiring a public relations firm 'to laud their sense of corporate responsibility'.[27]

Not surprisingly, codes continue to proliferate as transnational corporations feel they have no choice, whether it is motivated by the need to repair a damaged brand, to fend off government regulation, to seek redemption for past sins or to help open up new markets. Whatever the trigger, all have been keen to make a virtue out of necessity.

It is not all bad news. There are also successes. But these are seldom, if ever, driven by altruism or a sincere desire to behave virtuously, but by basic business logic, as Aneel Karnani explained in the *Wall Street Journal*:

> Very simply, in cases where private profits and public interests are aligned, the idea of corporate social responsibility is irrelevant: Companies that simply do everything they can to boost profits will end up increasing social welfare. In circumstances in which profits and social welfare are in direct opposition, an appeal to corporate social responsibility will almost always be ineffective, because executives are unlikely to act voluntarily in the public interest and against shareholder interests.[28]

Indeed, a lucrative industry has been built up by management consultants advising corporations as to how they can best profit from their CSR programmes. Management guru and professor at Harvard Business School, Michael Porter, has been a leader in the field, having developed strategies that exploit CSR as 'a source of opportunity, innovation, and competitive advantage'.[29] In addition, the very halo that accompanies CSR can, in itself, be used as a marketing tool to raise goodwill, which in turn can be translated into extra sales.

Citizen Inc.

While the traditional core of CSR programmes is to 'do no harm', the Sullivan Principles presaged the next stage of CSR of 'doing good' by making the world a better place. For Leon Sullivan that meant that corporations should actively confront apartheid beyond the workplace. They were reluctant at first, limiting their activities to desegregating workplaces and promoting black employees into management. Their position changed after years of escalating pressure by Sullivan and US pension funds. On 2 June 1986, the American Chamber of Commerce in South Africa, with the support of such companies as IBM, Coca-Cola, CitiBank and Union Carbide, ran full-page newspaper advertisements in major South African newspapers calling for the freeing of political prisoners and the legalisation of outlawed organisations, concluding that apartheid is 'totally contrary to the idea of free enterprise'.[30]

By the 1990s, as companies engaged in campaigns to improve the communities around them, the term 'corporate citizenship' began to enter the conversation.[31] Sometimes, it was merely rebranding of narrow CSR programmes, but in other cases companies actually embraced Sullivan's paradigm that they had a moral obligation to do good by confronting injustice and improving the world around them.

The corporate citizenship movement received a fillip during the rise in protests against neoliberal policies associated with corporate-dominated globalisation around the turn of the century. With many CEOs shaken by the iconic Battle of Seattle, some businesspeople decided the best approach was to empathise with protesters. Shell's chairman, Sir Mark Moody-Stuart, for example, announced that 'we share the objective of the recent demonstrators in Seattle, Davos and Prague'. He did not, however, support their calls for deglobalisation. His alternative solution was to help the poor raise themselves up by participating in the global economy, and he believed that corporations had a moral obligation to help them.[32] For IBM president, Sam Palmisano, the future was grim if the inequities embedded in economic globalisation were not addressed. '[D]iscontent with globalization would only grow', he warned, which could see global markets stifled as governments introduce protectionist regulations. 'Worse, they might gravitate toward more extreme nationalism, xenophobia and anti-modernism.'³³ Corporations, Palmisano believed, have a major role to play.

> Government leaders will find in business willing partners to reform health care and education, secure the world's trade lanes, and electronic commerce, train and enable the displaced and dispossessed, grapple with environmental problems and infectious diseases, and tackle the myriad other challenges that globalization raises.³⁴

Like a number of leading global firms, IBM has an active portfolio of programmes that are designed to mitigate the dark side of globalisation. One such programme is 'Smarter Cities', in which IBM experts and technology are offered to improve the liveability of cities. Other corporate citizens have also taken up the challenge, and an increasing number of firms actively tackle problems such as illiteracy, poverty and other social ills. As William Clay Ford Jr. of the Ford Motor Company explained, 'I believe very strongly that corporations could be, and should be, a major force for resolving environmental and social concerns in the 21ˢᵗ century.'³⁵

Questions have been raised on the legitimacy of corporations addressing such problems, which are traditionally regarded as the preserve of governments. The *Financial Time*'s Martin Wolf argues that, 'If we want to pursue social goals the right way is openly, through the political process where the pros and cons can be argued out explicitly.'³⁶ Frederick Hayek also saw CSR as a serious risk. If corporations are allowed to support 'socially desirable purposes' they acquire 'arbitrary and politically dangerous powers ... [over] cultural, political, and moral issues'.³⁷

Comments from some on the left are equally hostile, with the NGO Corporate Watch arguing that CSR is often used to assert corporate domination over the economy, concluding that 'Regulation, including rules on: how corporations can be structured, as well as on the impacts they can have on the environment and society, and their dealings with their workforce and other stakeholders, is the only way that a democratic society can control what is acceptable and unacceptable in corporate behaviour.'³⁸

Kofi Annan, who was a great admirer of Leon Sullivan, saw no such problems expanding the corporate citizenship movement. Soon after becoming secretary general of the United Nations, Annan asked Leon Sullivan to draft a set of global principles, drawing universal obligations out of his earlier code. In November 1999, the Global Sullivan Principles were launched. They set out norms 'to support economic, social and political justice by companies where they do business', including respect for human rights and equal work opportunities for all peoples.³⁹ Such norms are important because 'Governments can't do it all',

Sullivan explained. 'Corporations must contribute to the culture of peace.'[40] This code was the start of a larger campaign by the United Nations to give globalisation a human face by infusing universal values through the private sector.

Notes

1 L.H. Sullivan, *Moving Mountains, The Principles and Purpose of Leon Sullivan* (Valley Forge: Judson Press, 1998), p. 6.
2 L.H. Sullivan, interview in Philadelphia, Marshall University (1996).
3 Quoted by Eric Augenbraun in '"Stand On Your Feet, Black Boy!": Leon Sullivan, Black Power, Job Training, and the War on Poverty', in *2009–2010 Penn Humanities Forum on Connections* (1 April 2010).
4 L.H. Sullivan, interview in Philadelphia, Marshall University (1996).
5 E. Holsendolph, 'A Profile of Leon Sullivan', *Black Enterprise* (May 1975), pp. 47–51, quote on p. 48.
6 L.H. Sullivan, *Build Brother Build* (Philadelphia: Macrae Smith, 1969), p. 43.
7 L.H. Sullivan, interview in Philadelphia, Marshall University (1996).
8 M. Sager, 'A Tribute to the Rev. Leon Sullivan 1922–2001', *Rolling Stone* (July 2001), pp. 87–98, quote on p. 88.
9 V.P. Franklin, 'Pan-African Connections, Transnational Education, Collective Cultural Capital, and Opportunities Industrialization Centers International', *Journal of African American History*, 96:1 (2011), 44–61.
10 Dick Gregory quoted by Mike Sanger in 'A Tribute to the Rev. Leon Sullivan 1922–2001', p. 95.
11 'The Black on GM's Board', *Time* magazine (6 September 1976), pp. 54–5.
12 L.H. Sullivan, *Moving Mountains*, p. 26.
13 L.H. Sullivan, *Moving Mountains*, p. 27.
14 R.K. Massie, *Loosing the Bonds* (New York: Doubleday, 1997), pp. 387–8.
15 S.P. Sethi and O.F. Williams, *Economic Imperatives and Ethical Values* (Boston: Kluwer Academic Publishers, 2000), p. 13.
16 Letter from Union Carbide's W.B. Nicholson to Sullivan, dated 18 April 1977 and quoted by S. Prakash Sethi and Oliver F. Williams in *Economic Imperatives and Ethical Values*, pp. 62–3.
17 M. Parks, 'Time to Negotiate, S. Africans Told: But Botha Won't Spell Out Reforms, Dashing Hopes for Early End to Strife', *Los Angeles Times* (16 August 1985).
18 'A Deadline for Ending Apartheid', *Philadelphia Inquirer* (7 May 1985).
19 K.E. Holmes, 'Sullivan Recounts Pushing S. Africa Toward Democracy: The Philadelphia Minister Used Economic Pressure Against Apartheid. Hundreds of Companies Signed On', *philly.com* (10 May 1994).
20 K.E. Holmes, 'Sullivan Recounts Pushing S. Africa Toward Democracy'.
21 S.P. Sethi and O.F. Williams, *Economic Imperatives and Ethical Values*, p. 380.

22 M. Muller, *The Baby Killer: A War on Want Investigation into the Promotion and Sale of Powdered Baby Milks in the Third World* (London: War on Want, 1977).
23 International Baby Food Action Network, *Breaking the Rules, Stretching the Rules* (Penang, Malaysia: IFBAN, 2004).
24 Anon., 'Drug Companies Accused of Endangering Developing Countries', *British Medical Journal*, 304:6839 (1992), 1398.
25 S. Gamper-Rabindran and S.R. Finger, 'Does Industry Self-Regulation Reduce Pollution? Responsible Care in the Chemical Industry', *Journal of Regulatory Economics*, 43:1 (2013), 1–30.
26 G. Orwell, 'Reflections on Gandhi', *Partisan Review*, 16:1 (1949), 85–92, quote on p. 85.
27 J.E. Stiglitz, *Making Globalization Work* (New York, London: W.W. Norton, 2007), p. 199.
28 A. Karnani, 'The Case Against Corporate Social Responsibility', *Wall Street Journal* (23 August 2010), p. R1.
29 M.E. Porter and M.R. Kramer, 'Strategy & Society: The Link Between Competitive Advantage and Corporate Social Responsibility', *Harvard Business Review*, 84:12 (2006), 78–92, quote on p. 80.
30 Anon., 'U.S. Concerns Urge End to Apartheid', *New York Times* (3 June 1986).
31 Corporate citizenship went mainstream when President Bill Clinton gave a keynote speech at the Conference on Corporate Citizenship held in 1996 in Washington, DC, in which he identified, 'community welfare' as one of the 'essential elements' of corporate citizenship. See *Weekly Compilation of Presidential Documents*; 32: 20 (20 May 1996), 862.
32 Mark Moody-Stuart quoted by David Henderson in *Misguided Virtue: False Notions of CSR* (London: Institute of Economic Affairs, 2001), p. 125.
33 S.J. Palmisano, 'The Globally Integrated Enterprise', *Foreign Affairs*, 85:3 (2006), 127–36, quote on p. 135.
34 S.J. Palmisano, 'The Globally Integrated Enterprise', 135.
35 William Clay Ford Jr. quoted in a press release titled 'Princeton Receives $20-million Grant to Address Greenhouse Problem', issued by the Office of Communications at Princeton University on 25 October 2000.
36 M. Wolf, 'Response to Confronting the Critics', in Ella Joseph and John Parkinson. 'Confronting the Critics', *New Academy Review* 1:1 (2002), 21–7, quote on p. 27.
37 F.A. Hayek, 'The Corporation in a Democratic Society: In Whose Interest Ought It and Will It Be Run?', in F.A. Hayek, *Studies in Philosophy, Politics and Economics* (London: Routledge & Kegan Paul, 1967), pp. 300–12, quote on p. 305.
38 Corporate Watch, 'What's Wrong with Corporate Social Responsibility? The Arguments Against CSR'. Retrieved from: www.corporatewatch.org/?q=node/2688%3f (accessed 19 January 2015).
39 L.H. Sullivan, *The Global Sullivan Principles* (New York: United Nations, 1999).
40 K. Silverstein, 'Sullivan Principles: Corporations Must Contribute to the Culture of Peace and Help End Gun Violence', *Forbes* magazine (25 December 2012).

12

Assault on the summit

> We are told that when Jehovah created the world he saw that it was good. What would he say now? (George Bernard Shaw, 'Stray Sayings')

Outward bound

When the foundations of the international liberal order were laid in the 1940s, there was one notable omission: protection of the natural environment. If considered at all, it was treated as a local concern.

During the 1960s, Maurice Strong was one of a handful of public figures who disagreed, arguing that many environmental problems are global and need to be solved through international cooperation. This mission became his life's work, which he vigorously pursued both in public, as a powerful UN mandarin, and in his work with non-governmental organisations and in books and articles he wrote.

He first attracted public attention when he ran two mega-conferences that put the environment firmly on the international agenda. Without a hint of hyperbole, a *New York Times* editorial referred to Maurice Strong as 'Custodian of the Planet',[1] and *Maclean's* magazine hailed him as an 'evangelist for a cleaner world' in its 1992 Honor Roll of prominent Canadians.[2] And United Nations Secretary General Kofi Annan paid Strong this tribute:

> If the world succeeds in making a transition to truly sustainable development, all of us will owe no small debt of gratitude to Maurice Strong, whose prescience and dynamic presence on the International stage have played a key role in convincing governments and grassroots alike to embrace the principle – if not yet the practice – of adopting a new, long-term, custodial approach to the global environment.[3]

Maurice Strong was born on 29 April 1929. While still a baby, his father, Frederick, lost his job as a telegraph operator with the Canadian Pacific Railway, plunging the family into poverty. They lived in the rural town of Oak Lake, located in south-west Manitoba (Canada), where unemployment was high during the Depression. Like many others, Frederick struggled to find another job. And so the family had to survive on the meagre food Frederick bartered for backbreaking work on local farms. Wild chokeberries, saskatoons, dandelions and pigweed that his mother, Mary, harvested from her garden and the nearby forest added to their meagre daily sustenance. Struggling to pay the rent, the family moved from one rundown house to another, with most lacking electricity, heat and plumbing. In winter, Maurice would scavenge coal off train tracks by day, and at dawn would light the indoor stove to first thaw out the family's clothing and then defrost the water pump.

Their one luxury was books, and his college-educated mother read to Maurice from her favourites: Tennyson, Longfellow and Shakespeare. 'Her love of ideas gave me a permanent interest in the wider world.'[4]

Maurice's outlook was also shaped by his school principal, Clarence Heapy, who held strong views on poverty and injustice. Describing the boy, Heapy recalled that Maurice 'was always darting here and darting there, full of creative ideas ... He had the urge to see everything and do everything.'[5] Undoubtedly influenced by his old headmaster, Maurice Strong once described himself as 'a socialist, only in the sense that I believe that the purpose of economic life is to meet the social needs of people'. As a successful businessman later in life, he qualified this statement, adding, 'I'm a capitalist in that I believe that's the best way to do so. Capitalism is not an end in itself but a means of creating and managing wealth to meet social objectives.'[6]

During summer, Maurice would escape to the countryside, where he wandered alone among the rolling foothills just north of his home, with its forests of oaks, aspen and poplars, and prairie of meadow grasses. 'I'd watch how nature's cycles worked, how the sap rose in the spring, the ebbs and flows and how everything fitted together, how harmoniously it all worked.' This left him wondering: 'If nature could be so right, how could human society be so wrong?'[7]

At other times, he would sit on the banks of the lake daydreaming of the day he would build a boat that would take him away from Oak Lake to foreign climes. And as he roamed the four corners of the world, he would fight poverty and injustice. His commitment to protecting the environment came later.

In 1946, Maurice secured a job with Vincent Mining Corporations as an accounting clerk. Although just 17 years old, he exhibited a natural aptitude for business and was soon entrusted with much more responsibility than his youth and inexperience warranted. In an effort to appear older, he grew a wispy moustache, to which he added gravitas by darkening it with shoe polish.

While Maurice displayed considerable promise in business, he felt that his destiny lay elsewhere. And so, in the fall of 1947, he headed to New York City, where he landed a temporary job with the newly formed United Nations, as an assistant pass officer who checked security clearances. In his diary, he remarked, prophetically, 'I'm most impressed with the United Nations and convinced that therein lies the key to my future.'[8]

Without a formal college degree, Strong realised he would advance no further in the UN bureaucracy. Thus, after only two months he left, proceeding next to Winnipeg, where he became a stock broker, specialising in oil and mining securities. He then moved to Alberta, where an oil boom was in full swing. Working as a director for the newly formed Dome Mines, Strong demonstrated his prodigious knack for making money. Over the next decade or so, Strong earned a reputation as a shrewd, even ruthless, businessman, and by the end of the 1960s, he was independently wealthy.

Soft-spoken, hair thinning, short, and apple-faced, his moustache had thickened and darkened of its own accord, and it no longer needed cosmetic enhancing. In his prime he looked more like a suburban stationmaster than a high-powered executive, albeit one with an expensive taste in suits. With an abundance of old-world charm, Strong created lasting friendships and surprisingly few enemies.

In September 1966, having spent the past decade building his reputation as an astute businessman, Strong agreed to head Canada's External Aid Office,[9] and during the next four years, Canadian aid to foreign countries grew from $C80 million to $C400 million. While in this position, he discovered that poverty could not be treated in isolation: 'In handling foreign aid, I became increasingly aware of the importance of interdependence on [the] earth, and ... of conducting ourselves on this planet in a way that corresponds with the realities of the physical world.'[10] Making this connection would be important to the next phase of his career.

Base camp

At the start of 1971, Strong was handed his dream job when the UN appointed him secretary general responsible for organising the first ever international UN Conference on the Human Environment, planned for Stockholm in June 1972.

From day one, a number of developing countries announced that they saw little point in attending. They feared the conference would recommend new environmental rules that would limit their ability to exploit their natural resources and prevent them from building their industrial capacity. Brazil led the opposition, with its planning minister, Paulo Vellosa, claiming, 'Brazil can still afford to import pollution', and going on to argue that the country's only ecological problem was poverty.[11] In other words, their problem was too few factories, not too many. Developing countries also feared that rich countries would use environmental problems as a pretext to impose non-tariff barriers against their products because they had been manufactured by 'polluting' industries.

In response, Strong argued that protection of the environment should not constitute a barrier to development, but rather should complement it. To attract the support of developing countries, he decided he needed a conceptual framework – a common language – that would draw the rich and poor countries together towards a common cause.

To this end, in June 1971 Strong invited twenty-seven experts and intellectuals to attend an informal meeting in Founex, a pleasant little village just outside of Geneva. Over two weeks of intense discussion and debate, they produced a report that made an important distinction between rich and poor countries. Whereas in industrialised countries, the environment is often damaged by production and consumption patterns, for the rest of the world, environmental problems result from underdevelopment and poverty. This conclusion led them to call for the integration of development and environmental policies.[12] The Founex report was, for Strong, 'a milestone in the history of the environmental movement, an absolutely seminal document'.[13]

Keen to sell the ideas contained in the Founex report, Strong spent most of the next twelve months jetting around Asia, Latin America and Africa to persuade governments, particularly from developing countries, to send delegates to Stockholm. Strong's breakthrough came when Indira Gandhi met him in New Delhi. 'If the developing countries sit out the conference', he warned the Indian prime minister, 'it would leave the issue in the hands of the industrialized countries'. Flattering Mrs Gandhi, he suggested: 'Why not come to the Stockholm Conference yourself, as you are the best possible person to articulate the concerns and interests of the developing world?'[14] It worked, and when she announced she was going to Stockholm, many other developing countries followed suit.

Strong's next priority was to involve two other parties in the conference: the business community and the non-government sector. Their participation would contribute valuable knowledge and experience. Moreover, he hoped that they would pressure governments to adopt strong measures to protect the environment.

His invitations were welcomed by NGOs to the extent that around 170 attended. On the other hand, the business sector was not interested, with many corporations hostile to the environmental agenda. Still, Strong managed to convince the International Chamber of Commerce (ICC) to show up and made room on the agenda for Walter Hill, its secretary general, to address the summit. In a lacklustre eight-minute speech, Hill had little to contribute other than a few platitudes.

The opening session went some way to calm fears of poorer countries that the conference would be dominated by the developed countries. Welcoming 1,200 delegates from 113 countries on the afternoon of 5 June, Strong set the tone: 'Broadly interpreted, the human environment impinges upon the entire condition of man, and cannot be seen in isolation from war, and poverty, injustice and discrimination, which remain abiding social ills on planet earth.'[15] This theme was taken up by Gandhi, who posed the loaded question: 'Are not poverty and need the greatest polluters?'[16] The Founex report was also tabled, which provided further proof that the environmental agenda would no longer ignore development.

When the conference ended on 16 June, delegates had agreed to twenty-six principles. The most far-reaching of these placed limits on national sovereignty. In rather torturous language, Principle 21 states:

> States have ... the sovereign right to exploit their own resources pursuant to their own environmental policies, and the responsibility to ensure that activities within their jurisdiction or control do not cause damage to the environment of other States or of areas beyond the limits of national jurisdiction.[17]

This principle became the cornerstone of environmental governance by empowering international environmental treaties to promote global interests over national interests.

Conference delegates also endorsed an action plan containing 109 recommendations, which addressed issues like education, research, monitoring and exchange of information, although it offered few practical solutions to major problems.

The conference's other noteworthy achievement was the creation of the United Nations Environment Programme (UNEP). It would provide an institutional foundation for global environmentalism, though its birth did not come without complications.

Behind the scenes, a handful of countries plotted to hobble UNEP before it was even launched. A journalist for the *New Scientist*, Mick Hamer, uncovered a note in British archives that described the machinations of an 'informal and confidential' cabal of senior bureaucrats from Britain, the United States, Germany, Italy, Belgium, the Netherlands and France, which went by the name of the 'Brussels group'. In July 1971, this group met to consider the possible formation of an international environment body, almost a year before the Stockholm conference. 'The group was concerned that environmental regulations would restrict trade and also wanted to stop UNEP having a large budget to spend as it saw fit', reported Hamer.[18] One of those participants, in a confidential briefing to the British government, conceded that a 'new and expensive international organisation must be avoided, but a small effective central coordinating mechanism ... would not be welcome but is probably inevitable.'[19]

When UNEP was established, it had a modest budget and no role in managing, coordinating or monitoring environmental treaties. Instead, it devoted most of its time to disseminating information on environmental threats – outcomes that would have not displeased the Brussels group.

The location of UNEP's headquarters proved to be highly contested, with ten governments stepping forward. Location became an acute North/South issue, according to John McDonald, who represented the US in these negotiations. After the names of New York, Geneva and Vienna were withdrawn, the choice was between Kenya and India. '[I]t was quite a sight to see the ambassadors of the two countries arguing with each other as they walked down the hall', recalled McDonald. 'The Indian Ambassador was approximately five feet, one inch tall and weighed about one hundred pounds. The Kenyan Ambassador was approximately six feet, seven inches tall and weighed about three hundred pounds.' Matters turned ugly when the Kenyan president, Jomo Kenyatta, passed on a message to Indira Gandhi that unless the Secretariat was located in Nairobi, he would kick every Indian out of Kenya, much like Idi Amin had done with the Indians in Uganda several months earlier. The threat worked and Mrs Gandhi withdrew the Indian offer to host the new environmental body.[20]

Strong was supportive of locating UNEP in a developing country. 'There is little doubt that if UNEP had gone to New York or Geneva, the poorer countries would be nowhere as involved as they are', he explained. 'Before Stockholm, they were not much interested. Today, it is the exact opposite.'[21] The downside of Nairobi was that its communications infrastructure was unreliable, and the difficulties of keeping in touch with other UN agencies and donor countries compromised UNEP's effectiveness.

High road to Rio

Appointed UNEP's first secretary general, Maurice Strong moved into his new offices in Nairobi on 2 October 1973. 'From inception', Strong explained, 'it was clear that UNEP's role was as a leader, catalyst and coordinator – as a bridge between science and policy, between governments and non-governmental activists, and between environment and development'.[22]

His first priority was to help developing countries set up environmental ministries so that they could follow up the recommendations that came out of Stockholm. He also set about cultivating important stakeholders.

Strong started with NGOs, telling them: 'When decisions are made to carry out particular programmes, many of them will depend on complementary or supporting action on the part of NGO's.'[23] To strengthen links with this community, Strong appointed a member of his staff to work full-time with NGOs to encourage their input into UNEP projects.

Strong also believed that UNEP needed to engage corporations because they have considerable expertise and resources, which he hoped could be tapped to solve environmental problems. This was a hard sell, as many firms felt persecuted by activists and oppressed by local environmental regulations. There were, however, a few enlightened business leaders who did not share these feelings, such as mining executives, Ian K. MacGregor and Taylor Ostrander. Following a conversation with Strong, they decided to create the International Center for Industry and Environment, which would link UNEP and the business sector. With members drawn from the ICC, a number of international industrial associations, several transnational corporations and national chambers of commerce, it opened offices in Paris and Nairobi in 1973.

Strong was also keen to devise a common language that would link protection of the environment with development, building on the work started at Founex. At UNEP, he promoted the concept of 'eco-development' and then 'development without destruction', but neither term caught on. UNEP also funded the International Union for the Conservation of Nature (IUCN) to produce a World Conservation Strategy report, which, he hoped, would reconcile developers and conservationists. By the time it was published in March 1980, Strong was chairman of the governing council of the IUCN, and was pleased to see that its authors had recognised that conservation and development should be promoted as compatible objectives, coining the term 'sustainable development' to describe this relationship.[24] Unfortunately, this concept was poorly sketched out and, much to Strong's disappointment, the IUCN did not pursue it further.

In December 1983, Strong was delighted by the UN's invitation to join its World Commission on Environment and Development, chaired by former Norwegian environment minister and later prime minister, Gro Harlem Brundtland. This provided him with another opportunity to pursue the work started at Founex.

The Commission released its report, *Our Common Future*, in April 1987. At its core lies the concept of 'sustainable development', defined as 'development which meets the needs of the present without compromising the ability of future generations to meet their own needs',[25] thus setting out conditions in which economic growth would not damage the environment. In just a few years this term gained wide currency.

Our Common Future enjoyed wide appeal because it worked on a number of levels. Developing countries liked it because it identified poverty and underdevelopment as problems that needed urgent attention. Environmental activists saw it as a beacon of environmental liberalism, in which the markets and the economy needed to work within the limits imposed by the natural environment. It also resonated with progressive business leaders because the report argued that the environment could be protected without needing to stifle economic growth.

To flesh out concrete plans for a transition to more sustainable forms of development, the Commission recommended that the UN convene another international summit within five years, which happened to coincide with the twentieth anniversary of the Stockholm Conference. Once again, Maurice Strong was asked to organise it. At the urging of Brazilian president, Fernando Collor de Mello, the summit was held in Rio de Janeiro. This was an inspired choice, allowing a developing country that had once been hostile to act as the host.

Strong was delighted to see that environmentalists were fully engaged in the run-up to the summit and needed no further encouragement. But he was less certain about the business community. The ICC had moved on since Stockholm, and had developed its own environmental policies, but it had to tread carefully as many of its members remained hostile.

So, on his own initiative, Strong decided to help build a business coalition that would champion sustainable development. He took the first step in Bergen (Norway), where he had been invited to attend the Industry Forum on Environment in May 1990. At the conference dinner, held on the *Statsraad Lehmkuhl*, a 100-year-old three-masted barque chartered for the occasion, Strong made sure he sat next to Stephan Schmidheiny. Born in Switzerland and head of Asea Brown Boveri Group, a multibillion-dollar enterprise, Schmidheiny possessed the qualities Strong was looking for: respect in the business community and commitment to environmentalism. Moreover, his networks within the business community were extensive.

After discussing his plans for the upcoming Earth Summit, Strong pressed Schmidheiny: 'I need someone like you to rally support in the business community, because if this is going to be only a conference of governments, nothing will get done.' At first, Schmidheiny was reluctant, even though he was enthusiastic about where Strong wanted to take the summit. Undeterred, a few weeks later Strong called on Schmidheiny at home and refused to leave until Schmidheiny agreed.[26]

Once committed, Schmidheiny energetically took to the task. Capitalising on the apprehension among corporations towards the environment movement, he pitched much the same argument wherever he went. 'We have two options', he told anxious CEOs. '[E]ither we resist and we will suffer, or we anticipate the changes and we will have more profits and more personal satisfaction.'[27]

After many air-miles, on 12 April 1991, Schmidheiny assembled thirty-five CEOs in The Hague. By the end of the meeting, they agreed to form the Business Council for Sustainable Development (BCSD), with the core message: 'Business will play a vital role in the future health of this planet.'[28] By the time the Earth Summit started, its membership had grown to forty-seven and it had a budget of £4.7 million at its disposal.

Reaching for the summit

The Rio summit, otherwise known as the United Nations Conference on Environment and Development, opened on 3 June 1992. Delegates from 178 countries attended, 108 of whom were heads of state or government, making it the greatest show on earth.

Strong launched the summit on a sober note, reflecting that in 'Stockholm we thought we did it, but we didn't. Now we don't have another 20 years to squander.'[29]

As expected, political leaders all wanted to address the conference, and the line-up was impressive: George Bush Sr., Indian prime minister, P.V. Narasimha Rao, and president of the European Commission, Jacques Delors, to name a few. One of the more charismatic leaders to attend was Fidel Castro, but he would test Strong's diplomatic skills. The Cuban leader was renowned for lengthy speeches lasting up to four hours, yet Strong had allocated just seven minutes to each speaker. 'Mr. President', he whispered as Castro's turn approached, 'when you speak, you are very eloquent. But you are also very long. This time you need to be very eloquent and very brief.' Grinning, Castro replied: 'You'll see.'[30] To everyone's surprise, Castro spoke for a shade under five minutes, but the revolutionary leader did not disappoint expectations. 'Less luxury and wastage in a few countries would amount to less poverty and hunger in a large part of the world', he thundered.[31]

Like Stockholm, Strong was able to attract NGOs and around 1,400 attended. Most were headquartered in *Parque do Flamengo*, inconveniently located forty kilometres from the main conference centre. Setting up tents in the park, NGOs organised their own Global Forum and staged marches and photo opportunities. Despite attracting media attention, Larry Williams from the Sierra

Club concluded, 'I believe we had almost no impact',[32] which was backed by Fred Pearce, a journalist from the *New Scientist*, who reported that NGOs 'appeared marginalized, their lobbyists wandering round in ever increasing gloom'.[33]

By contrast, the corporate sector had a most worthwhile conference. The ICC was convinced it had dodged a bullet, as 'there was at one time the real possibility that the conference might be pushed to lay down detailed guidelines for the operations of transnational corporations'. Instead, they were pleased to see that the summit 'acknowledged the important role of business'.[34] There was a price to pay for their cooperation: that any final text from the summit that referred to transnational corporations be linked to self-regulation. To this end, the BCSD and ICC were successful, and to showcase its alternative to government regulations, the BCSD showcased examples of how corporations were reducing their impacts on the environment with the publication of *Changing Course*, authored by Schmidheiny.[35] This book allowed the BCSD to argue that corporations were now part of the solution.

Schmidheiny's book also provided the clearest description of the principles on which corporate environmentalism is based. Corporations, he argued, were best placed to deploy technology that would make more efficient use of resources and reduce their ecological footprint, through voluntary corporate social responsibility programmes. He also made a case that sustainable development was dependent on trade expansion and economic growth. For governments to harness the potential of corporate environmentalism, Schmidheiny argued that they needed to 'deregulate markets, privatize enterprises, and stabilize basic economic conditions'.[36]

While corporate environmentalism was showcased in Rio, its critics, like Professor Timothy Doyle from the University of Adelaide, asserted that it represents a mischievous strategy 'to beat the environmentalists at their own game (but on newly defined terms and agendas); to subvert them, to divide them, to supplant them, to *appear* to be greener than the green'.[37]

When the summit came to a close on 14 June, Strong judged it a mixed success. He was pleased that the summit launched framework conventions on climate change and biodiversity (with the US being the only country that refused to sign the agreement) and had a hand in starting the process that produced the Convention to Combat Desertification. He also welcomed Agenda 21, a detailed action plan for the twenty-first century (hence its name), which provided a roadmap to sustainable development. In his closing remarks to the summit, Strong said that Agenda 21 'stands as the most comprehensive, the most far-reaching and, if implemented, the most effective programme of international action ever sanctioned by the international community'.[38]

Coming down to earth

After Rio, as had occurred post-Stockholm, many governments failed to act on many of their commitments, and when they did, such as ratifying a new environmental treaty, they included loopholes to cater for national and vested interests. In addition, they lacked teeth, and in the absence of sanctions, governments were able to easily skirt around agreements or even ignore them with impunity.

While the summit popularised the principle of sustainable development, it was seldom implemented as the Brundtland Commission had hoped. Instead, governments and organisations that found the Commission's definition too restrictive, simply came up with their own self-serving definition. Rather than becoming 'part of the common everyday lexicon of humankind', Jim MacNeill complained that '[o]nly in a Humpty Dumpty world of Orwellian doublespeak could the concept be read in the way some would suggest'.[39] Rather than driving radical change, as Strong had hoped, 'sustainability' often masked the pursuit of business as usual by governments and businesses.

Despite these setbacks, the irrepressible Strong renewed his efforts to encourage NGOs and the corporate sector to pressure governments to live up to their pledges. He also believed that norms, in the absence of strong international laws to protect the environment, provided a way to civilise the behaviour of governments and corporations. In addition, he looked to non-government actors to engage in direct action to repair environmental damage.

One such norm, which was close to his heart, was the Earth Charter. In 1994, he and Mikhail Gorbachev launched the charter, which sets 'out the basic principles to guide the conduct of nations and peoples towards each other and towards the planet'.[40] It was less a package of solutions than a set of 'moral, spiritual and ethical principles' for the care of the earth, which Strong hoped, would 'become like the Ten Commandments, like the Universal Declaration of Human Rights, ... a symbol of the aspirations and the commitments of people everywhere'.[41] Strong then tried to have the Earth Charter adopted at Rio without success, and again at the next two summits, with no more success. The Earth Charter has since been used mainly as an educational resource.

Strong was also keen to encourage the business community to increase its contributions to sustainable development, and to this end, he worked his networks in the World Economic Forum, the World Business Council for Sustainable Development (WBCSD) and the Trilateral Commission.

The most active was the WBCSD, which had been formed in 1995 from an amalgamation of the BCSD and ICC's environmental arm. It centred its strategy on building voluntary partnerships between business, governments and members of civil society, with the WBSCD acting as broker.[42] These ideas would have a profound influence on the next Earth Summit (also known as the World Summit on Sustainable Development or WSSD), planned for 2002 in Johannesburg.

In the run-up to the next summit, Strong's dream of having business, civil society and governments working in harmony were well and truly dashed, as NGOs reviled corporate environmentalism, believing that it was an elaborate Trojan Horse for neoliberal policies.

The Johannesburg summit was headed by Nitin Desai, who had served as Strong's deputy at Rio. Unlike Strong, his credibility among NGOs was low, and the Amsterdam-based Corporate Europe Observatory attacked him for having 'whole-heartily embraced the world's most powerful corporate lobby groups such as the ICC and the WBCSD ... making business his closest ally'.[43] Their frustration was compounded when the preparatory meetings refused to include bold targets to reduce greenhouse gases, a new Earth Charter and guidelines to hold corporations accountable for their environmental performance. This was hardly Desai's fault, and he was in a difficult position. Governments were unwilling to make new commitments, having failed to live up to promises made in both Stockholm and Rio. The agenda was bereft: no multilateral treaties ready to be signed; no new targets; and no major new initiatives. Much of what was on the table was recycled from commitments made elsewhere, or was so vague as to have little value. Lacking Strong's drive, skill or creativity, Desai had not been able to push governments into adopting a more ambitious agenda. And with little else on the table, he was left promoting offerings from the WBCSD, which became known in Johannesburg as type-II commitments.[44] These were partnerships between governments, international organisations, the private sector, local communities and NGOs.

When the summit opened in Johannesburg on 26 August 2002, it was larger than Rio, with over 10,000 delegates representing 180 countries and around 8,000 from the non-governmental sector in attendance. The notable absentee was George W. Bush, who, unlike his father, showed little interest in the environment. The event was well covered, with around 4,000 members of the press in Johannesburg, who breathlessly reported the various announcements during the event, without realising many were recycled or were so vague as to have little import. There were also demonstrations by environmental and human rights activists, which gave TV cameras some action and colour for evening newscasts. With little other news to report, when around 220 partnerships were announced, with a promised $235 million in resources, they were extensively covered by the media.

On closer examination, many of the partnerships that governments committed to during the summit were existing programmes, recycled for the occasion.

Hilde Johnson, Norwegian minister for international development, described them as 'putting "green paint" on old projects'.[45]

The partnerships offered by corporations were dismissed by Greenpeace's Andre Carothers, who complained that they were little more than 'commerce with a human face'.[46]

By the end of the summit, it was clear that governments were unwilling to make new policy commitments, strengthen the network of multilateral environment agreements, or reform governance. Instead, Jonathan Lash, president of the World Resources Institute, observed a worrisome trend in the 'new way of governing the global commons, ... [with] a shift from the stiff formal waltz of traditional diplomacy to the jazzier dance of improvisational solution oriented partnerships'.[47]

Dismissing such criticism, the business sector hailed the summit an unqualified success. 'We were actually accused by some people of hijacking the summit', the president of the WBCSD, Björn Stigson, remarked. 'That is, I think, a good example of business leadership.'[48] Maria Livanos Cattaui, secretary general from the ICC, added: 'The result was a stunning success, with widespread acceptance of the key role business has to play in creating a sustainable future.'[49]

In a triumph of hope over experience, and despite the Johannesburg summit having made little measurable impact on the state of the world's environment, the UN announced that Rio+20 would be held in June 2012, which happened to be the twentieth anniversary of the Rio Earth Summit.

In the run-up to Rio+20, it was clear that global environmentalism was in even worse shape than it had been when the last summit had been held, being structurally weak and lacking clear direction. To address these problems, preparatory meetings canvassed the possibility of producing a roadmap for a green economy with concrete goals and ways of measuring progress; upgrading UNEP status to a specialised agency of the UN, modelled after the WTO; strengthening the Sustainable Development Council; and issuing Sustainable Development Goals with measureable targets. Most of these were dropped or weakened in the run-up to the summit by China and the G-77 of developing countries for various reasons, although a major concern was that these reforms compromised their sovereignty. They were also unhappy about the refusal of rich countries to help fund their transition to a green economy, or support transfers of environmentally friendly technologies to developing countries. With the preparatory meetings deadlocked, little of substance was on the table, and whatever commitments survived were badly compromised.

When the summit opened on 20 June 2012, Barack Obama, David Cameron and Angela Merkel were notable absentees, and with little of substance to discuss the event was limited to just three days. With little to report, media attention was focused on voluntary commitments, which gave the impression that progress was being made. They included: the adoption of sustainable principles by the insurance industry; an undertaking made by eight transnational banks to help fund sustainable transport; a plan by the International Trade Union Confederation outlined to use its pension funds to create green jobs; and a further 200 commitments were made by major firms during the Corporate Sustainability Forum.

As a result, the final document, titled *The Future We Want*,[50] contained little of substance and certainly no binding targets with specific deadlines. Instead, the fifty-three-page document is mainly filled with empty platitudes and restates many of the promises made elsewhere.

After the summit ended, Strong did not bother to hide his despair, calling the summit's proposals a 'weak' collection of 'pious generalities'.[51] Others agreed. UNEP's executive director, Achim Steiner, concluded: 'We can't legislate sustainable development in the current state of international relations.' The World Wide Fund for Nature lambasted a 'colossal failure of leadership and vision'; Care International called it a 'charade'.[52] The editorial in the centre-left daily, *Süddeutsche Zeitung*, was disappointed by the summit. What 'should have provided a new spark, has instead shined the spotlight on global timidity ... Even the conference motto – "The Future We Want" – sounds like an insult. If this is the future we want, then good night.'[53] For *Guardian* journalist George Monbiot, Rio+20 'marks, more or less, the end of the multilateral effort to protect the biosphere'.[54]

With the Johannesburg and Rio+20 judged failures by many, the question needs to be asked whether it is worth organising another mega-conference. And if there are no more summits, where will the drive come to reform governance structures and set the global environmental agenda? Reform, in particular, is overdue as most multilateral environmental agreements are poorly framed, managed, resourced and coordinated. Moreover, without sanctions, countries feel free to disregard the spirit of agreements, if not their substance, to pursue national interests. Unless another avenue is found to rebuild its architecture, it is unlikely that the environmental agenda can progress, and it risks becoming a backwater in the global order.

Notes

1   Editorial, 'Custodian of the Planet', *New York Times* (15 October 1975).
2   C. Mollins, 'Evangelist for a Cleaner World', *Maclean's* magazine (18 December 1992).

3   K.A. Annan, 'Foreword', in M.F. Strong, *Where on Earth Are We Going?* (Toronto: Alfred A Knopf, 2000), p. ix.
4   M.F. Strong, *Where on Earth Are We Going?*, p. 52.
5   H. Westrup, *Maurice Strong* (Brookfield, CT: The Millbrook Press, 1994), p. 13.
6   Maurice Strong interviewed by Leo Hickman in 'Maurice Strong on Climate "Conspiracy," Bilderberg and Population Control', *Guardian Environment Blog* (23 June 2010). Retrieved from: www.theguardian.com/environment/blog/2010/jun/22/maurice-strong-interview-global-government (accessed 30 March 2015).
7   M.F. Strong, *Where on Earth Are We Going?*, p. 50.
8   E.J. Kahn Jr., 'Profiles: Environmentalist', *New Yorker* (3 June 1972), pp. 45–6, 48, 51–2, 54, 59–62, 65–75, quote on p. 70.
9   Strong reorganised the External Aid Office and it changed its name to the Canadian International Development Agency.
10 E.J. Kohn Jr., 'Profiles: Environmentalist', p. 66.
11 Paulo Vellosa quoted in Ulrich Beck *Risk Society* (London: Sage Publication, 1992) p. 43.
12 Founex, *Development and Environment*, Report and Working Papers of Expert Committee by the Secretary General of the United Nations Conference on the Human Environment held in Founex, Switzerland between 4 and 12 June 1971 (Paris: Mouton, 1972).
13 M.F. Strong, *Where on Earth Are We Going?*, p. 125.
14 S. Johnson, *UNEP: The First 40 Years: A Narrative* (Paris: United Nations Environment Programme, 2012), p. 33.
15 Opening Statement by Maurice Strong, secretary general of the conference, delivered at the UN Conference of Human Environment in Stockholm on 5 June 1972.
16 Speech delivered by Indira Gandhi to the plenary session of the UN Conference of Human Environment in Stockholm on 14 June 1972.
17 Principle 21, UN Conference on the Human Environment, Stockholm, 5–16 June 1972, UN Doc. A/CONF.48/14.
18 M. Hamer, 'Plot to Undermine Global Pollution Controls Revealed', *New Scientist* (5 January 2002), p. 7.
19 S. Johnson, *UNEP*, p. 19.
20 J.W. McDonald, *The Shifting Grounds of Conflict and Peacebuilding: Stories and Lessons* (Lanham, MD: Lexington, 2008), p. 113.
21 Maurice Strong quoted by Roger Lewin in 'Environment in a Developing Would', *New Scientist* (15 March 1973), 632–3.
22 M.F. Strong, 'The Way Ahead', *Our Planet*, 8:5 (January 1997).
23 Maurice Strong quoted by Anne Thompson Feraru in 'Transnational Political Interests and the Global Environment', *International Organization*, 28:1 (1974), 31–60, quote on p. 42, based on transcript from 'Report on NGO Conference on the Human Environment', New York, 17, 18, 19 October 1972.
24 R. Allen, *How to Save the World: Strategy for World Conservation* (London: Kogan Page, 1980).

25 World Commission on Environment and Development, *Our Common Future* (New York: Oxford University Press, 1987), p. 43.
26 L. Timberlake, *Catalyzing Change: A Short History of the WBCSD* (Geneva: WBCSD, 2006), p. 7.
27 M. Simons, 'Ecological Plea from Executives', *New York Times* (8 May 1992).
28 S. Schmidheiny, *Changing Course: A Global Business Perspective on Development and the Environment* (Cambridge, MA: MIT Press, 1992), p. ix.
29 G. Marx, 'Earth Summit Called First Step', *Chicago Tribune* (15 June 1992).
30 S. Johnson, *UNEP*, pp. 134–5.
31 Speech delivered by Fidel Castro to the plenary session of the United Nations Conference on Environment and Development in Rio on 5 June 1992.
32 Global Forum, 'UNCED Evaluated by American NGOs', *Earth Island Journal*, 7:3 (Summer 1992), 28.
33 F. Pearce (1992) 'Earth Summit: Earth at the Mercy of National Interests', *New Scientist* (20 June 1992), p. 12.
34 J.-O. Willums and U. Golüke, *From Ideas to Action: Business and Sustainable Development: The ICC Report on the Greening of Enterprise 92*. No. 504. ICC Pub. (Oslo: Ad Notam Gyldendal, 1992), pp. 21–2.
35 S. Schmidheiny, *Changing Course*.
36 S. Schmidheiny, *Changing Course*, pp. 81 and 178.
37 T. Doyle, 'Sustainable Development and Agenda 21: The Secular Bible of Global Free Markets and Pluralist Democracy', *Third World Quarterly*, 19:4 (1998), 771–86, quote on p. 772.
38 Closing address delivered by Maurice F. Strong at the United Nations Conference on Environment and Development in Rio on 14 June 1992.
39 An acceptance address titled 'The Forgotten Imperative of Sustainable Development', delivered on 20 April 2006 by Jim MacNeill on receiving the 2006 Elizabeth Haub Prize for Environmental Diplomacy.
40 M.F. Strong, 'The Way Ahead'.
41 Interview with Maurice F. Strong on 'A People's Earth Charter' (5 March 1998).
42 G. Davis, *Exploring Sustainable Development: Global Scenarios 2000–2050* (Conches-Geneva: World Business Council for Sustainable Development, 1997).
43 Anon., 'Rio +10 and the Privatisation of Sustainable Development', *Corporate Europe Observer*, Issue 11 (May 2002).
44 'Type-I' commitments were pledges made by governments on new treaties, targets and the like.
45 H.F. Johnson, Intervention at WSSD, Prep. Com. IV, Denpasar, Indonesia, 6 June 2002.
46 A. Carothers, 'Merchants at the Helm of UNCED', *Earth Island Journal*, 7:3 (Summer 1992), 37.
47 World Resources Institute, 'WRI Expresses Disappointment Over Many WSSD Outcomes', News Release (4 September 2002).
48 L. Timberlake, *Catalyzing Change*, p. 50.

49 International Chamber of Commerce 'The World Business Organization in 2003' (Geneva: ICC, 2003).
50 Conference on Sustainable Development, *The Future We Want*. Outcome of the Conference held in Rio de Janeiro (Brazil) between 20 and 22 June 2012, A/CONF.216/L.1.
51 Maurice Strong quoted by Geoffrey Lean in 'Rio+20 Earth Summit Is a Washout', *The Telegraph* (22 June 2012).
52 F. Pearce, 'Beyond Rio, Green Economics Can Give Us Hope', *The Guardian* (29 June 2012).
53 *Süddeutsche Zeitung* editorial translated and quoted by Charles Hawley in 'The World from Berlin: "Rio+20 Has Become the Summit of Futility"', *Spiegel Online International* (21 June 2012).
54 G. Monbiot, 'After Rio, We Know: Governments Have Given Up on the Planet', *The Guardian* (26 June 2012), p. 25.

13

Civilising globalisation

Political economy is a mere skeleton unless it has a little human covering and filling out, a little human bloom upon it, and a little human warmth in it. (Charles Dickens, *Household Words*)

Out of Africa

Expectations could not have sunk lower than when Kofi Annan took up his position as secretary general of the United Nations in January 1997. The organisation had rarely lived up to its promise and, with the spread of globalisation, was wallowing in irrelevancy.

In a quiet revolution, Annan turned the UN around, showing that its value went beyond peacekeeping; under his leadership, the UN embarked on a campaign to civilise globalisation by spreading its benefits more broadly, particularly to the poor. In pursuing this objective, he reached out to civil society, business and other international agencies, urging them to work together to make the world a better place. In this way, Annan made the UN relevant to the challenges of the twenty-first century.

Recognising his contribution to the transformation of the UN, the Norwegian Nobel Committee singled out Annan for 'bringing new life to the organization'[1] when it awarded the UN the Peace Prize in 2001. Canadian writer and politician Michael Ignatieff described him as 'an entrepreneur of moral standards',[2] and *Time* magazine observed that Annan was on a mission to create 'a moral world order'.[3]

Kofi Atta Annan was born in the Gold Coast (now called Ghana) on 8 April 1938. Despite descending from chiefs of the Fante tribe – his uncle and both his grandfathers were tribal chiefs – Kofi Annan described himself as being 'atribal in a tribal world'.[4] His mother was Rose Eshun, and his father, Henry Reginald Annan (referred to deferentially as 'HR'), was a prominent business executive who worked for the United African Company, the African subsidiary of the Anglo-Dutch corporation Unilever. His father, whose first two names were a legacy of British colonialism, decided to give their children African names. He called his eldest son: 'Kofi', which means 'Friday', the day he was born, and his middle name 'Atta' signifies he was a twin to his sister, Efua Atta.

HR, a dignified patrician whose authority was absolute, heavily influenced Kofi. As a strict disciplinarian, HR held informal inquisitions after dinner in which his children were expected to own up to acts of tomfoolery and naughtiness. He used these sessions for moral instruction, not as occasions for punishing them. Kofi learned the value of honesty and the virtue of admitting his mistakes from these sessions. While such sessions were uncomfortable, Kofi was able to relieve the tension with a joke, making his father laugh.

Kofi admired his father's ability to straddle different worlds without compromising his integrity, as he explained in his autobiography.

> To him there was no contradiction of being African in identity and European in outlook, a nationalist as well as a traditionalist, a proponent of political change and an upholder of those values of respect, dignity, discipline and hard work that had sustained his own life and career.[5]

When he was fifteen, Kofi enrolled at Mfantsipim, an all-boy's boarding school in the hilly area near the town of Cape Coast. At school, Kofi faced the rigours of an English-style private school, designed to forge character. Every morning his house master would wake him up at 5:30 a.m. to take a bracing cold shower. Then he and the other boys lined up before the housemaster, who checked their cleanliness, down to their fingernails. Afterwards, he sat down to a hearty breakfast of porridge, toast, marmalade and tea, right out of *Tom Brown's Schooldays*.

He was popular at school, recalled classmate Akipataki Akiwumi-Thompson. 'Kofi was very affable and jovial, full of wit and character. He was always making us laugh.' Kofi also displayed early signs of being a natural diplomat. For example, it was tradition at school for upperclassmen to have the authority to punish juniors for minor infractions, from talking after lights-out to horsing around. Kofi became adept at talking his way out of trouble. 'By the time he was finished, he could calm them down and persuade them not to punish him', says Akiwumi-Thompson.[6]

Growing up, young Kofi found his world rapidly changing. After the Second World War, nationalists protested – sometimes violently – against British colonial rule. When Kwame Nkrumah won the first election in 1951, Great Britain reluctantly allowed his government a high level of autonomy, and in 1957 the Gold Coast achieved full independence. Nineteen years old at the time, Kofi Annan enthusiastically welcomed the changes that were taking place.

The colonial power was handed over to the country, to what we call 'freedom fighters.' People were released from jail and became prime ministers and presidents. So I grew up believing that change is possible, that everything is possible. That one can dare to try to make a difference.[7]

While the first years of independence were an exciting time, Kofi dreamt of horizons outside Africa. The opportunity came when a talent scout from the Ford Foundation identified him as a future leader. By providing Kofi Annan with a scholarship, the Foundation allowed him to continue his studies in the United States.

In the fall of 1959, Kofi Annan arrived at St Paul, Minnesota, where he enrolled in an economics course at Macalester College. There, he encountered a segregated America and on occasions came face-to-face with racism. On one road trip outside Minnesota, Kofi needed a haircut. When he entered the hairdresser, he was told, 'We don't cut niggers' hair', to which the young man calmly replied, 'I'm not a nigger, I'm an African.' Charmed by Kofi's quiet dignity, the hairdresser said, 'That's O.K., come on, sit down.'[8]

Although he was one of the few black students at Macalester, he had little trouble fitting in and even tried out for the school's football team. While he was fast, his slight, five-feet-seven-inch frame made him look like a toothpick among the 300-pound tree trunks, who would have crushed him on the first tackle. 'It was okay so long as I kept running and no one caught up with me', he recalled. 'Otherwise, I was like a piece of paper. I weighed 138 pounds ... So I gave up after 15 minutes.'[9]

While he had no trouble adapting to his new surroundings, the Minnesota winter, with temperatures often dipping well below freezing, tested him. 'One thing I swore never to wear was earmuffs, until one day I had gone out to get something to eat and almost lost my ears.' Putting aside his vanity – he saw earmuffs as inelegant and ugly – Annan goes on to admit, 'I went and bought the biggest pair of earmuffs I could find.' Appreciating the amusing side of this incident, Annan later remarked that '[t]he lesson I walked away with was don't go to a place and pretend you know better than the natives'.[10]

Friends he met at the university remember a lithe, athletic man with soft brown eyes and deep baritone voice. Confident, charming and an amusing conversationalist, Kofi never lacked female company. It also helped that he was a graceful dancer.

In 1961, with his earmuffs safely packed and now sporting a goateed beard, Kofi Annan moved to Geneva to continue his studies at the Institut Universitaire de Hautes Études. There, he mixed with an idealist group of Africans who endlessly debated 'how we were going to change the world', recalls Annan. 'It was sort of the folly and dreams of the young.'[11]

After graduating a year later with a bachelor's degree in economics, Annan started out on the lowest rung of the UN bureaucracy as an administrative and budget officer with the World Health Organization. By 1974, after a few other jobs within the UN and in Africa, Annan moved to the UN headquarters in New York, taking various administrative positions within the personnel and budget departments. Even as he progressed steadily up through the bureaucracy, Annan longed to break into the frontlines of UN operations. His shot came in 1993 with his appointment to the high profile position of undersecretary general for peacekeeping.

The American candidate

As head peacekeeper, Annan experienced modest successes and disastrous failures. In 1994, he neglected to alert the Security Council that only urgent action would prevent a massacre of Rwandans. As a result, over 800,000 perished. The following year, he failed to protect civilians in UN safe zones during the war in Bosnia.

At the time, Kofi Annan largely escaped opprobrium. Instead, the secretary general, Boutros Boutros-Ghali, took most of the criticism. US politicians, in particular, delighted in taking pot-shots at the haughty Egyptian as a way of reminding him he was not sufficiently 'pro-American'.[12] Hitting back, Boutros-Ghali pointed out that the US wanted a secretary general who was 'morally superior and generally passive', and he was convinced that his 'activism' was why the US had taken a dislike to him.[13]

In early 1996, a small group of officials met in Washington to work on a plot to deny Boutros-Ghali a second term. One of the conspirators, Richard A. Clarke, a member of the National Security Council, provided an account of how they executed the plot.

> Albright [secretary of state] and I and a handful of others (Michael Sheehan, Jamie Rubin) had entered into a pact together in 1996 to oust Boutros-Ghali as Secretary General of the United Nations, a secret plan we had called Operation Orient Express, reflecting our hope that many nations would join us in doing in the U.N. head. In the end, the U.S. had to do it alone (with its U.N. veto) and Sheehan and I had to prevent the President from giving in to pressure from world leaders and extending Boutros-Ghali's tenure, often by our racing to the Oval Office when we were alerted that a head of state was telephoning the President. In the end Clinton was impressed that we had managed not only to oust Boutros-Ghali but to have Kofi Annan selected to replace him. (Clinton told Sheehan and me, 'Get me a crow, I should eat a crow, because I said you would never pull it off.')[14]

Boutros-Ghali suspected that Annan was plotting with the Americans but he had no hard evidence proving so. Years later, one of the conspirators, Michael Sheehan, confessed that Annan 'generally knew what was happening and we kept him informed'.[15] What is also clear is that Kofi Annan never actively campaigned against his boss.

The ensuing campaign turned ugly as US officials used the press to spread scuttlebutt to discredit Boutros-Ghali. At the same time, Annan's friends and supporters started dropping his name as a possible candidate, while Annan diplomatically remained aloof of the fray.

For a while, the conspirators made little headway, as it became clear Boutros-Ghali had powerful supporters. Even President Clinton had second thoughts, but under pressure from Madeleine Albright, he agreed to veto Boutros-Ghali's re-election. When the first vote was taken on 29 November 1996, it was fourteen to one in favour of the incumbent, with the US exercising its veto. In successive ballots, four other names were included, one of which was Kofi Annan. While Albright admits that Annan was her preferred candidate, she astutely kept her choice quiet because she knew it would be the kiss of death to Annan's chances.[16]

Based on his record, there was no obvious reason for the US to have supported Kofi Annan. He had an undistinguished career as a bureaucrat, most of it in administration, and suffered some significant failures in peacekeeping. Nevertheless, the Americans saw much they liked in the quiet-spoken Ghanaian, as one former official of the US mission to the UN explained: 'Kofi Annan was an extremely nuanced, extremely serious man with whom we agreed most of the time.'[17] In addition, the US hoped that Annan, as an insider, would possess the knowledge to reform the UN, something Boutros-Ghali had failed to do during his term. Finally, his American sponsors knew he had spent a good period of his adult life in New York and admired the American way of life.

Annan's cause was assisted by the unwritten rule-of-thumb for selecting secretary generals. An unexceptional career is no barrier, but can, in fact, be an advantage. An acceptable candidate should not threaten the political interests of the major powers, and Annan was sufficiently innocuous to avoid strong objections from any member of the Security Council. As an added bonus, the Great Powers believed that he would not rock the boat.

Over the next two weeks, Boutros-Ghali lost ground and when the next vote was taken on 12 December, Annan led fourteen to one. It was impossible to ignore the lone 'no' vote because it came with a veto. France argued that the secretary general should come from a French-speaking African country. In response, Annan joked to friends that perhaps he should start speaking English with a French accent. Nevertheless, Annan was in a good position to satisfy

French demands. Not only was he fluent in English, he could also converse in French and several African languages. Eventually, France fell in line with other members of the Security Council, and five days later Kofi Annan was elected as the UN's seventh secretary general, becoming the first black African to hold the job.

The means of his election, which resulted from arm-twisting by the US, led some to mutter that he would be an 'American poodle'.[18] Despite the bitter taste his election left, Kofi Annan's subsequent career showed that he was willing to stand up to his sponsor when necessary. For example, he chided Congress for failing to pay its membership dues, defied George W. Bush over his invasion of Iraq and criticised the US for not supporting the UN's peacekeeping efforts in Somalia. Annan has also used the media to caution America against turning its back on the UN, as he did in 2001 when he told journalist Gregory Maniatis:

> The U.S. is the only superpower in the world. ... It has been very successful, and sometimes success has its own hubris. The temptation to do it alone is a very strong one. But as the world becomes more interdependent, there are quite a lot of issues no one country can handle. We need to accept that in certain situations the collective interest is the national interest.[19]

The UN that Annan stepped into had been paralysed for most of its existence by the Cold War. Little got through the Security Council, where vetoes by the major powers were de rigueur, and the original idea of the 'four policemen', which had been in the minds of the UN architects, had never worked.

Realising that he could do little to alter the attitudes of the UN's members, Annan looked to new areas in which he could extend its influence. While peacekeeping remained the bread-and-butter of the UN, Kofi Annan decided to shift its centre of gravity away from being solely dependent on its members. In an interview he gave in 2000, Annan told *The Nation*: 'I believe that in the past we have concentrated too much on state sovereignty, and now there is a need for a new consensus', he explained.[20] To build this new accord, Annan encouraged new partnerships between UN agencies and powerful non-state actors and used these relationships to inject UN values into the emerging global architecture.

Early in his term, Annan hired John Ruggie, who had taught political science at Columbia University, as his assistant secretary general for strategic planning – a post created specifically for him. Annan was impressed by Ruggie's published works on 'embedded liberalism',[21] which he believed provided him with the intellectual framework he needed to revitalise the UN.

Ruggie argued that the Bretton Woods compromise was built on embedded liberalism, which balanced liberalisation of the international economy, built on a stable monetary system and free trade, with domestic programmes that included social safety nets, full employment and wealth redistribution. This was an international liberal order built on 'socially sustainable markets'.[22]

The embedded liberal compromise was undermined by neoliberal insurgency, which strengthened market liberalisation while at the same time shrinking social programmes, privatising government services and deregulating large parts of the national economy. For developing countries, the Washington Consensus ensured they did not escape these neoliberal prescriptions, which often led to further inequality and poverty.

Annan hoped that the UN could put together a new compromise in which the UN and the private sectors could give 'global markets a more human face'.[23]

Ruggie's job was to translate these ideas into practical programmes, and during his time at the UN he worked on two important initiatives: the Millennium Development Goals and the Global Compact. Ruggie hoped that these programmes could be moulded into 'something akin to an embedded liberalism compromise ... pushed into the global arena', and in place of national governments, Ruggie believed that 'the corporate connection is a key element in that process'.[24]

Together, they represent prime examples of the UN's efforts to civilise globalisation and are lasting legacies of Annan's time at the head of the UN.

Millennium fever

Soon after Annan became secretary general, he revamped UN programmes designed to help those living in abject poverty.

This problem had become more urgent since the end of the Cold War, as the US and European countries slashed foreign aid once they no longer needed to bribe unaligned countries to support them in their fight against the USSR. As a result, aid from rich countries fell from $84 billion in 1992 to $68 billion in 1997. This made no sense to Annan, who observed that, 'unprecedented wealth is being created but large pockets of poverty remain endemic'.[25]

The UN's record tackling poverty was not good. Having worked inside the bureaucracy for so long, Annan was familiar with the shoals that had sunk earlier attempts, and moved quickly to sweep away potential obstacles and put together a programme that would make a real difference.

Annan first turned his attention to the UN's own backyard, in which its numerous agencies seldom coordinated their programmes. Having decided that his main priority would be poverty, Annan chose the United Nations Development

Programme (UNDP) to coordinate related programmes among the thirty-two agencies that had a stake in the issue.

He next turned to stopping wasteful turf wars that occasionally broke out between UN agencies and the Bretton Woods institutions. On 10 April 1997, Kofi Annan arranged a breakfast meeting with James Wolfensohn, president of the World Bank, and Michel Camdessus, managing director of the IMF. The three men discovered they had much in common and emerged with an informal commitment to deliver 'an unprecedented level of cooperation' to tackle poverty and its root causes.[26]

Over the next two years, the three institutions collaborated closely, and Annan decided to include their recommendations in the Millennium Summit, a special meeting of the General Assembly planned for 2000.

Held in New York on 8 September, Kofi Annan capitalised on the hype of a new millennium to present the General Assembly with the Millennium Declaration that outlined bold new directions for the UN in the twenty-first century. Ruggie's influence is evident, as its recommendation is infused with the language of embedded liberalism:

> The central challenge we face today is to ensure that globalization becomes a positive force for all the world's people, instead of leaving billions of them behind in squalor.[27]

In broad terms, the solution was to make 'globalization ... fully inclusive and equitable'.[28]

One section of the declaration was dedicated to dealing with 'development and poverty eradication', committing the UN to 'spare no effort to free our fellow men, women and children from the abject and dehumanizing conditions of extreme poverty'.[29]

At the end of the session, leaders of 147 countries signed the Declaration, and soon after, all other members of the UN supported its recommendations, as did twenty-three international organisations.

Annan knew member countries had seldom honoured prior pledges, which had undermined earlier attempts of the UN to rally the world community to tackle poverty. This time, however, he was optimistic, acknowledging he had employed subterfuge to lock them in.

> Between this universal simplicity and the commitment to a quantifiable set of targets, the member states thus bound themselves within the shackles of an incredibly powerful global idea. Many of them did so unwittingly, I suspect, not realizing the strength of what they had brought to life and expecting it to suffer the same quick death that had overtaken so many other UN declarations.[30]

For a while it looked like he was wrong, as the excitement generated during the Millennium Summit quickly dissipated.

Seeing the development programme could end up in the dustbin, sharing the fate of many previous UN declarations, Jan Vandemoortele, director of UNDP's Poverty Group, and Michael Doyle, who had replaced John Ruggie, were determined to rescue the Declaration from oblivion. In early 2001, they convened an informal group of experts drawn from UN agencies, the World Bank, IMF and OECD to produce a practical package to ensure progress made at the Millennium Summit was not lost. This group flew under the radar and was not subject to the intense lobbying that had preceded the Millennium Summit. Starting with eight sentences from the Millennium Declaration that addressed targets, the group massaged them into a coherent package that was simple, concise, easy to communicate, politically palatable and based on sound methodology.

After six months, this group produced the Millennium Development Goals (MDGs), a set of eight major goals, eighteen targets and forty-eight indicators to measure progress. Commitments to halve the proportion of people with daily incomes of less than a dollar and those suffering from hunger drew the most attention, as did goals to reduce child mortality by two-thirds and achieve universal primary education. Other goals addressed the environment, gender inequality, health and development partnerships.

Not everyone was happy, and the final document reflected tension between embedded liberalism and neoliberalism. Vandemoortele, in particular, criticised the final package because it narrowly defined poverty in terms of income, 'undermining the main purpose of the MDGs, which was to expand the development narrative beyond the narrow growth paradigm', in which '[p]overty will automatically be reduced by the trickle-down effect'. He goes on to concede that the economic rationalists from the World Bank and IMF had come out on top as the 'poverty debate has been dollarized, and the MDG discourse has been donorized'.[31]

Once the MDGs were drafted, Kofi Annan faced the tricky problem of securing support from the General Assembly. Unlike the Millennium Declaration, the MDGs were more specific and had been produced with limited consultation, therefore running the risk of facing opposition. Annan decided to slip the MDGs into a *Road Map*, a report the General Assembly had asked him to prepare that would describe how the UN would monitor implementation of the Millennium Declaration.[32] Released on 6 September 2001, Annan cunningly attached the MDGs as an annex, and 'although no explicit mention was made of the MDGs, they got an implicit blessing from the UN members states', reported Vandemoortele.[33]

The UN, however, did not possess the resources to implement the MDGs on its own, and so the *Road Map* called for a high-level meeting to determine how the development agenda would be implemented. In March 2002, the UN hosted the International Conference on the Financing of Development, which was held in Monterrey, Mexico. Those attending included the heads of UN agencies, the World Bank, IMF and WTO, along with fifty heads of government. President George W. Bush even made a rare appearance at an international event. NGOs and business associations were also given opportunities to contribute to the discussion.

The presence of political leaders at Monterrey helped secure real commitments to fund implementation of the MDGs. The European Union pledged an additional €8 billion a year in aid, while the US promised an additional $5 billion, which was probably a direct result of 9/11, as the Bush Administration needed a sweetener to enlist developing countries to join his war on terrorism. Together, these commitments fell well short of the extra $54 billion needed,[34] but it was assumed that the remainder would come from private investments and economic growth generated from free trade and market liberalisation.

At the end of the conference, the heads of the international agencies stood shoulder to shoulder, declaring it a success. Kofi Annan described the Monterrey Consensus as a 'historic compact'. Mark Malloch-Brown, the UNDP administrator, hailed the agreement as 'an extraordinary turnaround, not just financially, but politically'. Horst Köhler, managing director of the IMF, welcomed the agreement as an innovative balance between two principles: 'self-responsibility in developing countries' and 'solidarity on the part of the international community'. While James Wolfensohn portrayed Monterrey as the start of a 'partnership between leaders of the developing and developed world ... united by a global responsibility based on ethics, experience and self-interest'.[35]

Outside government circles, the MDGs received some good reviews. According to Sakiko Fukuda-Parr, a development economist, the goals 'have created a new narrative of international development centered on global poverty as a compelling moral concern for the world at large'.[36] The president of the International Chamber of Commerce, Richard McCormick, also applauded the Monterrey Consensus, explaining that the 'only long term and sustainable source of development finance is private sector investment – both domestic and international'.[37]

The MDGs also had their critics. John Foster of the North-South Institute in Canada called the Monterrey Consensus the 'Washington Consensus in a sombrero',[38] arguing that it was just another means of imposing the neoliberal agenda. Professor Ashwani Saith, from Erasmus University Rotterdam, agreed that the MDGs supported 'the mainstream neoliberal strategic and policy framework, significantly emphasising the responsibility of the poor countries themselves in addressing their development agendas, making external assistance contingent on such efforts, and at the same time heavily underscoring the role of the private sector in the development process'.[39]

The MDGs have since built up sufficient momentum to survive their critics and, while they have not yet met their targets, progress has been made. They are now a permanent feature of the global architecture, and Annan's successor at the UN, Ban Ki-moon, has continued the programme beyond 2015 and will include sustainable development goals in the updated package.

While imperfect, the MDGs represented a brave attempt to create new norms around poverty alleviation, which Annan hoped would become an important part of 'a global social movement'.[40]

Open for business

Another important priority for Annan was addressing the harmful behaviour of transnational corporations by having them embrace the norms and values that the UN had developed. He wanted to make them better global citizens.

Engaging them was no simple task. Since the 1960s, antipathy between the UN and the business community had festered, 'marked by discontent, disillusionment, and discord', according to an intellectual history of the United Nations.[41]

The private sector was unhappy because it was convinced that the UN was anti-business. One reason that this idea became fixed in the minds of businesspeople was that the UN bureaucracy was careful not to take sides in the Cold War, which pitted market-based systems of the west against planned economies of communist countries. In 1974, relations deteriorated markedly as a bloc of recently decolonised countries used their numbers in the General Assembly to create a Commission on Transnational Corporations; its major task was to draft a code of practice to control their behaviour. Even after Boutros-Ghali closed down this agency in 1992, the business sector was not convinced that this peace offering represented a genuine change of heart.

Moving quickly to repair relations, on 1 February 1997, Annan told the annual meeting of the World Economic Forum in Davos that he was determined to draw the UN and the private sector closer together. He surprised his mainly business audience when he went on to tell them that 'market capitalism has no major ideological rival', and that 'human ingenuity and enterprise will take us forward in to a new golden age'. He also issued a warning: 'If it cannot promote both prosperity and justice, it will not have succeeded.'[42]

Annan's underlying message was that unless the private sector accepted that they needed to act morally, then economic globalisation would be doomed, overwhelmed by a growing army of discontents. The solution was for transnational corporations to allow their better angels guide them, and in return the UN would work with the business community 'to bring 60 per cent of the world's population into the market'.[43] This was quite an about-face for the UN, with the new secretary general signalling that the UN was offering qualified support for economic liberalisation, which it believed could improve the lot of the poor and disadvantaged.

The obvious partner for the UN was the ICC, which was the only business organisation with global reach. Over the next two years, Annan assiduously courted the ICC with a view of entering into a formal relationship.

The nature of this relationship became clear in January 1998, when Annan used his next appearance at the World Economic Forum to sketch out how the two might work together. Annan proposed 'to unite the power of markets with the authority of universal ideals', meaning those contained in various principles within in UN treaties and declarations. In this way he hoped to civilise globalisation.

> Let us choose to reconcile the creative forces of private entrepreneurship with the needs of the disadvantaged and the requirements of future generations. Let us ensure that prosperity reaches the poor. Let us choose an enlightened way forward towards our ultimate, shared goal: a global marketplace that is open to all and benefits all.[44]

Annan did not have to wait long for the ICC to respond. On 5 February 1998, ICC secretary general, Maria Livanos Cattaui, wrote an op-ed piece for the *International Herald Tribune* in which she acknowledged that the ICC and the UN now saw the world in much the same way.

> What makes the dialogue possible is the perception by both sides that open markets are a precondition for spreading more widely the benefits of globalization, for integrating developing countries into the world economy, and for improving living standards of all the world's peoples, and in particular the poor.[45]

In 1998, Annan asked Ruggie to develop a concrete plan to formalise the relationship. The result was the Global Compact, which Kofi Annan announced at the 1999 meeting of the World Economic Forum:

> I call on you – individually through your firms, and collectively through your business associations – to embrace, support and enact a set of core values in the areas of human rights, labour standards, and environmental practices.[46]

After the Davos meeting, the UN released more details about the programme, which included a list of nine (later ten) international values that corporations could sign up to. The programme's objective is to spread best practices of socially responsible behaviour among corporations. Members report how they have implemented the UN values, giving case examples that might be useful to others.

At first, the ICC was uncertain whether to support the programme, worried that it could mutate into a legally binding code of conduct, even though the UN promised that the Global Compact was and would remain a voluntary programme.

Perversely, the turning point for the Global Compact occurred in November 1999 during the WTO Ministerial Conference, when massive protests in the streets of Seattle resulted in the conference ending prematurely. This event convinced many business leaders that unless globalisation was given a human face, the backlash against it might spread. Soon after, a number of companies lined up to join the programme. At its official launch, on 26 July 2000, the CEOs of forty-seven companies joined Annan to announce their support for the Global Compact. Over the next few years, the programme steadily expanded, and by 30 November 2014, the Global Compact boasted 8,285 business members and 4,448 non-business participants, based in more than 140 countries.[47] To put this in proportion, there are over 80,000 transnational corporations in the world today.

The Global Compact, for Annan, represented a ground-breaking rapprochement with the business sector.

> This would have to be a two-way street; we at the United Nations would abandon our past prejudices against the private enterprise, but in return I believe that global success would have to rethink its role, as well as its objectives, if we were to put global markets on a fair and sustainable footing.[48]

In the years that followed, many of Annan's public pronouncements showed how far the UN had embraced the business agenda. By championing the voluntary nature of the Global Compact, a secretary general Annan provided tacit support for self-regulation and corporate social responsibility programmes. He also promoted the paradigm that corporations should work to help solve problems like environmental degradation, access to medical services and inequality. Finally, Annan defended economic liberalisation, arguing that 'the poor are poor not because of too much globalization, but because of too little – because they are not part of it, because they are excluded'.[49]

Not everyone believed that the Global Compact was sufficiently rigorous to compel corporations to moderate their behaviour and live up to the values promoted by the UN. Two of its detractors were Kenny Bruno and Joshua Karliner, who wrote in their book *Tangled Up in Blue* that the programme was 'leading down a slippery slope toward the partial privatisation and commercialisation of the UN system itself'.[50] The Corporate Europe Observatory agreed, accusing the Global Compact of 'smuggling a business agenda into the United Nations'.[51][52] There was also criticism of the programme's inability to hold corporations accountable, with business ethicist Prakash Sethi remarking that the Global Compact 'provides a venue for opportunistic companies to make grandiose statements of corporate citizenship without worrying about being called to account for their actions'.[53] Without objective monitoring, it is unclear if the Global Compact has actually done much to civilise its major economic players: transnational corporations.

For all its limitations, Annan used the Global Compact to demonstrate that the UN is relevant to globalisation. Having realised that transnational corporations were seldom, if ever, subject to hard international laws, Annan wanted to show that norms were a credible alternative and that the Global Compact could be used to effectively spread UN values through the corporate sector.

While once governments were the main agent that delivered the social side of the embedded liberal compromise, since the 1980s, governments have substantially reduced their commitment to social programmes. This has forced international agencies like the UN to turn increasingly to transnational corporations to deal with a wide range of global problems, from tackling Ebola in Africa, to fighting corruption, to delivering vaccines to the poor.

This shift in strategy can be seen in the promotion of the MDGs and Global Compact, which has seen a substantial rise in the number of public–private partnerships. No agency was more enthusiastic in pursing such partnerships than the WHO under the leadership of Gro Brundtland, and it provided a test bed for this new type of cooperation.

Notes

1. Norwegian Nobel Committee, 'The Nobel Peace Prize for 2001', Press Release (12 October 2001).
2. M.G. Ignatieff, 'The Confessions of Kofi Annan', *New York Review of Books* (6 December 2012).
3. J.C. Ramo, 'The Five Virtues of Kofi Annan', *Time* magazine (4 September 2000), pp. 50–7.
4. Kofi Annan quoted by Stanley Meisler in *Kofi Annan* (New Jersey: John Wiley & Sons: Hoboken, 2007), p. 11.

5   K.A. Annan, *Interventions* (New York: Penguin, 2012), p. 15.
6   Quoted by Stanley Meisler in *Kofi Annan*, p. 14.
7   Anon., 'Kofi Annan', *Hello* magazine (undated).
8   P. Gourevitch, 'The Optimist', *New Yorker* (3 March 2003), pp. 50–73, quote on p. 64.
9   Kofi Annan quoted by Stanley Meiser in *Kofi Annan*, p. 17.
10 Kofi Annan quoted by Thomas G Weiss, Tatiana Carayannis, Louis Emmerij and Richard Jolly in *UN Voices* (Bloomington: Indiana University Press, 2005), p. 90.
11 P. Gourevitch, 'The Optimist', pp. 50–73.
12 L. Brown 'The Ignoble Abuse of the Noble UN', *Christian Science Monitor* (21 July 1999), p. 9.
13 B. Boutros-Ghali, *Unvanquished* (New York: Random House, 1999), p. 268.
14 R.A. Clarke, *Against All Enemies: Inside America's War on Terror* (New York: Free Press, 2004), pp. 201–2.
15 J. Traub, *The Best Intentions* (New York: Farrar, Straus and Giroux, 2006), p. 65.
16 M.K. Albright, *Madam Secretary* (New York: Miramax Books, 2003), p. 210.
17 J. Traub, *The Best Intentions*, p. 64.
18 A. Adebajo, 'African Prophet or American Poodle?' *Africa Review of Books*, 5:1 (2009), 8–9.
19 G.A. Maniatis, 'On Top of the World', *New York Magazine* (19 November 2001), pp. 42–7.
20 I. Williams, 'Kofi Annan: A "Moral Voice"', *The Nation* (19 June 2000), pp. 20–4, quote on p. 20.
21 J.G. Ruggie, 'International Regimes, Transactions and Change: Embedded Liberalism in the Postwar Economic Order', *International Organization*, 36:2 (1982), 379–415.
22 J.G. Ruggie, 'Taking Embedded Liberalism Global: The Corporate Connection', Miliband Public Lecture on Global Economic Governance, delivered at the London School of Economics and Political Science on 6 June 2002.
23 Address by Kofi Annan at the ceremony of adherence to the Global Compact, delivered in Madrid on 1 April 2002.
24 J.G. Ruggie, *Taking Embedded Liberalism Global: The Corporate Connection*. Institute for International Law and Justice, New York University School of Law (2003), pp. 93–129, quote on p. 122.
25 K.A. Annan, 'The Quiet Revolution', *Global Governance*, 4:2 (1998), 123–38, quote on p. 124.
26 K.A. Annan, *Interventions*, p. 221.
27 *United Nations Millennium Declaration*, UN Resolution A/RES/55/2 (New York: United Nations, 18 September 2000).
28 *United Nations Millennium Declaration*, UN Resolution A/RES/55/2.
29 *United Nations Millennium Declaration*, UN Resolution A/RES/55/2.
30 K.A. Annan, *Interventions*, p. 227.
31 J. Vandemoortele, 'The MDG Story: Intention Denied', *Development and Change*, 42:1 (2011), 1–21, quote on p. 18.

32 K.A. Annan, *Road Map Towards the Implementation of the United Nations Millennium Declaration*, Fifty-sixth session of the General Assembly, A/56/326 (8 September 2001).
33 J. Vandemoortele, 'The MDG Story: Intention Denied', 6.
34 United Nations, *Report of the International Conference on Financing for Development*, A/CONF.198/11, Monterrey, Mexico (22 March 2002).
35 Quotes taken from Jean-Philippe Thérian 'Towards a New Synthesis in Development Politics?', paper presented at the forty-eight annual convention of the International Studies Association held in Chicago between 28 February and 3 March 2007, pp. 9–10.
36 S. Fukuda-Parr, *Recapturing the Narrative of International Development*. United Nations Research Institute for Social Development, UNRISD Research Paper No. 2012–5 (July 2012). The quote is from p. iii.
37 Final plenary communique to the UN Conference on Financing for Development, delivered on behalf of the business interlocutors by Richard D. McCormick in Monterrey on 22 March 2002.
38 F. Haffajee, 'Monterrey Meet – "Washington Consensus in a Sombrero"', *Third World Network* (16–31 March 2002).
39 A. Saith, 'From Universal Values to Millennium Development Goals: Lost in Translation', *Development and Change*, 37:6 (2006), 1167–99, quote on p. 1170.
40 K.A. Annan, *Interventions*, p. 227.
41 L. Emmerij and R. Jolly, 'The UN and Transnational Corporations', UN Intellectual History Project, Briefing Note Number 17 (July 2009).
42 Secretary General, in address to World Economic Forum, Press Release SG/SM/6153.
43 Kofi Annan's address to World Economic Forum, delivered in Davos on 31 January 1997. Press Release SG/SM/6153.
44 Kofi Annan's speech, 'Markets for a Better World', delivered to the World Economic Forum on 31 January 1998. Press Release SG/SM/6448.
45 M.L. Cattaui, 'Get the UN and Business Talking', *International Herald Tribune* (5 February 1998), p. 8.
46 Kofi Annan's address to World Economic Forum, delivered in Davos on 31 January 1997.
47 UN Global Compact Bulletin, December 2014.
48 K.A. Annan, *Interventions*, p. 219.
49 K.A. Annan's address to the Millennium Forum, delivered in New York on 22 May 2000. Press Release SG/SM/7411 GA/9710.
50 K. Bruno and J. Karliner, *Tangled Up in Blue* (San Francisco: CorpWatch, 2000), p. 3.
51 Corporate Europe Observatory, 'The ICC and Corporate Cooptation of the UN''' Factsheet #2, 2000.
52 Corporate Europe Observatory, 'The ICC and Corporate Cooptation of the UN', ICC Factsheet #2 (2000).
53 S.P. Sethi, 'Global Compact Is Another Exercise in Futility', *The India Express* (7 September 2003), p. 8.

14
Health of nations

As a woman I have no country. As a woman I want no country. As a woman, my country is the whole world. (Virginia Woolf, *Three Guineas*)

'My name is Gro!'

When Gro Harlem Brundtland became director-general of the World Health Organization in 1997, she found an organisation that had badly lost its way and, through her reforms, gave it hope.

Like Kofi Annan, Brundtland was committed to help civilise globalisation. She did this by increasing resources devoted to improving health, particularly among the poor. Her success owes much to her ability of reframing health as an economic issue. This allowed Brundtland to convince the private sector that partnering with the WHO was in its commercial interests; to show donor countries that investment in health programmes was a cost effective way to support development and help people out of poverty; and to justify regulating tobacco marketing by exposing its real costs on the world's community.

While many of her reforms generated controversy, at the end of Brundtland's term, Richard Horton, editor of the prestigious medical journal *The Lancet* and erstwhile critic conceded that:

> for the first time since its creation in 1948, WHO now occupies a decisive position in the global political debate about health and human development ... [and Gro Brundtland] has successfully restored WHO's international credibility, an achievement that seemed almost impossible 5 years ago. WHO has become an agency to be reckoned with.[1]

Gro Harlem was born on 20 April 1939, in Bærum (Norway). A year later Germany invaded, and during the Nazi occupation, her parents, Inga Brynolf and Gudmund Harlem, worked for the Underground. When they were tipped off that they were on a Gestapo death list, they fled to Stockholm. They stayed with Inga's mother, Margareta Sandberg, who was a radical lawyer, feminist and advocate of free love. Her grandmother was an important role model for the young girl and she 'managed to convey both a kind of independence and also the feminine values'.[2] Growing up, Gro's parents were determined that she understood that she had the same abilities and responsibilities as her brothers – an uncommon view in the 1940s.

When she was just thirteen, Gro's parents encouraged her to read philosophers like Marx, Kant, Hegel and Nietzsche, whose ideas she and her family fiercely debated over the dinner table. Politically sophisticated, during her adolescence Gro joined various youth organisations associated with the labour movement. With such an upbringing, Gro predictably matured into a young woman who firmly believed in equality of the sexes, displayed a strong independent streak and possessed canny political instincts.

At university, her friends met her announcement that she had fallen in love with Arne Brundtland with disbelief. He was a high-profile conservative and an unlikely match. They married on 9 December 1960 and had four children, timing them between exams, as Gro Brundtland completed her medical education, first at the University of Oslo and then at Harvard.

Back in Norway, she held various positions in the medical system in Oslo, which allowed Brundtland to immerse herself in her two main interests: women's and children's health. As a young doctor working for the Oslo Municipal Board of Health, Brundtland defied the rules by passing out free contraceptives to poor women. In her subsequent political career, she would vigorously campaign for sex education, ready availability of contraceptives and the rights of women to legal abortions.

In August 1974, Prime Minister Trygve Bratteli summoned Brundtland to a meeting. Expecting him to discuss her campaign for abortion rights, she was surprised when he invited her to become minister for the environment.

As Brundtland's political career took off, she wondered whether she could balance all the expectations on her time. As she explained:

> Can I do it without taking away from my family and my role as mother? But to say no meant that women would be held back, because men do not say no to such opportunities when they have families. The first thing I did was ask my husband. He said he could do more.[3]

In agreeing to take the lion's share of household chores and child rearing, Arne set one condition: he would run the household his way. 'My philosophy was that the house should be clean enough to be healthy, dirty enough to be happy', he explained.[4]

Arne's support helped Brundtland concentrate on her career, but it did not change his political views. He remained active in the Conservative Party and worked for the right-wing foreign policy think tank, Norsk Utenrikspolitisk Institut. Norwegians were amused to read in Arne's newspaper columns, occasional denouncements of his wife's policies. Nevertheless, while their politics differed, Arne provided Gro with valuable advice on international issues. As he told *Time* magazine, 'My field is analysis of international relations. Her field is doing international relations. That makes for very good morning seminars.'[5]

In her first ministerial position, Brundtland displayed considerable strategic skills as she shifted the debate away from the intrinsic value of nature, to linking environment threats to their effect on human beings: their health, well-being, and enjoyment of the natural world. In this way, she garnered public support for strengthening regulations and overcame opposition from vested interests.

Recognised as a rising star in the Labor Party, Brundtland emerged as its deputy leader in 1975 and four years later she became the party's leader. In 1981, Norwegians elected Gro Brundtland as the country's first female prime minister. At forty-two, she was also the youngest person to hold that office in Norway. From day one as prime minister, Brundtland demonstrated that she would do it her way. Uncomfortable with the formalities that came with high office, before anyone could call her 'Madam Brundtland', she would break in with: 'My name is Gro.'

On the job, she displayed keen intelligence and open-mindedness, but lacked a sense of humour, to the point that aides would have to nudge her to laugh when a visiting dignitary cracked a joke. She also possessed a fearsome temper when crossed and could curse like a navvy. A formidable politician, *The Independent* newspaper described her as 'a Viking warrior incarnate, smiting others not with the sword but with the strength of her beliefs'.[6]

Her first term as prime minister lasted only eight months, but she won office again on three other occasions: 1986–89, 1990–93 and 1993–96. During her time in power, she pursued causes close to her heart: extending parental leave, criminalising sexual harassment and expanding access to childcare. In addition, she came to international attention when, in 1986, she appointed eight women to her eighteen-person cabinet, which demonstrated her commitment to gender equality.

Despite her social democratic roots, in 1989 Brundtland supported changes to her party's constitution, removing references to socialism. She caused further consternation among the left-wing of her party when, during the economic downturn in the 1980s, she privatised state-owned enterprises and trimmed the welfare state. Her parliamentary opponent, Jan Syse, called this strategy 'Stealing Conservative clothes while we were out into the bathroom'.[7]

Brundtland explains her approach to politics differently. 'It is a combination of being willing to state things that many people are not ready to take yet – that's why I say there's a revolutionary part in me – but I am also a pragmatist. I do want to have followers so that we can get change.'[8] Despite her protestations, leftist critics accused her of pursuing neoliberalist policies.

While still serving in the Norwegian parliament, Brundtland's international reputation grew as she contributed to a number of high-profile committees. These included the Independent Commission on Security and Disarmament (1980) and the World Commission on Environment and Development (1983–87). She also spoke at international events: the Earth Summit in Rio in 1982, the UN Population and Development Conference in Cairo in 1994 and the UN's Fourth World Conference on Women held in Beijing in 1995. These forays into international affairs raised her profile outside Norway.

By 1996 Brundtland dominated Norwegian politics like no prime minister before her and was affectionately known as *landsmoderen* (mother of the nation). Alluding to her political stature, cartoonists often depicted Lilliputian politicians scuttling around her feet. Despite her popularity, with a rating hovering around an astonishing 90 per cent, she did what many politicians seldom do: she resigned at the top of her game. On 25 October 1996, Brundtland handed the reins over to Thorbjørn Jagland. After leaving the job, she enjoyed relating a conversation between a five-year-old boy and his father. 'Daddy', asked the child, 'on television today they said that a man was Prime Minister. Is it possible that a man can be Prime Minister?'[9]

Now free of any obligations, Brundtland and her husband retired to their cottage on Lake Mylla, where Arne carefully placed on her desk 500 sheets of clean white paper – his way of saying that she could spend the next few years fussing over her memoirs, with enough time out to spoil her grandchildren.

Soon, Brundtland's name was associated with a number of high-profile jobs, including heading the UN, the International Labor Organization and NATO. The one closest to her heart was that of director-general of WHO, which had become vacant when Hiroshi Nakajima decided not to seek a third term. In late 1997, she threw her cap into the ring. After campaigning around the world, on 27 January 1998, Brundtland emerged as the first female to head a major UN agency.

The best of times, the worst of times

Brundtland started the job burdened by history. In its short life, WHO had gone from being the jewel in the crown of the UN to a basket case. In the run-up to the election, editor of the prestigious *British Medical Journal*, Richard Smith, wrote an editorial that bluntly warned that the WHO needed to 'change or die'.[10] In her book *Betrayal of Trust*, health writer Laurie Garrett lamented the organisation's slow decline:

> The World Health Organization, once the conscience of global health, lost its way in the 1990s. Demoralized, rife with rumors of corruption and lacking leadership, WHO floundered.[11]

How had the WHO gone from being a valued and vigorous agency to barely surviving on life-support?

Conceived in San Francisco, at the same time as the UN, the WHO owed its early success to its structure. 'WHO is not a political body', explained Dr Karl Evang, one of its architects, 'We must all think and feel one for all and all for one.'[12] To protect its reputation as a technical agency, the WHO's governing body, the World Health Assembly, consists of health ministers who are free to vote as they please, not according to the dictates of their government. In this way, the architects of the WHO hoped to keep politics out.

In the early days, the WHO tackled smallpox, diphtheria, tetanus, whooping cough, poliomyelitis measles, malaria, tuberculosis, syphilis, women's and children's health, nutrition and environmental sanitation. Despite its modest budget, during the 1950s and 1960s, the WHO was one of the few success stories within the UN family, an achievement largely attributed to its ability to deliver worthwhile programmes on the ground.

It was its third director-general, Dr Halfdan Mahler, who had most profoundly changed the strategic direction of the WHO. At a WHO conference held in Alma-Ata (Kazak Soviet Republic, now Kazakhstan) during September 1978, he set out to reframe the global health problems within a wider context. Part of its final declaration stated:

> The Conference strongly reaffirms that health, which is a state of complete physical, mental, and social wellbeing, and not merely the absence of disease or infirmity, is a fundamental human right and that the attainment of the highest possible level of health is a most important world-wide social goal whose realization requires the action of many other social and economic sectors in addition to the health sector.[13]

In the years that followed, Mahler started to talk about 'a new development order' in which he argued that health could not be addressed without tackling social ills, such as the:

pernicious combination of unemployment and underemployment, economic impotence, scarcity of worldly goods, a low level of mostly irrelevant education, poor housing, poor sanitation, malnutrition, ill health, social apathy and, above all, the lack of will and initiative to make change for the better.[14]

Many western countries, however, felt uneasy about the WHO's new preoccupation with social reform, equity and human rights. They were convinced that the WHO had lost its way in an ideological cul-de-sac. In response, they started to divert some of their aid to other international organisations. The World Bank, in particular, benefited, as it showed that it was in tune with the neoliberal orthodoxy that had taken hold in the 1980s. Through its structural adjustment loans, the bank forced developing countries to introduce fees on its health services and rely more heavily on the private sector.

Mahler also oversaw programmes that incurred the displeasure of the powerful pharmaceutical industry. In particular, the International Federation of Pharmaceutical Manufacturers Association took umbrage when, in 1977, the WHO introduced a shortlist of essential drugs designed to help poor countries reduce imports of costly non-essential drugs. They saw this programme as an attack on the free market, and its mood did not improve when Mahler accused the industry of 'drug colonialism'.[15]

After Ronald Reagan's election as president, corporations with a grievance against the WHO found that they had a sympathetic ear in the White House. Angry with the WHO's perceived anti-business agenda, in 1982 the Administration froze the level of its contributions. In 1985, the US went further by unilaterally reducing its annual contribution by 20 per cent and further slashed its contributions in 1986 and 1987. Other major donors followed suit. At one point, the US even threatened to leave the WHO altogether.

When Mahler left the WHO in 1988, his successor faced a host of problems: donors were unhappy with the direction the WHO was pursuing; drug companies were convinced that the organisation was hostile to business; tight budgets that resulted in programmes being wound down; and the US was openly hostile and threatened to withdraw its membership.

The election of Dr Hiroshi Nakajima, however, did not bode well for the WHO. An unpopular choice, he only managed to win the vote through the efforts of the Japanese government, which exerted undue pressure on developing countries, including threats to withdraw trade concessions and aid if they did not vote for its candidate.

On taking office, Nakajima immediately scaled back the WHO's more controversial programmes. Nakajima also moderated his rhetoric so as not to upset commercial interests, and a number of programmes that might have drawn criticism were placed on the backburner. Nakajima's management skills were poor and during his watch the organisation fell victim to cronyism and corruption. In addition, his poor English thwarted his efforts to communicate a coherent vision for the WHO, which 'floundered in a maze of incomprehension'.[16]

Brundtland's challenge was to fill the policy vacuum created by Nakajima, repair relations with key stakeholders, restore the organisation's credibility and reassert the WHO's authority over the global health agenda.

Opening Pandora's Box

One of Brundtland's priorities was to engage with stakeholders, and during her term Brundtland enthusiastically forged partnerships with other international agencies, NGOs, charitable foundations and drug companies. Explaining her strategy, she told the World Health Assembly in May 1998:

> The private sector has an important role to play both in technology development and the provision of services. We need open and constructive relations with the private sector and industry, knowing where our roles differ and where they may complement each other. ... [W]hether we like it or not, we are dependent on our partners to achieve health for all.[17]

There were other reasons why the WHO embraced partnerships, as Dr David Nabarro, Brundtland's executive director and *chef de cabinet*, explained:

> We certainly need private financing. For the past decade governments' financial contributions have dwindled. The main sources of funding are the private sector and the financial markets. And since the American economy is the world's richest, we must make the WHO attractive to the United States and the financial markets.[18]

As many of these partnerships involved the pharmaceutical industry, Brundtland was able to show that the WHO was no longer anti-business.

One of the first was the Global Alliance for Vaccines and Immunization (GAVI). Launched in January 2000, GAVI supplied vaccines to protect children against a variety of preventable, life-threatening diseases, including diarrhoea and pneumonia. Its partners consisted of governments, research institutions, NGOs, philanthropists like the Gates Foundation, the pharmaceutical industry, the World Bank, and the UN's Children's Fund (UNICEF). In its first decade, GAVI successfully raised $2.9 billion, immunised more than 250 million children and prevented over 5 million deaths.

With so many partners, Brundtland positioned the WHO at the centre of such programmes by adroitly exploiting the organisation's strengths: its technical expertise and access to global health networks.

GAVI became the flagship of WHO's new approach to health, and Brundtland seized every opportunity to talk it up. Political scientists from the University of Oslo, Benedicte Bull and Desmond McNeill, however, cast doubts over the programme's lasting value.

> It is relatively clear that the pharmaceutical companies have benefited greatly from the expansion of the market due to increased funding for vaccination resulting from GAVI's activities; the prices still reflects supply and demand and the limitations of the current patents system, rather than any form of corporate philanthropy.[19]

Looking at the broader context, Carol Bellamy, executive director of UNICEF, saw dangers in chasing such public–private partnerships.

> [I]t is dangerous to assume that the goals of the private sector are somehow synonymous with those of the United Nations, because they most emphatically are not.[20]

As the WHO sets international standards, norm and health policies, its growing dependence on private funding made it vulnerable to inappropriate influence from the corporate sector. Pursuing this argument, *The Lancet*'s Richard Horton concluded that under Brundtland, the 'demands of the private sector trump public-health principles'.[21]

A test of how the WHO might handle potential conflicts arose in November 2001, when the WTO started a new round of negotiations in Doha. In the run-up to this meeting, developing countries presented proposals to relax the Agreement on Trade-Related Aspects of Intellectual Property Rights so that the poor could afford essential drugs still in patent. Such reforms were preferable to relying on charitable donations from pharmaceutical companies that might be terminated at any time, should a sponsor lose interest.

For the pharmaceutical industry, this was a serious threat to their profits and it lobbied hard to protect the integrity of TRIPS because, as Pfizer chairman William C. Steere Jr. explained, the industry 'lives and dies on intellectual property'.[22]

The WHO was caught in the middle, with both sides eager to secure its support. Reflecting on its conduct during the Doha negotiations, Horton observed, 'WHO's voice has been almost silent.'[23] Jamie Love, director of the Consumer Project on Technology, even accused Brundtland of forsaking the needs of poor countries.

[S]he was both intimidated by the USA, the European Commission, and big drug companies, and unrealistically impressed by the goodwill of the drug companies, and not impressed enough by what our side was doing at the time. We had built a strong social movement, and Brundtland's efforts were harmful, not helpful, because she was becoming part of the big pharma PR machine.

He further suggested that behind the scenes, 'Gro was working closely with the drug companies, and trying to work out tiered pricing deals to undermine the compulsory licensing initiatives and the Doha negotiations. She was working with Merck, GSK [GlaxoSmithKline] and [Bill] Gates on this.'[24]

Brundtland's failure to challenge the drug companies also attracted internal criticism. In 2002, Daphne Fresle, a former top official in the WHO office that monitors worldwide pharmaceutical use, resigned in protest at the agency's unhealthy relationship with drug makers. She was 'appalled … by WHO's unwillingness to speak with a strong public health voice on issues which are of such vital importance to the developing countries who should be the main concern of this organization'. Fresle further complained that the WHO had abandoned its traditional goal, 'health for all', by kowtowing to powerful countries and transnational drug companies.[25]

NGOs have also criticised the reliance on partnership programmes. For example, Lisa Hayes from Health Action International attacked partnerships, claiming that pharmaceutical companies that give 'money to WHO programs or working with the organization could be seen as a way to deflect criticism about corporate strategy or drug prices for essential medicines'.[26]

For once, drug companies' lobbying proved unsuccessful, and on 14 November 2001, WTO members signed the *Declaration on the TRIPS Agreement and Public Health*, which stated: 'We agree that the TRIPS Agreement does not and should not prevent members from taking measures to protect public health.'[27] Two years later, TRIPS was grudgingly reformed to allow less developed countries better access to affordable drugs.

Brundtland's heavy reliance on partnerships was also blamed for distorting the WHO's priorities.[28] Important areas, such as maternal and child health, nutrition, food safety, and preventable diseases like obesity and alcohol abuse, received less attention than infectious diseases due to the lack of cashed-up partners to fund such programmes. Brundtland, however, saw little choice but to push ahead with WHO's partnership programme, believing that she could manage its downsides.

During her tenure, which finished in 2003, WHO entered into seventy-nine partnerships and supported a number of joint projects that came out of the UN's Global Compact. These ventures helped generate an extra budgetary income of $1.5 billion in 2001, almost double that of the $842 million in contributions from member countries. Even after Brundtland left office, private donors continued to make up the bulk of the WHO's budget.

The economics of health

As important as partnerships with the private sector were to Brundtland, she also resolved to reconnect with rich donor countries, whose contributions had dropped off alarmingly during the 1990s. Only with their engagement could major inroads be made to improve global health, particularly among the poor.

One reason that health had lost ground was because the WHO's traditional power base had little control of the purse strings, as Brundtland explained:

> I knew as a political leader that if these poor health ministers are going to deal with all these important issues on their own, with no support from the finance minister, from the prime minister, they are lost. The way of moving health onto the political agenda within countries and internationally was part of my profile.[29]

She also needed a better way to market health, which, under Dr Mahler, had been framed as a human right. Such an argument might appeal to ideologues from developing countries, but it did not resonate with donor countries. To shift health into the mainstream, Brundtland believed that the WHO needed to put together a compelling case 'that sound investments in health can be one of the most cost-effective ways of promoting development and progress'.[30] To succeed, she knew she would have to challenge the economic orthodoxy by arguing that rather than 'being an unproductive consumer of public budgets, health is now gradually seen as a central element of productivity itself'.[31]

To build the case around this proposition, in January 2000 Brundtland launched the Commission on Macroeconomics and Health, complaining that too 'few finance officials and development economists have so far explored the potential importance of health investment as an instrument for reducing poverty'.[32] Brundtland asked eminent development economist, Jeffrey Sachs, to head her newly formed Commission. Other members of the Commission included former ministers of finance and economists from the World Bank, IMF, WTO and UNDP. There were, however, comparatively few public health experts on the Commission.

Raking over historic records from the previous two centuries, the Commission discovered that health interventions had contributed to the economic take off by various countries. This data suggests that improving health is an effective strategy to help people out of poverty. The Commission then went on to quantify the cost effectiveness of different interventions.

The Commission's report, *Macroeconomics and Health: Investing in Health for Economic Development*, was published in December 2001.[33] Designed to appeal to donor countries, it demonstrated that modest increases in aid would save 8 million lives per year by 2010. Furthermore, it showed that 'improvements in health translate into higher incomes, higher economic growth and reduced population growth'.[34] By increasing aid from $6 billion to $27 billion per year by 2007, the Commission predicted a payoff of more than $360 billion per year by 2015–20.

The report provided another justification for increasing aid. Infused with the language of embedded liberalism, it suggested that action for health will help 'address the strains and inequities of globalization', and that by building 'a partnership of rich and poor of unrivaled significance, offering the gift of life itself to millions of the world's dispossessed … [it would prove] to all doubters that globalization can indeed work to the benefit of all humankind'.[35]

For Brundtland, the report was important because it challenged the 'anachronistic' notion that good health would follow economic growth and higher income levels. Known as the 'trickle down' effect, this argument was promoted by mainstream neoliberals. Instead, she promoted an alternative proposition: '[A] healthy population is as much a prerequisite of growth as a result of it.'[36] Giving every appearance of being a chicken-and-egg argument, the Commission's report allowed Brundtland to refute the proposition that wealth-creates-health by arguing that health-creates-wealth.

This important distinction illustrates how Brundtland was willing to cannily adapt to the prevailing neoliberal environment, but on her own terms. Associate Professor Nitsan Chorev from Brown University describes the strategy employed by the WHO:

> While embracing economic reasoning, prioritizing cost-effective programs, and accepting market-driven solutions and business-friendly arrangements, however, the WHO bureaucracy was also able to strategically reinterpret the neoliberal prescriptions so that the new policies incorporated the bureaucracy's own goals.[37]

Brundtland's efforts undoubtedly helped draw the attention of political leaders to the economically debilitating effects of ill health. As a result, donor governments have a renewed confidence in the WHO and have steadily increased their contributions to health, although nowhere near that envisaged by the Commission.

Facing off Big Tobacco

Economic arguments were also an important part of Brundtland's attack on tobacco marketing, an issue that she had long been passionate about. As far back as 1983, the tobacco industry became aware of her campaign against smoking in Norway. In an internal memorandum, one of its executives warned: 'We need to watch her; if she goes global, it could be bad for business.'[38]

Like many projects she inherited from her predecessor, little had been done, even though the Tobacco Free Initiative had been on the WHO's work programme since 1996, when the World Health Assembly called for the development of a public health treaty to curb the spread of tobacco addiction. Determined to see this project through, Brundtland fast-tracked negotiations, setting a deadline of 2003.

As a health problem, tobacco use is the largest preventable cause of disease and death, causing about 5 million deaths annually. With tobacco companies aggressively moving into developing countries where anti-smoking legislation seldom exists, the toll is expected to rise to 8.4 million by 2020.[39]

This trend is a direct result of globalisation, with tobacco companies actively lobbying for greater trade liberalisation. 'As international tariff barriers are eliminated, access to important global markets for our brands is certain to improve', predicted an internal document by British American Tobacco (BAT). '[T]he WTO's binding rules for "fair play" in international trade are of real practical significance to BAT.'[40] As trade barriers disappeared, the large tobacco companies successfully challenged the monopolies of national tobacco companies. Once established, they employed sophisticated marketing techniques to substantially increase the number of smokers in developed countries, particularly among the young.

For Brundtland, a new anti-tobacco treaty would counter the undesirable impacts of economic liberalisation, and it demonstrated her support for the UN's efforts to civilise globalisation.

Brundtland also realised that any move to regulate tobacco marketing could be used by the WHO's enemies to suggest a relapse to its anti-business attitudes. To counter this possibility, Brundtland shrewdly painted the tobacco industry as a pariah by pointing out that a 'cigarette is a euphemism for a cleverly crafted product that delivers just the right amount of nicotine to keep its user addicted for life before killing the person'. Speaking at the Ninth International Conference of Drug Regulatory Authorities in Berlin, she continued this line of attack:

> The tobacco companies will inevitably tell you they are selling a simple agricultural product – chopped up tobacco leaves rolled into a paper tube. This is categorically

untrue. Cigarettes are one of the most highly engineered consumer products available ... the problem is the product itself.[41]

The WHO responded to this preventable plague with the Framework Convention on Tobacco Control (FCTC), which introduced measures to deter smoking. The treaty restricted the tobacco companies' ability to recruit new smokers by placing limits on advertising and promotions, as well as discouraging the habit in existing smokers by introducing compulsory health labels and advocating higher sales taxes on cigarettes.

Over the next five years, the tobacco companies waged an intense campaign to defeat the FCTC. As in past campaigns, they used surrogates (such as tobacco farmers) to wage the war against the WHO; funded research to cast doubts on the effectiveness of tobacco controls; and launched a scare campaign that claimed that tobacco controls would reduce employment and damage economies.

To give itself the best chance of success, the WHO managed to co-opt the World Bank to its cause. Up until the early 1990s, the bank supported tobacco growing and manufacturing, which it argued contributed to the productive base of developing countries. This changed in 1994, when a World Bank study revealed that tobacco produced an annual global loss of $200 billion.[42] In May 1999, the World Bank followed this report with *Curbing the Epidemic*, which concluded that the FCTC would improve health without harming economies in most countries.[43] This economic analysis was an important weapon in the WHO's armoury, and when this report was launched at the fifty-second meeting of the World Health Assembly, it helped win support for the FCTC. Above all, the report indicated that only a handful of countries would be disadvantaged and recommended measures to counter negative impacts.

Realising that the World Bank report was critical to the success of the FCTC, the tobacco companies commissioned economists and think tanks, in particular the Institute of Economic Affairs in London and the Liberty Institute in New Delhi, to critique *Curbing the Epidemic*. Had the source of funding been declared, it would have undermined its authority.[44] As it turned out, asking well-known neoliberal think tanks to undertake the analysis was a mistake, as they were seen as ideologues that wanted to get rid of most regulations.

Having encountered dirty tricks from the tobacco companies in Norway, Brundtland suspected that the industry was executing a largely convert campaign against the FCTC. To counter this threat, she appointed a panel of experts to expose its skulduggery. In 2000, Brundtland released the panel's report, which accused tobacco companies of deliberately trying to subvert the WHO in an 'elaborate, well financed, sophisticated and usually invisible' campaign. It went on to show that the tobacco companies spent vast amounts of money:

diverting attention from the public health issues raised by tobacco use, attempting to reduce budgets for the scientific and policy activities carried out by WHO, pitting other UN agencies against WHO, seeking to foster views that WHO's tobacco control program was a 'First World' agenda carried out at the expense of the developing world, distorting the results of important scientific studies on tobacco, and discrediting WHO as an institution.[45]

Outmanoeuvred by Brundtland, the industry made one last desperate effort to derail the FCTC. An internal document from Philip Morris, dated January 2000, proposed a self-regulatory regime that 'may in itself divert the Organization [WHO] from moving more rapidly against the industry'. It was also an opportunity to divide and conquer.

> A negotiated regulatory regime that might be global in scope and application would inevitably have to take into account the views of the governments of many of these developing countries, which have constituencies which are far less in tune with the more irrational of our critics in the developed world.[46]

On 11 September 2001, the major tobacco companies released their alternative, *International Tobacco Products Marketing Standards*, which promised to implement a voluntary programme to limit marketing activities that targeted young people. A quick analysis of the code showed that it was vague and was much weaker than existing legislation in many countries.

As battle-hardened as they were, tobacco lobbyists found that they had been cleverly outflanked by Brundtland. On 21 May 2003, the World Health Assembly adopted the WHO's Framework Convention on Tobacco Control, and it entered into force in 2005. By 19 October 2014, it had been embraced by 177 countries.[47]

The FCTC broke new ground for the WHO. Using the long-neglected article 19 of its charter, the WHO created a set of international rules that legally bound its members, although there are no sanctions for countries that ignore the FCTC. Nevertheless, it represents a potentially powerful governance feature to the global architecture, as Brundtland explained:

> This global treaty – the first ever under the auspices of WHO – could mark the beginning of a new phase in building an effective rules-based international system for combating the many other global health challenges we face.[48]

It is much too early to decide whether the FCTC represents a new model for spreading the rule of law to non-economic areas, but if it does, it should significantly strengthen the global architecture.

Notes

1. R.C. Horton, 'WHO: The Casualties and Compromises of Renewal', *The Lancet*, 359: 9317 (2002), 1605–11, quote on p. 1605.
2. Gro Brundtland quoted by Fred Hauptfuhrer in 'On Top of the World', *People* magazine (20 April 1987), pp. 35–9, quote on p. 37.
3. B.O. Solheim, *On Top of the World: Women's Political Leadership in Scandinavia and Beyond* (Westport, CT: Greenwood Publishing Group, 2000), pp. 78–9.
4. C. Mosey, 'The Iron Lady v Superwoman', *The Observer* (7 September 1986), p. 14.
5. N. Gibbs, 'Norway's Radical Daughter', *Time Magazine World* (24 June 2001).
6. L. O'Hanlon, 'Profile: Too Big for Her Roots', *The Independent* (11 September 1994).
7. Jan P. Syse quoted by Harald Kjølås in 'Gro Harlem Brundtland', *Allkunne nynorsk kulturhistorie*. Entry updated on 1 July 2013. Retrieved form: www.allkunne.no/default.aspx?menu=85&id=3718 (accessed 30 March 2015)
8. A. Young, 'PM to Welcome a Personal Hero', *New Zealand Herald* (7 June 2005).
9. G.H. Brundtland, *Madam Prime Minister* (New York: Farrar, Straus and Giroux, 2002), p. 452.
10. R. Smith, 'The WHO: Change or Die', *British Medical Journal*, 310: 6979 (1995), 543–4.
11. L. Garrett, *Betrayal of Trust: Collapse of Global Health* (New York: Hyperion, 2000), p. 8.
12. Dr Karl Evang inaugural address to the second World Health Assembly, quoted by Amy L.S. Staples in *The Birth of Development* (Ohio: Kent State University Press, 2006), p. 148
13. Declaration of Alma-Ata 'Health for All by the Year 2000', International Conference on Primary Health Care, Alma-Ata, USSR, 6–12 September, 1978.
14. Twenty-Third Meeting of the Pan-American Health Organization held in Washington, DC on 29 September 1975.
15. M. Silverman, P.R. Lee and M. Lydecker, *Prescriptions of Death* (Berkeley: University of California Press, 1982), p. 133.
16. F. Godlee, 'WHO in Crisis', *British Medical Journal*, 309: 6966 (1994), 1424–8.
17. Speech delivered by Gro Brundtland to the Fifty-first World Health Assembly in Geneva on 13 May 1998.
18. David Nabarro quoted by Jean-Loup Motchane in 'Health for All or Riches for Some: WHO's Responsible?', *International Journal of Health Services*, 33:2 (2003), 395–400, quote on p. 396.
19. B. Bull and M. McNeill, *Development Issues in Global Governance: Public-Private Partnerships and Market Multilateralism* (London and New York: Routledge, 2007), p. 84.
20. Statement issued by Carol Bellamy titled 'Public, Private and Civil Society' released at the Harvard international development conference on 'Sharing Responsibilities: Public, Private and Civil Society', at Harvard University, Cambridge, MA, on 16 April 1999.
21. R. Horton, 'WHO: The Casualties and Compromises of Renewal', *The Lancet*, 359:9317 (2002), 1605–11, quote on p. 1607.

22 B. Gellman, 'A Turning Point that Left Millions Behind', *Washington Post* (28 December 2000), p. A1.
23 R. Horton, 'WHO's Next Director-General: The Person and the Programme', *The Lancet*, 360:9348 (2002), 1799–800, quote on p. 1799.
24 J.P. Love, personal communication (30 August 2012).
25 Letter from Daphne A. Fresle to Dr Brundtland, dated 23 December 2001, and cited by Jean-Loup Motchane in 'Health for All or Riches for Some: WHO's Responsible?', 399.
26 L. Hayes, 'Industry's Growing Influence at the WHO', *Global Policy Forum* (15 February 2001).
27 World Trade Organization, 'Declaration on the TRIPS Agreement and Public Health', Ministerial Conference, Fourth Session. Doha, WT/MIN(01)/DEC/W/2 (2001).
28 E. Ollila, 'Global Health Priorities – Priorities of the Wealthy?' *Globalization and Health*, 1:6 (2005).
29 G.H. Brundtland, 'Role of WHO: A Leader's Perspective', talk delivered to the Harvard School of Public Health on 24 May 2011.
30 G.H. Brundtland, 'WHO – The Way Ahead', statement delivered by the Director-General to the Executive Board at its 103rd session in Geneva on 25 January 1999.
31 WHO, 'Turn the Tables on Ill Health and Poverty, says WHO Chief', Press Release (14 January 1999).
32 WHO, 'WHO, Internationally-Renowned Economists Launch Commission on Macroeconomics and Health', Press Release (18 January 2000).
33 WHO Commission on Macroeconomics and Health, *Macroeconomics and Health: Investing in Health for Economic Development* (Geneva: WHO, 2001).
34 WHO Commission on Macroeconomics and Health, *Macroeconomics and Health*, p. 3.
35 WHO Commission on Macroeconomics and Health, *Macroeconomics and Health*, introductory remarks.
36 G.H. Brundtland, 'The Globalization of Health', *Seton Hall Journal of Diplomacy and International Relations*, 4:2 (2003), 7–12, quote on p. 10.
37 N. Chorev, 'Restructuring Neoliberalism at the World Health Organization', *Review of International Political Economy*, 20:4 (2013), 627–66, quote on p. 628.
38 K. Senior, 'Brundtland's Legacy', *The Lancet Oncology*, 4:1 (2003), 3.
39 D. Bettcher, C. Subramanian and E. Guindon, *Confronting the Tobacco Epidemic in an Era of Trade Liberalization*, Commission on Macroeconomics and Health (Geneva: World Health Organization, 2001), Paper No. WG4:8.
40 British American Tobacco on International Trade [Draft III], Legacy Tobacco Documents Library, Bates 322253320-322253331 (undated).
41 Gro Brundtland quoted in a press release 'Cigarettes Should Be Regulated Like Other Drugs, says Director-General', Press Release WHO/26 (26 April 1999).
42 H. Barnum, 'The Economic Burden of the Global Trade in Tobacco', *Tobacco Control*, 3:4 (1994), 358–61.
43 P. Jha and F. Chaloupka, *Curbing the Epidemic* (Washington, DC: World Bank, 1999).
44 H.M. Mamudu, R. Hammond and S. Glantz, 'Tobacco Industry Attempts to Counter

the World Bank Report Curbing the Epidemic and Obstruct the WHO Framework Convention on Tobacco Control', *Social Science and Medicine*, 67:11 (2008), 1690–9.
45 Committee of Experts on Tobacco Industry Documents, *Tobacco Company Strategies to Undermine Tobacco Control Activities at the World Health Organization*. WHO Paper No. 7 (Geneva: World Health Organization, July 2000), p. 1.
46 Philip Morris, 'Why Look at Setting Up a Regulatory Body? The World Health Organization and Tobacco', Bates No. 2072183811/3823 (January 2000).
47 WHO, 'Parties to the WHO Framework Convention on Tobacco Control', updated on 19 October 2014. Data retrieved from: www.who.int/fctc/signatories_parties/en/ (accessed 4 January 2015).
48 G.H. Brundtland, 'The Globalization of Health', *Seton Hall Journal of Diplomacy and International Relations*, 4:2 (2003), 7–12, quote on p. 12.

Epilogue

> Keeping his eyes fixed upon the Castle, K. went ahead, nothing else mattered to him. But as he came closer he was disappointed in the Castle, it was only a rather miserable little tower pieced together from village houses, distinctive only because everything was perhaps built out of stone, but the paint had long since flaked off, and the stone seemed to be crumbling. (Franz Kafka, *The Castle*)

The success of postwar globalisation is not simply the result of the onward march of technology that has brought people and markets closer together, but a conscious decision by successive generations of architects to build institutions, rules and norms that would spread the rule of law. These formal and informal structures not only made the current era of globalisation unique, but were designed to make the architecture sufficiently robust to protect it from external threats.

The ascent of globalisation has certainly not been without its challenges, not least being the Cold War, the Nixon Shock and anti-globalisation protests that peaked with the Battle of Seattle. But on each occasion, new generations of architects stepped forward to improvise solutions, to strengthen its superstructure and even to expand its frontiers. Not every change has been for the better, and problems remain, particularly making globalisation deliver a fairer, more equitable, securer and more just world, but it also can claim many significant achievements, such as raising over a billion people out of extreme poverty and creating opportunities for public and private cooperation in addressing pressing global problems.

Entering the twenty-first century, globalisation faces a new set of challenges, any of which could bring about its end.

In the years since the fall of the Berlin Wall, US triumphalism has posed a grave threat to the rule of law, which went into overdrive during the presidency of George W. Bush. The result was an alarming rise in US unilateralism, which has gravely wounded the authority of global governance. 'What you're going to get from this administration is "à la carte multilateralism"', explained Richard Haass, who at the time was the State Department's director of policy planning.[1]

As it turned out, there was little on the multilateral menu that the US liked. During its two terms the Bush Administration withdrew from the Anti-Ballistic Missile Treaty, Kyoto Protocol and Comprehensive Test Ban Treaty; refused to accept amendments to strengthen of the Biological Weapons Convention; opposed the International Criminal Court and undermined its authority after it was created;[2] refused to ratify the Law of the Sea[3] and the Anti-Personnel Mine Ban Convention; gutted the treaty limiting the proliferation of small arms; and, after 9/11, defied protections for POWs contained in the Geneva Convention and flouted international law by transferring prisoners to countries like Egypt, Poland and Pakistan under the CIA's extraordinary rendition programme, where they were tortured.

When it came to the 'War on Terror,' the US announced that the game had totally changed – countries were either 'with us or against us',[4] and rather than seeking international consensus or even approval through the United Nations, the 'Bush administration was, in effect, announcing unilaterally the new rules of the global security order', posited political scientist John Ikenberry. 'The old liberal hegemonic rules, institutions, and bargains were giving way to new American-imposed global arrangements.'[5] Rather than international security being a collective responsibility, Bush placed his faith in 'coalitions of the willing' to attack global terrorism. Led by the US, such coalitions were formed to invade Iraq and Afghanistan, conduct drone attacks to destroy Taliban cells in a number of other countries and fly bombing sorties against the Islamic State (ISIL). Justifying such interventions, Haass explained: 'The Security Council is not the sole custodian of what is legitimate',[6] dismissing a key tenet of the global security order established in 1945.

The US was not alone in believing that international institutions were too timid, cumbersome and dysfunctional. Although usually for different motives, other countries have embraced 'coalitions of the willing' as a practical way to reduce protectionism, protect the environment, fight poverty and improve health. The difficulty with this strategy is that it is fragmenting the global polity and debasing the principle of collective responsibility embedded in the postwar order.

The economic order, in particular, is also fraying, with multilateral trade giving way to regional blocs. Such coalitions of the willing gained currency after it became clear that the Doha Round of multilateral trade negotiations were in dire straits and there was little prospect that the 159 of countries that made up the WTO would unanimously agree to major reductions in tariffs and quotas, particularly those protecting agricultural goods.[7]

This strategy drew fire from former WTO president Peter Sutherland, who argued that such blocs would damage the principles on which the global trading order was built: universal laws that are non-discriminatory. Sutherland worried that a 'spaghetti bowl' of regional agreements would result in 'damage to the credibility of the WTO' and have a lasting impact 'not merely on trade, but on political relationships more generally'. Ominously, he warned that the world could 'revert to earlier, more dangerous times',[8] alluding to the 1930s when competing trading blocs led the world into treacherous waters. At that time, Germany dominated the central European trade bloc, Britain was at the heart of the Commonwealth bloc, the US used reciprocal trade agreements with various Latin American countries to consolidate the western hemisphere bloc, and Japan was aggressively building its Greater East Asia Co-Prosperity Sphere. By the end of that decade, these blocs formed the core of military alliances that fought out the Second World War.

Unfortunately, there are worrying signs that regional trading blocs, like those in the 1930s, are once again contributing to political instability.

Take the example of the Trans-Pacific Partnership (TPP), which is being negotiated by the US, Japan, Australia, Vietnam, Mexico and a number of other countries in the Asia-Pacific region. The notable exclusion is China, which has good reason to believe that one of the purposes of the TPP is to isolate it economically and politically, in an attempt to check its rise as a superpower.[9] In response, China has put its support behind a rival trading bloc – the Regional Comprehensive Economic Partnership[10] – which includes sixteen Asia-Pacific countries,[11] but not the US. It is also creating a web of bilateral agreements, with the US once again a notable exclusion.[12]

On the other side of the world, the US and EU are negotiating a similar agreement, the Transatlantic Trade and Investment Partnership (TTIP), which shares strategic objectives with the TPP. According to the *Financial Times*:

> [T]he mooted EU–US deal is about writing the rules of global commerce before the Chinese can. It is also about making sure that trade between the two economies, which together now account for just under half of global gross domestic product, is as efficient as it can be so that they can compete in a bigger game with China.[13]

US Secretary of State Hillary Clinton called this agreement an 'economic NATO',[14] suggesting that the west was determined to exclude rather than accommodate a rising China. This view was reinforced by EU Trade Commissioner Karel De Gucht, who claimed that the agreement 'is about the weight of the western, free world in world economic and political affairs'.[15]

Any move to impose western values on the TTIP could backfire by 'inducing the Global South, Russia and Brazil to rally round the Chinese flag, just to thwart EU–US standard-setting ambitions', suggests Peter van Ham, senior research fellow at the Clingendael Institute.[16] The result might well be the rise of a unified anti-western bloc. Should this happen, argues Mark Leonard, director of the European Council on Foreign Relations, the world could enter a 'strange new form of bipolarity that will superficially resemble the Cold War more than the world of the past two decades' as western powers go about building 'a world without China' and China and its partners respond by creating 'a world without the West'.[17]

Once mega trade blocs form, there is an ever-present danger that friction between them could lead to open conflict, as has already occurred in the Ukraine. The European Union's expansion eastwards, in the wake of the fall of the Soviet Union, threatens Russia and frustrates its ambition to carve out its own sphere of influence by creating the Eurasian Economic Community and Customs Union among the former territories and satellites of the USSR. Having won over President Viktor Yanukovych, who was forging closer ties between the Ukraine and Russia, this policy was abruptly overturned in February 2014 when a popular uprising turned the Ukraine towards Europe. This policy was confirmed when pro-western Petro Poroshenko won the presidential election in May 2014. In this instance, what started as shadow-boxing between two trading blocs flamed into aggression, resulting in the annexation of Crimea by Russia and insurgency in the east of the country. This 'civil war' is being covertly incited by Russia, chillingly reminiscent of the proxy wars employed by the superpowers during the Cold War.

In a pale imitation of US unilateralism, China has started to assume the same privileges as an up-and-coming superpower by claiming vast parts of the East and South China Sea within territorial waters of Vietnam, Japan, Brunei, Indonesia, Taiwan, Malaysia and the Philippines. Rather than resolve this dispute by using international law, on 31 March 2014 Foreign Ministry spokesperson Hong Lei attacked the proposal by the Philippines to have the dispute arbitrated by the International Court of Justice, declaring that: 'It is a political provocation by abusing international legal means', and going on to ominously threaten the Philippines by telling its government that if they tried to stop Chinese occupation then it would 'have to take the consequences caused by its provocative actions'.[18] From these comments, other countries in the region realised that they could expect little comfort from international law in the face of Chinese aggression.

Another challenge to the cohesion and integrity of the postwar order is posed by the global financial crisis and its aftermath.

In November 2008, when it looked as if the world's economy could be entering into another Great Depression, President Bush summoned the leaders of the world's twenty largest economies to Washington to discuss a coordinated response to the crisis.[19] The next meeting of the G-20, as it became known, was held in September 2009 in London, where participants agreed to a package of well overdue regulatory reforms to the financial system.

This package also looked to reform the IMF by allowing emerging economies like China, India and Brazil a greater say in its governance, although it allowed the US to retain its de facto veto.[20] Even though this reform was supported by all members of the G-20, including Barack Obama, it was opposed by the US Congress, effectively vetoing the reform. US intransigence promoted Martin Parkinson, secretary of the Australian Treasury to warn that the IMF might soon find itself replaced by 'a growing web of sub-global overlapping forums, institutions and arrangements ... [that] present a risk to international cooperation – and at the very time when it's needed most'.[21]

As for the remainder of the package, over the next few years many G-20 members buckled under intense lobbying by the financial sector, leading to them to weaken or delay particular reforms and shelve the rest.

To make matters worse, under domestic pressure to stimulate employment, seventeen members of the G-20 implemented forty-seven measures that restricted trade at the expense of other countries or provided subsidies to help local firms, according to a 2009 World Bank report.[22]

There were other ways that some governments sought to unfairly support their exports. On 27 September 2010, the Brazilian Finance Minister Guido Mantega attacked China, who he claimed had started an 'international currency war'.[23] He was reacting to China's manipulation of the value of the Yuan against the US dollar. The currency war escalated when the US,[24] UK and Japan joined the fray by employing 'quantitative easing' – printing money to buy government bonds – to lower the value of their currencies. As a consequence, developing countries have been particularly hard hit as their currencies were forced to appreciate, unfairly damaging the competitiveness of their exports. This war has also poisoned trust between members of the G-20, who have been less willing to pursue coordinated policies to reform the global economy.

The result, according to a 2014 study conducted by academics Bin Gu and Tong Liu, is a 'tendency toward unilateralism and national divergence increases, forcing international financial regulatory efforts to retreat behind national borders, and resulting in a fragmentation of global financial markets'.[25] The Institute of International Finance described this trend as financial 'Balkanization' warning that such actions 'increase the fragility of the global financial system'.[26] In 2009, *The Economist* further suggested: 'Economic nationalism – the urge to keep jobs and capital at home – is both turning the economic crisis into a political one and threatening the world with depression.'[27]

One reason that political leaders are looking inwards is that they are responding to an upsurge of isolationism, nationalism and populism. On the streets, extremists have found a ready audience as they blame globalisation for the financial meltdown and austerity measures that followed, going on to scapegoat immigrants, in a xenophobic campaign reminiscent of the anti-Semitic movements of the 1930s.

The global financial crisis also showed up the weakness in another building block of the postwar order. Corporate social responsibility has been feted for creating voluntary norms that transnational corporations would use to impose self-restraint, and help soften the caprices of the free market. If 'responsibility' is synonymous with ethics and morality, then CSR did little to moderate the excesses of bankers, according to Leo Martin, former executive of the accounting firm KPMG.

The rise and rise of corporate responsibility reports might make the casual observer think there has been a revolution in responsible business behaviour. But the storm in the financial markets suggests otherwise, and the curve of the graph showing the number of scandals involving mis-selling, bribery, corruption and greenwash is rising strongly.[28]

Martin wryly observed that the very companies caught up in scandals were also writing corporate responsibility reports – and even winning awards for them. So rather than CSR being a sign of saintliness, many in the financial sector inadvertently brought down plagues onto the financial system of biblical proportions. The problem was that most of the codes and standards on which their CSR programmes relied dealt with issues like sexual diversity policies, limiting greenhouse emissions and charitable giving, but most were silent on how to employ ethical values in their day-to-day business decisions, and those that did were certainly not acted upon.[29] The problem runs deeper, according to Jonathon Porritt, author of *Capitalism As If the World Matters*. Singling out the banking industry, he says, 'there are also too many examples of corporate responsibility deployed by companies with fundamentally amoral business models that cannot stand up to scrutiny'.[30]

Another test for the global order is whether it can rally countries to cooperate on containing climate change.

At first, the signs were positive. In December 1997, 84 signed the Kyoto Protocol, and since then the number has grown to 193. While its targets were modest and it was riddled with loopholes, it nevertheless reflected a consensus among governments that this was a problem needing urgent attention. This consensus began to fall apart when President Bush withdrew his support from the Kyoto Protocol in March 2001, making the US the first major country to stand outside the agreement.[31]

A new round of negotiations started in Copenhagen (Denmark), and continued in Cancún (Mexico), Durban (South Africa), Doha (Qatar), Warsaw (Poland) and Lima (Peru). Unfortunately, progress has been slow and few concrete proposals have been agreed to so far. Realistically, there is little prospect that 196 will unanimously agree to strong measures necessary to achieve the goal set in Cancún in 2010 to limit global warming to 2°C by 2050. Working quietly behind the scenes are countries like Canada, Australia and Saudi Arabia, with large stocks of fossil fuels, which are likely to undermine any agreement that will affect their vested interests.

In anticipation of failure of these multilateral negotiations, a number of coalitions of the willing have sprung up. They include the Major Economies Forum on Energy and Climate, Asia-Pacific Partnership on Clean Development and Climate; the G-8[32] and G-20, which include climate change on their agendas; the Cities for Climate Protection whose 650 member municipalities commit to reduce urban greenhouse gas emissions; and the World Economic Forum and UN's Global Compact, which have brokered public–private partnerships to tackle climate change. There are also private coalitions, such as the E-8, comprising the world's largest electricity companies; the Worldwide Fund for Nature's Climate Savers programme that works with some of the world's largest companies including Sony, Coca-Cola and Nike; and the Investor Network on Climate Risk.

While each of these coalitions has made useful, albeit modest contributions, they have also unintentionally relieved pressure from the international community to come up with a collective and universal treaty on climate change. It also allows the unwilling to keep on damaging the climate while stealing markets from the willing, whose exporters are less competitive because they have to add the price of carbon to their manufacturing costs.[33]

The consequences of failing to stem climate change are dire, with UN Secretary General Ban Ki-moon referring to it as an 'existential threat'.[34] More immediately, it also poses significant risks to world security, according to a 2014 report produced by the Intergovernmental Panel on Climate Change. As sea levels rise, fresh water resources decrease and agriculture is disrupted, the report found that 'climate change can indirectly increase risks of violent conflicts in the form of civil war and inter-group violence by amplifying well-documented drivers of these conflicts such as poverty and economic shocks'.[35]

What we are seeing in the above instances is that globalisation is under severe pressure from a number of directions. As its architecture buckles and fractures, international affairs may well return to the old, inherently unstable and dangerous order based on bargaining between the major powers, with international disputes once again being resolved through the naked exercise of military, economic and political power.

These are particularly dangerous times as the world is going through one of its periodic power transitions with Sino-American, Sino-Japanese and US/European-Russian competition on the rise. It is significant that only once has such a power transition occurred peacefully: after the Second World War, at Bretton Woods, when the British accepted the US as its replacement as the world's major economic hegemon. The question is whether the postwar global order has the authority and determination to facilitate another such peaceful transition, this time from a unipolar world, with the US at its centre, to a multipolar world.

There are other dangers. With the world so interdependent, should de-globalisation accelerate, it will lead to economic distress should global trade contract, which in turn will increase unemployment and social unrest.

In addition, as interdependent economies decouple and multilateral institutions and agreements lose their authority, the world polity will lose its ability to resolve disputes through the rule of law and its capacity to address problems that demand international cooperation, climate change being the most pressing.

So, unless a new generation of architects steps forward to renovate its structures and address globalisation's flaws, de-globalisation may well pick up pace towards its logical and tragic conclusion.

Notes

1 T. Shanker, 'White House Says the U.S. Is Not a Loner, Just Choosy', *New York Times* (31 July 2001).
2 The US further coerced other countries to sign an agreement that they would not surrender any American to the International Criminal Court, which is a breach of the Rome Treaty under which the Court was created.
3 In this instance, both Presidents Bush and Obama supported the treaty's ratification, but it faced determined opposition in the US Senate from hard-line Republicans.
4 G.W. Bush, 'President Welcomes President Chirac to White House', Joint News Conference with French President Jacques Chirac and US President George W. Bush held in Washington, DC, on 6 November 2001.
5 G.J. Ikenberry, *The Crisis of American Foreign Policy: Wilsonianism in the Twenty-First Century* (New Jersey: Princeton University Press, 2009), p. 8.
6 H. La Franchi , 'Why Obama, When Moving to Punish Syria, Is Unlikely to Go It Alone', *Christian Science Monitor* (26 August 2013).
7 After thirteen years of bickering, in December 2013, the round ended with an agreement for little more than cutting customs red tape – satisfying nobody. By 2013, negotiations on regional agreements were well advanced.
8 P.D. Sutherland, 'The Bilateral Threat to Free Trade', *Australian Financial Review* (4 January 2013), 12.

9   G. Song and W.J. Yuan, 'China's Free Trade Agreement Strategies', *The Washington Quarterly*, 35:4 (2012), 107–19.
10 This Partnership is designed to accommodate Asia's less developed countries by allowing them to opt out of trade policies and protect vulnerable industries. It also aims to harmonise the noodle bowl of overlapping free trade agreements among South East Asian Nations' (ASEAN) members.
11 The initiate is being coordinated by the association of ASEANs.
12 By early 2012, China had signed bilateral and multilateral free trade agreements (FTAs) with: Hong Kong, Macau, Taiwan, ASEAN10, Pakistan, Chile, New Zealand, Singapore, Peru, and Costa Rica. China is also in the process of signing bilateral FTAs with several others including: Australia, Iceland, South Korea, Norway, Switzerland, the Gulf Cooperation Council (GCC), and the Southern African Customs Union (SACU). China has also been actively pursuing a trilateral FTA with Japan and South Korea.
13 S. Donnan, 'Crimea Focuses Minds on Geopolitical Undercurrent in US–EU Trade Talks', *FT.com* (13 March 2014).
14 Quoted by David Ignatius, 'A Free Trade Agreement with Europe?' *Washington Post* (5 December 2012).
15 R. Emmott, 'EU Trade Chief Hopes To Clinch U.S. Trade By Late 2014', *Reuters* (27 February 2013).
16 P. van Ham, 'The Geopolitics of TTIP', Clingendael Policy Brief, No. 23 (The Hague: Clingendael Institute, October 2013).
17 M. Leonard, 'Why Convergence Breeds Conflict', *Foreign Affairs*, 92:5 (2013), 125–35, quote on p. 134.
18 Foreign Ministry Spokesperson Hong Lei's Regular Press Conference on 31 March 2014. Transcript retrieved from: http://au.china-embassy.org/eng/fyrth/t1142811.htm (accessed 2 January 2015).
19 The G-20 of finance ministers had been meeting since December 1999, and was the brainchild of Canadian Prime Minister Paul Martin. It provided a forum for finance ministers and central bank governors from twenty major economies to meet and discuss the state of the international financial system. In 2008 it became a two tiered meeting, with a meeting of heads of state and a second meeting of finance ministers.
20 In this proposal, a number of emerging economies would increase their voting quota, mainly at the expense of European countries. For example, China would increase its quota from 3.81 to 6.39 per cent. The US would retain the largest quota on the IMF of 16.75 per cent, which gave it an effective veto as all decisions needed to be passed by an 85 per cent majority.
21 M. Parkinson, 'International Economic Cooperation – Is it at Risk?' Speech to the Centre for Strategic and International Studies, delivered in Washington, DC, on 10 April 2014.
22 E. Gamberoni and R. Newfarmer, 'Trade Protection: Incipient But Worrisome Trends', TradeNotes No.27 (Geneva/Washington, DC: International Trade Department, 2009) p. 1.

23 T. Webb, 'World Gripped by "International Currency War"', *The Guardian* (28 September 2010).
24 The US signalled that it was ending quantitative easing in October 2014.
25 B. Gu and T. Liu, 'Enforcing International Financial Regulatory Reforms', *Journal of International Economic Law*, 17:1 (2014), 139–76, quote on p. 169.
26 Letter from Timothy D. Adams, president and CEO of the Institute of International Finance to Mr Tharman Shanmugaratnam (chairman, International Monetary and Financial Committee) and Marek Belka (chairman, Development Committee), dated 16 April 2013.
27 Anon., 'The Return of Economic Nationalism', *The Economist* (9 February 2009), p. 9.
28 L. Martin, 'Right Now, Business Needs More Walk and Less Talk', *Ethical Performance* (November 2008), p. 2.
29 L. Markowitz, 'Can Strategic Investing Transform the Corporation?' *Critical Sociology*, 34:5 (2008), 681–707.
30 E. Marx, 'The Big Interview: Jonathan Porritt – When Real Progress Means Standing Still', *Ethical Corporation* (21 September 2009).
31 This policy has not been reversed, even though President Barak Obama supports the Kyoto Protocol, and an obdurate Congress has prevented the US from joining with other countries to support global action to stem climate change.
32 In 2014, it became the G-7, as Russia was excluded after its annexation of Crimea.
33 Many countries impose a cost of carbon to regulate their greenhouse emissions, either through a trading scheme or through a carbon tax.
34 UN Secretary General Ban Ki-moon address to World Economic Forum, 'Climate Change, Sustainable Development "Mutually Supporting"', delivered in Davos, Switzerland on 24 January 2014.
35 Intergovernmental Panel on Climate Change, *Summary for Policymakers* (2014), p. 20.

Index

9/11 37, 175–6, 218, 243

Acheson, Dean 36, 54, 64, 65, 66
Action Committee for the United States of Europe 67–9
Adenauer, Konrad 65, 68
Albright, Madeleine 212, 213
alter-mondialisation 174
   'mondialisation maîtrisée' 175
   'mondialisation humaine' 175
Annan, Kofi 189, 209–22
apartheid 179, 182–5, 188
Atlantic Charter 29, 30
Atlas Economic Research Foundation 94, 95
Atlas Network *see* Atlas Economic Research Foundation
Australia 34, 49, 167

Ball, George 63, 66, 68, 99–100, 103
Ban Ki-moon 219, 248
Bank for Reconstruction and Development *see* World Bank
Barroso, José Manuel 73
BCSD *see* Business Council for Sustainable Development
Bellamy, Carol 232
Bhagwati, Jagdish 152
Boutros-Ghali, Boutros 212–13, 219
Bové, José 173–4, 175
Brazil 147, 149, 194, 199, 244, 246
Bretton Woods 4, 50, 51, 52, 79–80, 81, 84, 104, 113, 150, 214, 249
   conference 48–9, 52
   Final Act 49
   liberal order 9, 42, 50, 95
   rule of law 50
Brittan, Leon 144, 149
Brundtland, Gro
   background 225–8

   health 222, 228, 231–8
   World Commission on Environment and Development 198, 202
Brundtland Commission *see* World Commission on Environment and Development
Bruno, Kenny 222
Bush, George H. W. 37, 200
Bush, George W. 37, 38, 203, 214, 218, 242–3, 245, 247
Business Council for Sustainable Development 200–2

capital
   currency 3, 10, 49, 117, 120, 121
   currency war 246
   Eurodollars 80, 117–18
   Eurozone 72–3
   floating exchange rate 79–80, 120–1
   managed exchange rate 45, 49, 79
   movement of 46, 50, 81–2, 118, 120
   reserve currency 49, 79, 80, 117
   speculation 45, 50, 82, 116, 121, 122
Castro, Fidel 200
Cattaui, Maria Livanos 204, 220
Chenery, Hollis 130, 136
China
   global order 38
   IMF 246
   South China Sea 245
   trade 244–5
   unilateralism 245
   United Nations 30, 32
   World Bank 135
Chirac, Jacques 175
Churchill, Winston 29–30, 33, 63
Clarke, Tony 166
Clausen, Tom 100, 101, 135–7
Clayton, Will 52–4
climate change 4, 38, 107, 201, 243, 247–8

Index

Clinton, Bill 38, 121, 164, 212–13
Clinton, Hillary 244
Cold War 36, 51, 54, 64, 127, 131, 214, 215, 219, 242, 245
Comité d'action pour les Etat-Unis d'Europe see Action Committee for the United States of Europe
Conference on the Human Environment 194–6
Connally, Tom 24, 32, 34, 35
corporate social responsibility 107, 179, 185–9, 201, 221, 247
    Code of Pharmaceutical Marketing Practices 186
    International Code of Marketing of Breast-milk Substitutes 186
    Responsible Care® 187
corporations 4, 5, 54, 70, 81, 92, 100–1, 102, 103, 107, 109, 119, 121, 138, 149, 152, 153, 157, 163, 164, 168, 174, 175, 176, 179, 186, 187, 188–9, 190, 195, 198, 200, 201, 202, 203, 204, 219, 220, 221–2, 247
    corporate citizens 101, 188–9, 219, 222
    corporate environmentalism 201, 203
    corporate sovereignty 168
Cripps, Stafford 53–4
CSR see corporate social responsibility

De Gaulle, Charles 63, 65, 69
deglobalisation 188, 242–9
Dekker, Wisse 70, 71
Delors, Jacques 70–1, 72, 142, 200
Desai, Nitin 203
development 21, 50, 102, 127, 129–30, 132, 133, 167, 195–6, 197, 198–9, 216–19, 225, 229, 234–5
Dunkel, Arthur 143–4

Earth Charter 202, 203
environment 4, 5, 37, 96, 133, 163, 167, 174, 175, 176, 186, 189, 192–205, 217, 220, 221, 227, 243
Epstein, Richard 157–60, 161, 162, 165
Eurasian Economic Community and Customs Union 245
Eurodollar market 80, 117–18
Europe
    austerity 73, 247
    Europe des patries 69, 70
    European Coal and Steel Community 64–7
    European Court of Justice 66, 143
    European Economic Community 68

European Union 4, 73, 245
    Luxembourg compromise 69, 70
    Maastricht Treaty 72
    monetary union 71–3
    political threats 73–4
    Single European Act 70–1, 142
    Treaty of Rome 68
European Round Table of Industrialists 70, 71, 72, 143
Evatt, Herbert 34

Fabian Society 86, 87, 91
FDR see Franklin Delano Roosevelt
Feketekuty, Geza 148
Fisher, Antony 83, 90–5
Framework Convention on Tobacco Control 237–8
Freeman, Harry 148, 149, 150
Fresle, Daphne 233
Friedman, Milton 80, 81, 89, 92
Funk, Walter 42, 46

Gandhi, Indira 195, 196, 197
GATT 55, 143–4, 146, 147, 148, 149
Glass-Steagall Act 116–17, 123
Global Compact 215, 220–2, 233, 248
global financial crisis 4, 72–3, 107, 122, 124, 176, 245–7
global policy clubs 68, 104, 108, 109
Gorbachev, Mikhail 202
Gorlin, Jacques 146, 147
Greenberg, Hank 149, 150

Harris, Ralph 91, 92, 93, 95
Havana Charter 53–5
Hayek, Friedrich 5, 83–6, 92, 93, 94, 95, 150
    corporate social responsibility 189
    economics 5, 83, 84, 86, 87, 95–6, 168
    Road to Serfdom, The 86–8
    war of ideas 86, 89–91, 94–5
health 5, 96, 136, 176, 189, 217, 225, 226–38
Heritage Foundation 93–4, 161
Hill, Walter 196
Hines, John 182
Horton, Richard 225, 232
Hull, Cordell 24–33, 52–3
human rights 5, 37, 176, 189, 220, 229–30, 234
Hunold, Albert 88–9

ICC see International Chamber of Commerce
IEA see Institute of Economic Affairs

IMF 4, 49–51, 79–80, 81, 136, 137, 217, 218, 246
India 20, 132, 147, 149, 153, 246
Institute of Economic Affairs, 83, 91–3, 94
Intellectual Property Committee 146, 147
International Center for Industry and Environment 198
International Chamber of Commerce 147, 149, 166, 195–6, 198, 199, 201, 202, 203, 204, 218, 220–1
International Court of Justice 33, 245
International Criminal Court 38, 243
International Intellectual Property Alliance 146, 147
international liberal order 4–5, 9–10, 20, 83–4, 104, 145, 192, 215
International Stabilization Fund *see* IMF
International Trade Organization 9, 54–5, 145
International Union for the Conservation of Nature 198
ITO *see* International Trade Organization

Johannesburg Earth Summit *see* World Summit on Sustainable Development

Kantor, Mickey 141, 144
Keynes, John Maynard 9–10, 42–52, 83
  Economic Consequences of Peace, The 2–3, 44
  liberal order 4–5, 45–50, 84–6, 88, 131–2
Köhler, Horst 218
Krueger, Anne 136, 137
Kyoto Protocol *see* climate change

League of Nations 7–10, 15, 25, 35, 61
liberal order 45–50, 81, 95
  embedded liberalism 52, 67, 71, 73, 81, 214, 215, 216, 217, 222, 235
  rule of law 10, 21, 35, 37, 48, 50, 109, 150, 168, 238, 242, 249

MacGregor, Ian K. 198
MAI *see* Multilateral Agreement on Investment
Malloch-Brown, Mark 218
Mandela, Nelson 120, 185
McNamara, Robert 127–36, 138
  neoliberal policies 134–5
  political philosophy 129–30
  World Bank 130–5
MDGs *see* Millennium Development Goals
Meade, James 52
Meese III, Edwin 161

Mexico 118–19, 136, 162, 163
Millennium Development Goals 217–19, 222
Molotov, Vyacheslav 30, 36
Monnet, Jean 10, 59–69, 72, 74
  Action Committee for the United States of Europe 67–9
  Coal and Steel Community 4, 64–7
  Méthode Monnet 59, 61, 64, 72–3
Mont Pèlerin Society 89
Monterrey Consensus 218
Morgenthau Jr., Henry 46, 47, 48
Müntefering, Franz 120

NAFTA 162–5, 166, 167
neoliberal global order 5, 81, 145
neoliberalism 5, 55, 71, 80, 81, 82, 84, 86, 87, 88, 92, 93, 95, 107, 113, 119, 121, 122, 127, 145, 168, 175, 203, 215, 217, 218, 228, 230, 235
  constitutionalism 168
  rule of law 5, 87
  Washington Consensus 136–8, 215, 218
NGOs 109, 165, 186, 195, 198, 200–1, 202, 203, 218, 231, 233
Nixon Shock 79–80, 92, 102, 120, 242
non-governmental organisations *see* NGOs
North American Free Trade Agreement *see* NAFTA

Obama, Barack 246
OECD 103, 147, 148, 166, 167, 217
Ostrander, Taylor 198

Pakistan 132
Palmisano, Sam 188–9
Paris Peace Conference 8, 9, 10, 25, 43
Pasvolsky, Leo 24–6, 32
  San Francisco conference 34–5
  universalist v regional model 26–9, 31
Peccei, Aurelio 100, 101
Porritt, Jonathan 247
poverty 3, 5, 81, 129, 130, 132–3, 135–6, 138, 181–2, 189, 194, 195, 196, 199, 200, 215–19, 225, 234–5, 242, 243, 248
Pratt, Ed 146
Price, Dan 164–5
Principles of Equal Rights *see* Sullivan Principles
protests 174–6, 188, 242, 247
  Battle in Seattle 108, 174, 175, 188, 221
  extremists 247
  Occupy movement 176

Index

Reagan, Ronald 94, 136, 146, 161, 230
Rio Earth Summit 200–1
Rio+20 204–5
Rockefeller, David 100, 101–4
    Trilateral Commission, formation of 101–4
Rockefeller, Nelson 34
Roosevelt, Franklin Delano 9, 16, 17, 19, 24, 26, 27, 28, 29–32, 33, 35
Rotberg, Eugene 131
Ruggie, John 5, 52, 214–15, 216, 220
Russia 29, 30, 32, 36, 37, 38, 49, 51, 215, 244–5, 249

Sachs, Jeffrey 234
Seldon, Arthur 91
Schmidheiny, Stephen 199–200, 201
Schuman, Robert 64–5
Schuman Plan 65, 66
Schwab, Klaus 104–9, 119
    global governance 108–9
    World Economic Forum 104, 106–8
Sheehan, Michael 212–13
Shultz, George 80, 81
Silva-Herzog, Jesús 118
Singh, Manmohan 176
Soviet Union *see* Russia
Stalin, Joseph 3, 18, 30, 33
Stettinius, Ed 26, 32, 33, 34
Stiglitz, Joseph 137, 152, 164, 187
Stigson, Björn 204
Stockholm Earth Summit *see* Conference on the Human Environment
Strong, Maurice 192–203, 205
Sullivan, Leon 179–86
    Global Sullivan Principles 189–90
    South Africa 182–5
    Sullivan Principles 183–6, 188
sustainable development 103, 198–9, 201, 202, 204, 205, 219
Sutherland, Peter 71, 141–5
    trade negotiations 141, 143–5, 147
    trading blocs 243–4
    WTO 150–1, 152

takings
    bilateral investment agreements 167–8
    Multilateral Agreement on Investment 166–7
    NAFTA 162–6
    regulatory takings 157, 159, 160–1, 162, 165, 166, 167, 168

Takings 159, 162
Takings Project 160–2
Thatcher, Margaret 71, 81, 93, 95
Transatlantic Trade and Investment Partnership 244
trade negotiations
    Doha Round 232–3
    Uruguay Round 143, 146–7, 149, 150, 151, 152, 153, 166
Trans-Pacific Partnership 244
Trilateral Commission 68, 103–4, 202
    Between Two Ages 102
    Brzezinski, Zbigniew 102–3
Truman, Harry 9, 28, 33, 35–6, 55

Ukraine 245
UN Conference on Environment and Development *see* Rio Earth Summit
UNEP *see* United Nations Environment Programme
unilateralism 246
    China 245
    US 242
United Nations 5, 7, 29–38, 209–23, 234
    Commission on Transnational Corporations 219
    General Assembly 32, 35–6, 216–17, 219
    Security Council 30, 32–3, 36, 38, 213–14, 243
United Nations Conference on Sustainable Development *see* Rio+20
United Nations Environment Programme 196–8, 204
    Brussels Group 196–7
United States Coalition of Service Industries 149
USSR *see* Russia

Valenti, Jack 146
Van Doren, Irita 15–16, 20
Vandenberg, Arthur 22, 24, 32, 34, 35
Verhofstadt, Guy 175
Verne, Jules 1–2
Vinson, Fred 50–1
Von Mises, Ludwig 84, 89

War on Terror 218, 243
Washington Consensus 136–8, 215, 218
WBCSD *see* World Business Council for Sustainable Development
Welles, Sumner 26–9, 30–2, 34–5
White, Harry Dexter 42, 46–9, 51

WHO 186, 225, 228–36
   public-private partnerships 222, 225, 231–2, 233–4
   tobacco control 236–8
   TRIPS 232–3
   US hostility 230
Williamson, Edwin 163
Willkie, Wendell 13–22
   international order 13, 17, 18, 20–2
   One World 19–22
   political career 15–17
   trip around the world 17–19
Wilson, Woodrow 7–10, 25, 46
Wolfensohn, James 81, 175, 216, 218
World Bank 4, 5, 9, 22, 50–1, 81, 127, 129–38, 216, 217, 218, 230, 301, 237
World Business Council for Sustainable Development 108, 202, 203, 204
World Commission on Environment and Development 198–9, 202
   Our Common Future 199

World Economic Forum 104, 105–8, 109
   club for the elites 107, 109, 143
   global policy making 106–9
World Health Organization *see* WHO
World Summit on Sustainable Development 203–4
Wriston, Walter 5, 100, 101, 113–24
   attack on regulations 115–19, 122
   career 113, 114–20
   ideas on markets 119–22
WTO 55, 141, 143–5, 150–3, 173, 218, 232, 236, 243–4
   Antigua and Barbuda 151–2
   free trade 55, 145, 150–3
   GATS 147–50, 53
   TRIMS 153, 166, 167
   TRIPS 145–7, 152, 232–3

Yeutter, Clayton 146

Zanuck, Darryl F. 7–8